Llewellyn's
2005
Magical Almanac

Featuring

*Elizabeth Barrette, Shira Bee, Twilight Bard, Stephanie Rose Bird,
Nina Lee Braden, Mavesper Cy Ceridwen, Dallas Jennifer Cobb,
Nuala Drago, Ellen Dugan, Denise Dumars, Ember, Emely Flak,
Karen Follett, Lily Gardner, Magenta Griffith, Eileen Holland,
Christine Jette, Raven Kaldera, James Kambos, Jonathan Keyes, Laura
LaVoie, Sorita Loock, Anthony Louis, Kristin Madden, Muse,
Sharynne NicMhacha, Olivia O'Meir, Diana Rajchel, Janina
Renée, Steven Repko, Laurel Reufner, Sheri Richerson, Tannin
Schwartzstein, Sedwyn, Cerridwen Iris Shea, Lynne Sturtevant,
Tammy Sullivan, Julianna Yau, and S. Y. Zenith*

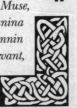

Llewellyn's 2005 Magical Almanac

ISBN 0-7387-0138-6. Copyright © 2004 by Llewellyn Worldwide. All rights reserved. Printed in the United States.

Editor/Designer: Michael Fallon

Cover Illustration: © Eric Hotz

Calendar Pages Design: Andrea Neff and Michael Fallon

Calendar Pages Illustrations: © Kerigwen

Interior Illustrations © Helen Michaels, pages: 17, 32, 61, 63, 77, 97, 112, 114, 125, 138, 136, 235, 252, 266, 270, 306–308, 309, 310, 312, 321, 339; © Wendy Froshay, pages: 23, 25, 50, 103–106, 157, 243, 296, 298, 343, 353, 355, 365

Clip Art Illustrations: Dover Publications

Special thanks to Amber Wolfe for the use of daily color and incense correspondences. For more detailed information, please see *Personal Alchemy* by Amber Wolfe.

You can order Llewellyn annuals and books from *New Worlds*, Llewellyn's magazine catalog. To request a free copy of the catalog, call toll-free 1-877-NEWWRLD, or visit our website at http://subscriptions.llewellyn.com.

Moon sign and phase data computed by Astro Communications Services (ACS).

Llewellyn Worldwide
Dept. 0-7387-0138-6
P.O. Box 64383
St. Paul, MN 55164-0838

About the Authors

ELIZABETH BARRETTE serves as the managing editor of *PanGaia* and assistant editor of *SageWoman*. She has been involved with the Pagan community for fifteen-plus years, and in 2003 earned ordination as a priestess through Sanctuary of the Silver Moon. Her writing fields include speculative fiction and gender studies. She lives in central Illinois and enjoys herbal landscaping and gardening. Visit her website at: http://www.worthlink.net/~ysabet/index.html.

SHIRA BEE considers nature her sanctuary and is fascinated by occult history. She holds a BA in creative writing and has been published in *New Witch* magazine, *SageWoman*, *Venus Magazine*, *Morbid Curiosity* #5 and #6, and morbidoutlook.com. She resides with her familiars in California.

TWILIGHT BARD has been walking the Wiccan path for more than twelve years. As a freelance writer of both fiction and nonfiction, her work is revolves around her three passions: parenting, homeschooling, and Pagan spirituality. She holds a degree in English secondary education and is currently homeschooling her own three little Witchlings.

STEPHANIE ROSE BIRD is an artist, writer, herbalist, healer, mother, and companion. She studied Australian Aboriginal art and ritual as a Fulbright Senior Scholar, and she is a faculty member in the painting and drawing department at the school of the Art Institute of Chicago. Her column "Ase! from the Crossroads" is featured in *Sage-Woman*. She has a book on Hoodoo forthcoming from Llewellyn.

NINA LEE BRADEN loves to officiate at handfastings whenever she gets the opportunity. In particular, she enjoys working with the couple to personalize a ceremony that will reflect their goals and beliefs. Nina Lee lives in Tennessee with her husband of seven years. When not reading, writing, editing, teaching, or studying, she enjoys playing computer games and going to movies.

MAVESPER CY CERIDWEN lives in Brasilia, the capital of Brazil. She has been involved in the craft for about twelve years and is one of the founders of the Brazilian Dianic Wicca Tradition. She is a proud mother of Sorcha Arkteia, and loves to breed dogs and cats. She is the president of Abrawicca, the Brazilian Association of Wicca, and she runs conferences and workshops in all Brazil to teach about Wicca. She has written a guide to the rituals of Brazilian indigenous goddesses and a work of comparative mythology.

DALLAS JENNIFER COBB weaves a magical life with her partner Bob and their daughter Terra. Living in a waterfront village, she is enchanted by Moon and water, beach and sky. While parenting is her top priority, she also writes, runs, gardens, and dreams in her spare time. She enjoys the harvests of rural life: more time, more peace, a contented family, and an enormous organic garden. She is a regular contributor to Llewellyn's almanacs.

NUALA DRAGO is an author, musician, folklorist, and self-initiate. She has been a lifelong student of ancient cultures and extinct languages. She enjoys training horses, spending quiet time with her many pets, collecting ancient herbal remedies, and looking for antiques.

ELLEN DUGAN, also known as the "Garden Witch," is a psychic-clairvoyant and practicing Witch of more than seventeen years. A regular contributor to the almanacs, Ellen is a master gardener, and she teaches classes on gardening and flower folklore at a local community college. She is the author of the Llewellyn books *Garden Witchery: Magick from the Ground Up* and *Elements of Witchcraft: Natural Magick for Teens.* With her husband, she raises three teenagers and tends to an enchanted garden in Missouri.

DENISE DUMARS is the cofounder of the Iseum of Isis Paedusis, an Egyptian religion study group chartered by the Fellowship of Isis. Her book *The Dark Archetype: Exploring the Shadow Side of the Divine,* coauthored with Lori Nyx, was published in 2003 by New Page

Books, as well as her collection of short stories, *Lovecraft Slept Here* (Wildside Press). Denise teaches college English and classes on Isian religion, aromatherapy, and magic at various New Age shops around Southern California.

EMBER is a poet and freelance writer inspired by a path of nature-centered spirituality. She enjoys music, reading, gardening, camping, and hiking. Her writing has appeared in *PanGaia, newWitch,* and various Llewellyn annuals. She lives in the Midwest with her husband and two feline companions.

EMELY FLAK has been a practicing solitary Witch for ten years. She is a freelance writer based in Daylesford, Australia, who is also employed as a learning and development professional. Much of her work is dedicated to embracing the ancient wisdom of Wicca for the personal empowerment of women in the competitive work environment.

KAREN FOLLETT has been a practitioner of witchcraft for over thirty years. Initiated in the Georgian tradition, she currently practices as a solitary. Karen is a psychic, empath, energy intuitive, and educator in the metaphysical arts and in the religion of the craft. By profession, she is a registered nurse who specializes in maternal and child health. She teaches childbirth classes at a local hospital. She is the wife to one husband, the biological mother to two young adult sons, and the adoptive mother to one dog and three cats.

LILY GARDNER has studied folklore and mythology since she learned to read. In addition to her contributions to the Llewellyn annuals, her short stories are beginning to show up in literary journals. Lily lives in Portland, Oregon and is a member of the Power of Three coven.

MAGENTA GRIFFITH has been a Witch more than twenty-five years, a high priestess for thirteen years, and a founding member of the coven Prodea. She leads rituals and workshops in the Midwest and

is currently librarian for the New Alexandria Library, a Pagan magical resource center (http://www.magusbooks.com/newalexandria).

EILEEN HOLLAND is a Wiccan priestess and a solitary eclectic Witch. She is the author of *The Wicca Handbook* (Weiser, 2000), *Spells for the Solitary Witch* (Weiser, 2004), and coauthor with Cerelia of *A Witch's Book of Answers* (Weiser, 2003). She is also the webmaster of Open Sesame (www.open-sesame.com) and a regular contributor to Llewellyn's annuals.

CHRISTINE JETTE is a registered nurse and holds a bachelor of arts degree in psychology. She is also a therapeutic touch practitioner, a member of the American Holistic Nurses Association, and a professional tarot consultant. Christine specializes in health readings combined with hands-on (energetic) healing. She teaches noncredit writing part-time at the University of Cincinnati, and also works as an RN in a traditional acute care setting. Christine lives in Cincinnati with her husband and three cats.

RAVEN KALDERA is a Neopagan shaman, homesteader, activist, musician, astrologer, and wordsmith who did time in many cities before finally escaping to the countryside.

JAMES KAMBOS is a writer and painter who has had a lifelong interest in folk magic. He has written numerous articles concerning the folk magic traditions of Greece, the Near East, and the Appalachian region of the United States. He writes and paints from his home in the beautiful Appalachian hills of southern Ohio.

JONATHAN KEYES lives in Portland, Oregon, where he works as an astrologer and herbalist and has written books on astrological health and on herbs. He is currently working on a book titled *Healers,* a series of interviews of various herbalists, *curanderos,* and medicine people from around the United States.

LAURA LAVOIE is a professional recruiter with a degree in anthropology. She has been practicing Paganism for ten years and served as vice president of the Western Michigan University student organiza-

tion, Ancient Altars, during her senior year of college. She is also a contributing columnist for *PanGaia* magazine. She lives in Atlanta, Georgia, with her husband Matt, and their cat Piglet.

SORITA LOOCK grew up in Cape Town, South Africa, but now lives happily in West London with her partner David Rankine. Sorita studied aromatherapy and herbalism and has trained in a range of alternative and healing practices. She is the creatrix of the Wiccan website www. Avalonia.co.uk, and has contributed articles to a range of Wiccan and Pagan websites and magazines. In addition to writing, Sorita teaches Wicca through an annual course she runs with her partner. She also runs workshops on psychic development, healing, and astral projection, and often gives talks about various aspect of Goddess spirituality.

ANTHONY LOUIS is a psychiatrist with an abiding interest in symbolism and mythology. He has lectured internationally and has published numerous articles on astrology and tarot. He is also the author of the books *Tarot Plain and Simple* and *Horary Astrology*, both published by Llewellyn.

KRISTIN MADDEN is a homeschooling mom who was raised in a shamanic home. She is the dean of Ardantane's School of Shamanic Studies and the founder of the Pathfinder Nature School. A Druid and tutor in the Order of Bards, Ovates, and Druids, Kristin also writes books and rehabilitates wild birds. Visit her online at http://www.kristinmadden.com.

MUSE lives in Colorado Springs, Colorado, with her dalmatian, MacLeod. Having studied alternative religions, spiritual practices, and magic since an early age, she has a fascination with the unseen world. Among many other things, she is an aspiring writer, a college graduate with a BA in European history, a graduate student in international business, and a professional in the field of e-commerce. Believe it or not, she still finds time to travel, do yoga, and read the latest Harry Potter book.

SHARYNNE MACLEOD NICMHACHA is a Celtic priestess and Witch, and direct descendant of Clan MacLeod—long recorded in oral tradition to have connections to the sidhe, or fairy folk. She has studied Old Irish, Scottish Gaelic, and Celtic mythology through Harvard University, where she has published a number of research papers. She teaches workshops and sings and plays bodran, woodwinds, and stringed instruments with the group Devandaurae (and previously with the Moors) and has recently published her first book.

OLIVIA O'MEIR is a writer and public relations specialist. She has been published in *The Beltane Papers* and *newWitch*. She began studying witchcraft in 1993 and discovered Wicca in 1997. After studying with a traditional Celtic coven, she remembered her love of ancient Mediterranean goddesses. Olivia leans toward the Dianic path, and currently she studies at Dianic University with Z. Budapest. She runs a small jewelry and woven crafts business called Apollo's Daughter (http://www.geocities.com/apollodaughter).

DIANA RAJCHEL, a.k.a. "Di," works full time for a major bank while trying to arrange her Pagan life around the demands of the 9-to-5 work week. She lives in the warehouse district of downtown Minneapolis, where she enjoys her favorite coffee shop, an apartment with a dishwasher, and close proximity to the Mississippi River. If you want to contact her or know more about her work, take a look at http://www.medeaschariot.com.

JANINA RENÉE is a scholar of material culture, folklore, mythology, ancient religion, psychology, medical anthropology, history, and literature. She is also the author of the Llewellyn books *Tarot Spells, Playful Magic, Tarot: Your Everyday Guide, Tarot for a New Generation*, and *By Candlelight: Rites for Celebration, Blessing, and Prayer.*

STEVEN REPKO is an elder and founding member of the Coven of NatureWise. He has studied the craft for more than three decades. An astrologer, medium, musician, and poet, he and his wife Bonnie are Pagan parents of three children, and owners of

Gem N Aries, a store in Mays Landing, New Jersey. They provide free online horoscopes and shopping at http://www.gem-naries.com/.

LAUREL REUFNER has been a solitary pagan for over a decade now. She is active in the local CUUPS chapter, Circle of Gaia Dreaming, and is often attracted to bright and shiny ideas. Southeastern Ohio has always been home, and she currently lives in lovely Athens County with her wonderful husband and two adorable heathens, er, daughters. Her website is found at www.spiritrealm.com/Melinda/paganism.html.

SHERI RICHERSON has more than twenty years of experience in newspaper, magazine, and creative writing. She is also a lifetime member of the International Thespian Society, and is a longtime member of the Garden Writers Association of America and the American Horticultural Society. Her favorite pastimes are riding horses and motorcycles, visiting arboretums, traveling, and working in her garden. She specializes in herb gardening and in cultivating tropical, subtropical, and other exotic plants.

TANNIN SCHWARTZSTEIN has dedicated a significant part of her life, both privately and professionally, to the pursuit of the spiritual arts. Tannin has studied diverse practices and paths such as chi gong, shamanistic energy techniques, Gnosticism, Afro-Caribbean religions, and even a pinch of ceremonial magic. She is the proprietor of Bones and Flowers, Worcester's only occult specialty store (www.bonesandflowers.com), and she is also a crafter in diverse media—such as acrylic, sculpture, ceramic, bone, and wood—and a legally ordained Pagan minister.

SEDWYN is an explorer of Celtic history, myth, and magic, and an initiate of the Hearth of Brigid Lyceum. She is an artist who works in photography and pastels, and who occasionally exhibits at a local gallery. Sedwyn enjoys leading workshops, rituals, and drumming circles.

CERRIDWEN IRIS SHEA is a tarot-reading, horse-playing ice-hockey addicted, Broadway dresser kitchen witch. She contributes regularly to the Llewellyn annuals, writes the tarot column "In the Cards" for *Fayth* magazine, and pens the occult horror serial *Angel Hunt* for www.keepitcoming.net. Her website is www.cerridwenscottage.com.

LYNNE STURTEVANT is a freelance writer specializing in folklore, mythology, fairy tales, and the paranormal. She has been a solitary practitioner following an eclectic path since 1970. She holds a bachelor's degree in philosophy and is a regular contributor to Llewellyn's annuals. Her work has also appeared in *Fate* magazine.

TAMMY SULLIVAN writes from her home in the beautiful foothills of the Great Smoky Mountains. She has been a practicing solitary Witch for over a decade. The mother of four teenagers, she is currently writing a spell book for teens.

JULIANNA YAU is a freelance writer and artist residing in Canada. She has published several articles Llewellyn's annuals.

S. Y. ZENITH is three-quarters Chinese, one tad Irish, and a full lifelong solitary eclectic Pagan. She has lived and traveled extensively in Asia to such countries as India, Nepal, Thailand, Malaysia, Singapore, Borneo, and Japan over two decades. She is now based in Australia where her time is divided between writing, experimenting with alternative remedies, and teaching the use of gems, holy beads, and religious objects from India and the Himalayas. She is also a member of the Australian Society of Authors.

Table of Contents

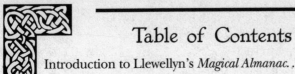

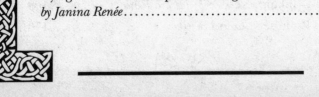

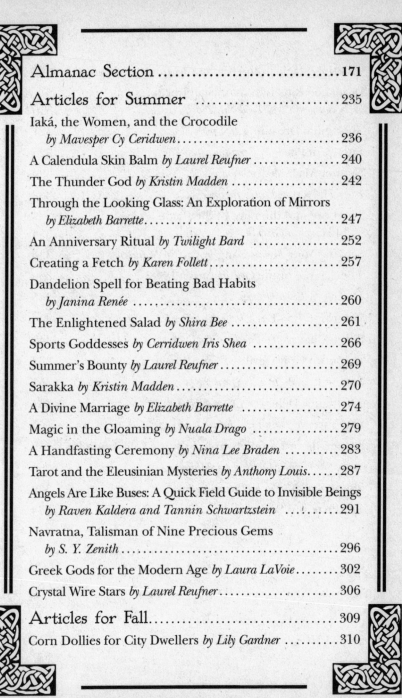

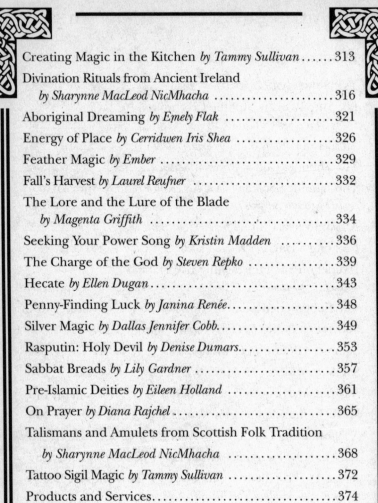

Introduction to Llewellyn's Magical Almanac

The *Magical Almanac* is fifteen years—one-and-a-half decades—old this year, and at the threshold of maturity. The offerings in this edition reflect a maturing world view among its authors, who in turn reflect the maturing magical and Pagan community.

In this edition, our authors are taking mature looks at magic in everyday life, and tapping into some of the world's most ancient knowledge—the magic and healing power of natural forces such as chocolate, the stars, angels, and the seasons, for instance, as well as the lore regarding knives, pennies, pine trees, and an array of gods and goddesses. We bring to these pages some of the most innovative and original thinkers and writers on these subjects.

This focus on the old ways—on the lore of men and women around the world who knew and understood the power of their ancestors—is important today, as we work to renew a world overwhelmed by problems—terrorism, water shortages, environmental degradation, internecine battles, and simple discourtesy. While we don't want to assign blame or cast any other aspersions, this state of affairs is not surprising considering so many of us—each one of us—is out of touch with the old ways. Many of us spend too much of our lives rushing about in a technological bubble—striving to make money, being everywhere but here, living life in fast-forward. We forget, at times, to stop, take a deep breath, and act our age.

Still, the news is not all bad. People are still fighting to make us all more aware of the magical, beautiful things in the world. Pagan and Wiccan communities, for instance, are thriving across the country and throughout the world. In this edition of the *Magical Almanac*, writers from far away as Australia, Canada, and England—as well as across the whole of the United States—contribute to an expanding volume of knowledge, lore, and magical ritual.

In the 2005 edition of the *Magical Almanac* we pay tribute and homage to a maturing understanding of the magic and beauty and balance of our ancestors, and to the magic of all the ages. This may sound a bit corny for some, and perhaps a bit too idealistic, too, but those who say so likely have never put what has been written in this almanac over the past fifteen years to good use.

Magic is an ancient tool whose time has come back around to help us restore balance in our lives. More and more people are using magic, celebrating the elements, praying to the Goddess and the various incarnations of the divine, and studying the myths and legends, lore and tales of the past. In the end, one person at a time, using ancient wisdom, we can make a new world.

Articles for Winter

How to Project a Persona through Aura Color Control

by Muse

There are times when it may be easier to have a different persona or personality trait. Do you get nervous during a job interview, and wish you had more confidence? Are you nervous on first dates, and want to learn how to calm yourself down? How about at a fancy party, do you ever want to seem more witty and interesting? We cannot change our personalities, per se, but we can affect how other people perceive us through aura projection.

Aura projection is the act of donning a new aura color in order to have a desired affect not only on the people around you, but also on yourself. It is a very easy practice, especially for people with meditation and visualization experience. The steps are simple:

1. Choose the appropriate color for your need. A basic list is below, but feel free to use your own knowledge of colors to expand it.

2. Relax and center yourself. Close your eyes if possible.

3. Starting from your solar plexus (the area just above your navel), imagine there is a tiny spec of your chosen color there.

4. Imagine that color growing and growing, filling your body, then expanding outside it about a foot. The color covers your natural aura.

5. You are now projecting a new aura color. Visualize and believe that that color will stay with you, projecting past your normal aura, until you consciously release it.

Color Associations

White: This is the color of innocence and purity. Use this color when you want to project kindness, sensitivity, and calm. White will make you seem peaceful to others, and it will calm nervousness in yourself. White is also a useful color to project when you want to go unnoticed—it makes you "invisible" in a crowd.

Blue: This is the color of strength and confidence. It is a fabulous color to project during a job interview. It will not only make you appear confident and competent to a potential employer, but it will make you *feel* more confident. I have also found this to be a great first-date aura color. It gives you that added boost of confidence, and it puts your partner at ease because it reduces emotional pressure on his or her psyche. This is also the color of protection. Use it when you are feeling unsafe.

Pink: This is the color of emotional love (as opposed to the passionate kind). Like white, it projects sweetness and kindness, but unlike white it also projects affection. Pink is a good color to use when you are trying to show a person you care about him or her. Use this color the first time you tell someone you love him or her, or when you have to say something difficult to a loved one whom you want to know such feelings are coming from your heart.

Green: This is the color of healing and nature. Project this color in a hospital or medical facility, and you will notice patients perking up and feeling better. This color is also good to project when you are not feeling physically healthy—it will decrease the amount of time it takes you to heal. Also use this color when you want to feel more connected to nature, such as on a hike. Green literally makes your aura blend with the natural world around you. It will also make animals more comfortable around you.

Red: This is the color of passion. People with red auras are seen as passionate and interesting. Project this color in a room full of people when you want to be noticed, and especially when you are looking for stimulating conversation. People with something to say will be drawn to your energy and enthusiasm. Red will make you feel more open-minded and more curious about the world around you.

Orange: This is a great color to use when you need to seem energetic. It not only makes people around you see you in a healthy, lively light, but orange will also make you feel more energetic just by it revitalizing energy.

Yellow: This is the color of intelligence. Project this color when you want to seem smart and bookish. Yellow is the color of the student and is good to use in the presence of a teacher or employer, as it will make you come across as willing and able to learn. This is also a good color to don when you are studying. Yellow will help you retain facts easier and aid in your understanding of the material.

New Aspects of Yourself

Projecting a new aura color can be an interesting and fun experience, akin to some of the shape-shifting exercises many cultures practice. You may find new aspects of yourself you did not know you possessed, and it may open you up to experiences you may have passed by previously.

Keep in mind that practicing aura color projection will not change you, but rather it will open you up to new ways of thinking and acting. It will never cause you to act in a way that is not naturally you, but it will cause you and the people around you to see you in a new light.

Aura color projection can be a positive experience and lead to great personal growth, and you may find new colors naturally appearing in your auric field after practicing aura color projection frequently.

Circle Power

by Emely Flak

"Everything the power of the world does is done in a circle."
—Black Elk, Oglala Sioux Holy Man

Mediterranean civilizations have given a great deal of culture to the world. This includes a rich heritage of magical concepts and artifacts that increase our ability to manage in the world. Among these are *malocchio,* or "evil eye," lore, and the many protection charms used to ward against the evil eye.

Mysteries of the Circle

If you ask a few people what a circle means to them, you will probably hear various responses. Some will speak of magic, of healing power, or perhaps of energy or the natural world. These diverse answers reflect the multidimensional understanding of the meaning of a circle. The circle, as a shape or symbol, invokes imagery of movement such as dance, spirituality, protection, energy, ritual, equality, continuity, creation, fertility, marriage, and celestial bodies.

The shape of the circle is visualized in ritual, and it is visible in the material world in objects such as the wedding ring and the Moon. Circles, and variations such as spirals and labyrinths, are found in ancient rock art tens of thousands of years old, proving that the symbol has long played a role in human culture and spirituality.

The natural world moves and exists in circles. A circle represents feminine energy, the egg, fertility, and Mother Earth. Our planet is a sphere, as are other heavenly bodies in the solar system. Our Moon travels in a circle around the Earth. In turn, our planet moves in a circle around the Sun. Our seasons are expressed as the wheel of the year. We experience the contrast of seasonal change when our planet completes each circular journey around the Sun. The wheel of the year represents the continuous organic cycle of birth, death, and rebirth. With no defined beginning or end, the wheel of the year, like the circle, symbolizes eternity.

In a Wiccan context, the circle means magic, protection, and ritual. A pentagram inscribed inside a circle becomes a pentacle, signifying unity and rebirth. As the integral component of Wiccan ritual,

the visualized circle protects and creates sacred space while containing the magical energy raised. The casting of the circle prepares the celebrant for the magical work ahead. To create the ritual circle, some Wiccans use visible markings such as chalk, flowers, or herbs. Others imagine the circle as separating their sacred space from the mundane world.

The circle sets boundaries for ritual, and it engenders the respect and focus of the group working within it. Calling the four quarters invites the four elements, and the athame projects the energy required for the manifestation of the elements. In the safety and sacred space of the circle, one enters an altered state of mind for manifestation, raising energy, and spell work. In visualization work, the circle is a symbol of protection.

Performing any religious work in a circle represents equality and esoteric spiritual authority. This is a stark contrast to the way mainstream religions worship in a church or synagogue, where the focus is on the minister who leads the prayer. Without a circle, this form of institutionalized ritual often leaves its followers spiritually disconnected and alone.

The Circle in Practice

In Native American practice, the medicine wheel is also known as the circle of knowledge. Here, it's believed that "medicine" equates to knowledge and enlightenment. The medicine wheel is a circle that offers diverse applications. It symbolizes animal totems, the four elements, and the four cardinal directions. As a model that also represents the four realms of spiritual, economical, psychological, and physical reality, it is a self-improvement tool. Medicine wheel circles from our Pagan past have left their mark today in the form of stones and rocks in various parts of the global landscape.

The circle dance that takes place as a part of ritual can be a grounding and therapeutic movement. A dance performed in a circle recreates a tribal feeling that synchronizes with the movements of the universe and with the rhythm of nature. In the Northern Hemisphere, a circle dance typically follows a clockwise direction to align with the direction of the Sun's movement. Conversely, in the Southern Hemisphere, circle dancers express their connection to their environment with counterclockwise movement.

A fast moving circle, in the form of a spiral dance, raises a cone of energy. This has been described as a way of singing to the Earth. In particular, the dancers connect with Mother Earth when they dance barefoot. This is a primal activity that connects us to our Pagan past.

Australian aboriginal ceremonial dances performed in a circle have left permanent imprints on the ground where grass never grows. To this day, many indigenous Australians believe it is taboo to enter this sacred circle. Interestingly, many movements in belly dance are circular and so honor the Great Mother Goddess. In particular, the circular hip movements connect the dancer's body with goddess energy and the spirit of the Earth.

A labyrinth is a circular path that has been used in walking meditation by many cultures. Traditionally, as a person walks toward the center of the labyrinth, he or she contemplates a problem. In the center, time is spent in reflection and solitude. On the walk back out, he or she carries the gift of knowledge.

In the contemporary world of business, a circle can make a difference. The meeting dynamics at a round table contrast significantly with those at square or rectangular tables. The round table promotes a climate of equality, paving the way for improved communication in a less threatening environment. This setting removes perceived barriers between the participants and the facilitator and encourages a shared learning environment.

Self-help and recovery groups often meet in a circle to capture a climate that promotes healing, trust, and recovery. The circle restores a sense of community and encourages people to contribute. In a circle, no one occupies a position of power or dominance over others.

As a healing tool, the circle can be nonreligious way for people to gather and communicate in sacred space. It unites people from a diverse range of cultural and religious backgrounds. Some therapists describe this form of healing as "circle work."

The mandala, created by Tibetan monks to honor the cycle of life, is shaped in a circle. *Mandala,* a Sanskrit word for "circle, community, and connection," is a symbol of the universe and of its omnipotent energy. Tibetan monks create a mandala as a work of art and for meditation using sand ground from brightly colored stone.

More recently, the ground stones are dyed to create stunning, vibrantly decorated circles. The use of the mandala for meditation and contemplation restores balance and inner peace. The Navajo Indians use mandala imagery and sand paintings for personal healing. Psychologist Carl Jung acknowledged the power of the circle as an archetype that could be used to cure modern psychological problems. Jung painted mandalas as a form of self-help therapy, and he promoted this art as therapy for his patients.

The circle is more than just a symmetrical shape. With its multidimensional interpretation and application, it plays a significant role in ritual, healing, and self-development. Rich in symbolism, it affirms our interconnectedness with the natural world and with each other.

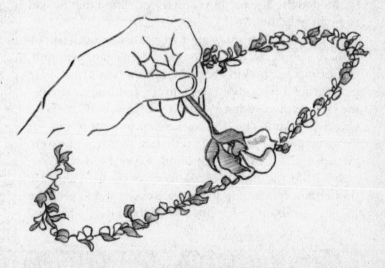

The Magic of Chocolate

by Lynne Sturtevant

Does chocolate possess magical properties? The people of ancient Mexico believed it did. For most of its long history, chocolate was consumed as a bitter and spicy ritual beverage. It was recognized as a powerful aphrodisiac that conferred both mental and physical vitality on those who consumed it. Brides and grooms drank chocolate on their wedding nights. Warriors drank it to enhance their strength before battles, and priests drank it to communicate with the gods.

Chocolate's mystical powers were linked to its supernatural origin. According to an Aztec legend, Quetzacoatl, the plumed serpent god of the air, gave it to the Toltecs—people who had lived in Mexico long before the Aztecs. Quetzacoatl assumed human form and traveled to Earth on a beam of light from the morning star. He was very tall and thin. His skin was pale and luminous, and his beard was long and white. Quetzacoatl's appearance frightened the Toltecs, but soon they realized that he had come to help them.

Under Quetzacoatl's guidance artists produced colorful masterpieces, architects designed elegant pyramids, and priests learned to chart the movements of stars. He taught the Toltecs about agriculture and how to predict the cycle of the seasons. When the crops were flourishing, Quetzacoatl told the Toltecs he had one more gift for them, something he had secretly removed from heaven. He opened his thin, white hand. Several glossy brown beans from the divine cocoa tree lay on his palm. He showed the Toltecs how to cultivate cocoa and to produce *xocolatl* (pronounced "chocoatl"), the sacred drink of the gods.

The other gods watched with anger as the Toltecs enjoyed the drink that had been exclusively theirs. They sent Tezcatlipoca, the god of darkness, disguised as a chocolate merchant to punish Quetzacoatl. Tezcatlipoca descended from heaven on the thread of a black spider's web. He tricked Quetzacoatl into drinking a poisonous cup of chocolate that made Quetzacoatl believe he had to leave his earthly kingdom.

Burning with fever and overwhelmed by sadness, Quetzacoatl made his way to the coast of Tabasco. Promising to return, he boarded a small raft, drifted out to sea, and disappeared over the horizon. The widespread belief that Quetzacoatl would eventually come back to Mexico lead to disaster for the Aztecs later on.

The Toltecs passed the technique of growing chocolate down from generation to generation. By the time the Aztecs arrived, chocolate plantations were thriving in Mexico's tropical areas. Magic and ritual surrounded the cultivation of cocoa trees. Men working on chocolate plantations abstained from sex for the first thirteen nights of the two weeks leading up to planting time. On the fourteenth night they would return to their wives. The next morning as the men sowed the beans, priests in feathered headdresses prayed to Quetzacoatl and waved smoldering cocoa branches over the fields.

Although chocolate was plentiful in the Aztec world, its distribution was tightly controlled. It was the ultimate luxury substance and status symbol. Only the very wealthy had regular access. Cocoa beans were so valuable they were used as currency. Archeologists have even found evidence of chocolate counterfeiters. They duped the unsuspecting by selling them cocoa beans filled with dirt.

The process of preparing chocolate for drinking was elaborate and time-consuming. It was critical that the guardian goddesses of cocoa bless the undertaking.

Tonacatecutli was the goddess of the beans, and Calchi-uhtlucue was the goddess of the water. Help was needed from both. The beans were fermented, cured, roasted, and then ground into an intensely bitter powder. The chocolate powder was mixed with water flavored with hot chilies. Sometimes vanilla or honey were added. The liquid was then poured from one cup to another until it became frothy. The chocolate's magic resided in the froth. Without it, the drink was powerless. If the cocoa goddesses were properly honored and the chocolate sufficiently frothy, Aztec priests believed they would hear Quetzacoatl whispering on the breeze as they sipped the foam.

The Aztec emperor Montezuma was a great believer in chocolate's power. He always drank a golden goblet of chocolate before visiting one of his many wives. Each goblet was used only once. When Montezuma finished drinking he tossed the goblet into a sacred lake next to his harem's quarters. This ritual was repeated several times a day. Though this story sounds apocryphal, archeologists found hundreds of golden goblets in a dried lake bed near the ruins of Montezuma's palace.

Montezuma not only believed in the magic of chocolate, he believed in the legend of Quetzacoatl's return. When the Spanish conquistador Hernan Cortez arrived in Mexico during Montezuma's reign, the Aztecs thought he was the returning serpent god. Cortez and his band of followers were tall compared to the Aztecs. They had white skin and long beards like Quetzacoatl, and they came from the sea. Montezuma welcomed them into his palace and even served Cortez chocolate from a golden goblet. By the time the Aztecs realized the conquistadors were not benevolent gods, it was too late. The destruction of the Aztec empire had already begun.

Cortez returned to Spain with the riches of the New World—including cocoa beans. He regaled the Spanish court with tales of chocolate's amazing ability to boost energy and libido. The beans were entrusted to groups of monks skilled in the cultivation and use of pharmaceutical herbs. The monks analyzed the cocoa beans and reported that chocolate soothed digestive difficulties, pepped up sluggish metabolisms, and cured tuberculosis.

The monks adapted the Aztec drink recipe to suit European tastes. They omitted the chilies, added sugar, cinnamon, and nutmeg, and served the drink hot. Before long, the monks and the Spanish royal family and court were as addicted to chocolate as the Aztecs had been. In those days, aristocratic women took their cooks and favorite foods with them when they married. Even though the king of Spain tried to keep the existence of chocolate secret, it spread across Europe with Spanish brides.

Drinking chocolate became all the rage. Chocolate houses, which coffee houses were later modeled after, opened everywhere. The fashionable ladies of Paris served it in their salons, and Casanova drank it before visiting his lovers. Monks and nuns consumed gallons of chocolate, and Catholic cardinals drank it as they elected new popes. However, not everyone within the church was enamored with chocolate. The Jesuits believed it was a diabolical and dangerous stimulant, and they forbade members from drinking it. They were forced to change their position when they began having trouble attracting new recruits. Attempts to ban chocolate surfaced from time to time, but the church consistently ruled in chocolate's favor. Catholic officials were simply unwilling to give it up.

In 1897, the Swiss invented the milk chocolate candy bar. Mass production techniques followed, and soon inexpensive chocolate was available to everyone. Chocolate lost its mystique. People considered it a junk food that caused acne and tooth decay. But today chocolate's reputation is changing. We learn it may actually be good for us. It is full of healthy antioxidants, and nutritionists recently acknowledged what chocoholics have always known—eating chocolate produces a mild euphoric state similar to the feeling of falling in love. The Aztecs knew chocolate was a precious gift from the gods. Perhaps modern science is finally catching up.

A Chocolate Ritual

If you are facing a dilemma, unable to choose between several options, or simply need to clarify your thinking, a chocolate ritual may help you sort things out. Silently ask the Aztec cocoa goddesses Tonacatecutli and Calchiuhtlucue to help as you prepare the following recipe:

1	cup of water
1	two-inch square of a plain dark chocolate
⅛	tsp. powdered cinnamon
⅛	tsp. vanilla extract
⅛	tsp. chili powder
⅛	tsp. hot sauce or tabasco sauce
	Honey (optional)

Bring the water to a boil and add the chocolate, breaking it into smaller pieces if necessary. Add the spices, and stir until the chocolate melts. If it is too bitter, add a few drops of honey. Light a chocolate-scented candle or chocolate incense. Drink the chocolate very slowly, taking the time to savor its complex fragrance and spicy flavor.

Aztec priests listened for Quetzacoatl's whisper as they drank chocolate. Quiet your mind and allow the chocolate to stimulate your subconscious. Possible solutions to your problem will surface as you sip.

Coventina,
Northumbrian Well Goddess

by Cerridwen Iris Shea

Goddesses of water, wells, and spring were revered in Celtic Britain. Near Carrawburgh, in one of the forts along Hadrian's Wall (not far from Hexham), there reside the remains of Coventina's sacred site. Sacred wells were often sites of healing, with offerings also made for fertility and safe delivery for childbirth. These are usually feminine associations. What makes Coventina's Well doubly interesting is that there is evidence she was also worshiped by Roman soldiers who were assigned to Hadrian's Wall.

At Carrawburgh are also a Roman fort and a temple dedicated to Mithras. Mithras was a Persian god of light, often shown slaying a holy bull. A cult of Mithras grew over the years, and he was often considered a soldier's god. Within a short distance of each other, close to Hadrian's Wall, are a temple to the Roman-appropriated Persian soldier's god and a temple to a Celtic goddess of a healing well. It is an example of the Mingler at work.

A Goddess's Origins

Coventina's origins are obscure. Sometimes she is called "goddess" and sometimes she is called "nymph." In Caitlin Matthews's beautiful *Celtic Wisdom Tarot*, Coventina is represented as Card 14 of the Major Arcana. She is called "The Mingler" in this deck, on a card that is called "Temperance" in many other decks. The goddess's name gives clues to her origins. *Co-* in Latin means "together," and *venio* means "a coming," so her name indicates a coming together, or mingling. In Gaelic, interestingly, *co-* (also *cho-*) means "equally." *Ti* means "any human being," and *tinn* means "sick" or "unwell." Several combinations of these words would make sense in the naming of Coventina's healing well.

Coventina's temple has ten remaining altar stones. Four of these were dedicated by auxiliary Roman infantry units. The stones had carvings of thanksgiving on them. The phrase (when translated) "fulfilling a vow" appears on several of the altar stones. We can only wonder what kind of vow this inscription

refs to. Were the stones made as a thanksgiving for answered prayers? When excavated, a large amount of Roman coins were found in the well. The soldiers may have performed their rituals to Mithras, but they did not lack gratitude toward Coventina.

Coventina in a Modern World

We can appeal to Coventina in several ways. One is to convert a bathroom into a temple to her. Create a place of healing waters, where you can relax and wash away a stressful day, or start your morning with invigorating waters. Use soothing colors and appropriate scents. Set up an altar or shrine. Remember to leave thanks and offerings as often as you leave requests. I make my own bath salts and oils, and I named one in her honor that is specifically tailored to relaxing and restoring sore, overworked muscles.

If you can't redesign your entire bathroom to recreate Coventina's temple, you can keep a candle or two that you only use when you wish to heal with waters. Dedicate special bath salts, oils, or soap to Coventina, and use them in your ablutions.

You can also obtain a tabletop fountain, decorate it with stones in soothing, healing shades, and dedicate it to Coventina as a healing fountain. It can become part of your regular working sacred space, or you can assign it a site of its own. Spend time here in contemplation, and let your soul heal after a rough day. Take time to build a relationship with Coventina, a goddess who has listened and responded to petitioners for centuries. Coventina's origins may be obscure, but her relevance is timeless.

Fire Legends and Fire Magic

by Sheri Richerson

Legends abound as to how fire came to be, but all agree that in the beginning humans did not have fire. Some say animals caught fire and gave it to us, some say trees caught fire and that is why you can get fire from rubbing two sticks together, and still others claim fire was a gift from the gods.

An Apache legend says that long ago, before there was fire, animals and trees spoke to one another. The Fox, cleverest of the animals, spent his time trying to devise a way to create fire. Fox also wanted to learn the cry of the geese. One day he visited the geese and persuaded them to teach him how to fly. The geese made Fox promise that he would not open his eyes while in flight. They made him some wings and Fox began to fly with them and to practice their cry.

One day, however, Fox forgot his promise to keep his eyes shut. As darkness descended they flew over a village of fireflies.

The glare from the fireflies was bright enough to make Fox open his eyes, and instantly his wings collapsed. He could not control his fall and landed in the center of the firefly village, where a great fire burned continually.

Fox convinced the fireflies to show him how to get out of the village. Two of the fireflies led him to a cedar tree, which they said would bend down upon command and catapult him over the wall whenever he desired. With that knowledge, Fox began to plan to capture fire and escape with it.

First, Fox found the spring where the fireflies got their

water. While he was there he discovered colored earth, which he mixed with the water to make paint.

On his return to the village Fox suggested to the fireflies that they could have a dance festival. Fox said he could make the music. The fireflies thought this would be great fun, so they gathered more wood to make a larger fire. While gathering the wood Fox secretly tied a piece of cedar to his tail. Fox then made the first drum, so that he could create music for the fireflies to dance to.

Fox vigorously beat the drum with a stick and moved ever closer to the fire. He pretended to tire and handed the drums to the fireflies so that they could make their own music. While he was doing this he thrust his tail into the fire, lighting the cedar that was attached to his tail. He then escaped the ceremony, saying it was too hot there for him. He ran to the cedar tree and commanded it to bend down for him. Fox ran as quickly as he could with the fireflies in pursuit. As he ran, brush and wood along his path were ignited by the burning cedar on his tail.

Fox finally tired. He saw a hawk and gave the burning bark to him and instructed him to scatter sparks over the earth, which he did. The fireflies followed Fox to his burrow. The fireflies punished Fox for stealing their fire by ensuring that he could never use fire for his own purpose.

Fire Rituals

While there are many more stories associated with fire, the properties of fire and the various elements are important to consider before performing any type of fire magic. The untamed spirit that resides in the flames of a fire is something that many of us would like to use in our everyday lives. However, centuries later, fire still remains a free and dangerous spirit that must be dealt with carefully.

The energy from fire is masculine, and its direction is south. The southern direction means that fire represents the Sun at its extreme southern declination. This is where the Sun is able to fully warm Mother Earth and infuse her with energy that will bring forth an abundant harvest. The masculine energy is yang, which is also a positive energy.

Once fire became available to man, many believed that it had numerous magical powers. Some of that belief came from the stories associated with how fire came to be, and some came from various ceremonies that involve the use of fire magic.

Fire creates the spiritual warrior in service to the highest light of truth. Fire is the force that brings us the true purpose of life. However, fire is also lethal. Fire clears the path that begins and ends with the self. On the other hand, fire is no respecter of life. It will destroy humans, animals, plants, and property indiscriminately.

Fire can bestow courage, and helps us preserve a high quality in life. Fire can inspire us to connect with others in both worldly and otherworldly ways. Many fire rituals enable us to charge our energies through physical sensations. Fire energizes our essential, personal self. It also provides the energies of rebellion and revolutionary spirit. Fire is a force that requires a purity of purpose and a purity of heart from its warriors. Fire is a celebration of life that inspires the next phase of the journey of self-transformation.

One legend that clearly shows the power of fire comes from the myths and legends of California and the Old Southwest. According to the legend there was a man who loved two women. The women both laughed at him and refused to marry him. The man, upset, headed north in order to make himself a boat. Once the boat was finished he set the world on fire.

Fire magic is most often used to effect necessary change, to purify, for activation or rebirth, or even to burn away an illness or wrongdoing. Fire is the element of the spiritual body and of the spiritual plane.

There is no doubt that there is something mythical, arousing, mysterious, and magical about fire. Fire is the energy of life. Fire is also nature's cleanser. Its flames move and flicker and impart a wonderful warm feeling. Fire is said to change the environment from a mundane, common one to one of adventure and romance.

There is an art to fire magic. Fire magic is best done outside. Following is a fire magic spell. Use this spell with a touch of caution, and remember whatever you do will come back threefold on you. The signs of the zodiac that are associated with fire are Leo,

Aries, and Sagittarius. The magical associations connected to fire include power, creativity, motivation, leadership, purification, strength, anger, authority, loyalty, health, and vitality.

The element of fire brings out something in people that causes them to do things that normally they would not think of doing. Fire represents the cycle of life but also destroys anything in its pathway. On the flip side, fire does allow for regeneration. When working with fire magic, results come quickly because of the force within the flames. Fire is the most physical of all the elements. Fire is often used in magic to burn away old desires and bring on new ones.

Fire Magic

You can experience the magic of fire by trying one of these simple ideas. Watch closely as fire consumes and transforms an object such as paper or wood. Be sure to do this in a safe area—such as a BBQ pit, fireplace, or other similar location. Think about how fire affects you and why fire exists. Think about how fire fits into your everyday life and how often you are exposed to this magical element. Feel the heat of the fire, and see the light it creates. Finally, try to attune to fire.

Candle flames are another good way to experience fire magic. Simply light a candle, and meditate on the flame. Meditating on the flickering flames can sometimes help one achieve a new outlook on life. The flames can spur creativity that has been bottled up for some time. Fire can also kindle sexual desires. This is why fireplaces are often used in bedrooms or in honeymoon suites.

For those of you who wish to use essential oils instead of an actual flame to bring the element of fire into your life, try the following blend. It is particularly fitting for those who are drawn to the dance of flames. Mix equal parts of the following essential oils: ginger, basil, cardamom, cinnamon, and sweet orange. Try adding a few drops to an essential-oil burner, to the dryer while drying clothes, or to a massage oil or a bathtub.

When creating a fire ritual, the first rule must be ensuring the safety of the surrounding area and participants in the ritual. When preparing the area, make sure the spot is twice as wide as the material that will be burned. It is also a good idea to clear the area of tall grass or other objects that could easily catch on fire.

Make sure you have a supply of water or a hose in the area, as well as some extra shovels just in case. Most importantly, do not use chemical accelerants on the fire.

Finally, remember the embers will be carried into the air, but at some point they will come back down. Make sure people watch for these falling embers so that they do not get burned.

Often, fire rituals are done during the harvest season. This not only offers a wide array of burnable products to work with but also opens up farm fields, which should give plenty of room to build the bonfire.

Many of us have experienced bad luck. Here is a fire magic spell that will help to eliminate any bad luck that comes our way.

After dark, light a fire in a cauldron or other firesafe container. Take a piece of plain white paper, and cut it into a three-inch by three-inch square. On this piece of paper write the words "bad luck," then list all of the bad things that have been happening in your life. With a black marker draw a big "X" across the paper. Throughout this ritual visualize the bad things going away and not returning. Place the paper in the fire. Repeat these words three times while watching the paper burn.

Fire burn bright,
Turn my darkness into light.
Take away my bad luck,
And bring me nothing but good luck.
With this fire burn bright,
Bring me good luck, bring me light.
So mote it be.

Continue to mediate on the spell, visualizing the outcome. If possible, stay with the fire and allow it to extinguish itself. If this is not possible, extinguish the fire when you are done.

Feng Shui Remedies

by S. Y. Zenith

For the Chinese, the art and science of feng shui has been a way of life since ancient times. The Great Wall of China is a monumental example of feng shui that has withstood the ravages of time.

Masters of feng shui adopt various forms of thought and practice. Some practices are derived from ancient methods, while others are expanded upon by a master's own interpretations and experiences. One doesn't have to be a feng shui master to utilize the mysteries of the philosophy. There are simple and practical methods useful to the layman.

Generally, one needs only the basic tools of good and mindful personal conduct, intuition, and instinct. The rest will fall into place in time through personal experience. A true and honest heart turns misfortune into good luck. Dark thoughts are like mirrors or ponds that reflect. Feng shui may be utilized to facilitate outer changes and bring about better fortunes. However, personal conduct is what sows seeds for reaping appropriate harvests.

Drawing Prosperity

When business stagnates, place a small round fountain near the front door and turn it on for several hours every day. The direction of the flowing water should be positioned toward the business premises, not outward. If the establishment has a foyer or reception area, place the fountain there. A large framed mirror hung opposite the front door will draw customers and finances. Pictures of pleasing landscapes can also be hung in the foyer.

Happy Plant

Plants are helpful in correcting unbalanced or negative vibrations. *Dracaena fragrans massangeana* is also known as the Chinese money tree. This plant is common in many Asian homes and businesses dating back thousands of years. If unable to find this particular plant, any plant with round leaves will effective. Take good care of the plant. As the leaves grow, finances will be given a boost. This plant should be placed near the entrance, in the living room and study, but not in the bedroom. It thrives best in diffused light and when fertilized sparingly.

The jade plant *(Crassula argentea)* is also commonly referred to as the money tree, and is highly favored for drawing good fortune. The Chinese rank jade as the most precious stone due to its green color (which symbolizes health and longevity). Jade is also known to deflect evil. Activate jade plant energies by placing a piece of red cloth on the spot where the plant is to be positioned. On top of the red cloth, place a round mirror. String together three I-Ching coins with red ribbon, and place them on top of the mirror. Put the potted jade plant on top of the coins.

L-Shaped Desks

L-shaped desks are likened to the form of the Chinese cleaver. It is believed that a person with such a desk would not find it difficult to convince customers. It also assists the person behind it in collecting money. However, an L-shaped desk can also make the occupant feel restless and irritable. The intensity of these feelings depends largely on the individual's inner well-being and ability to control negativity. To reduce or prevent negativity, place a quartz crystal or an amethyst near the computer and a round-leafed plant on the desk. If working for a company, place the desk in the corner diagonal to the entrance of the room where there is a clear view of everyone entering. It is a rule of thumb not to sit with the back facing the entrance.

The Bagua Mirror

The bagua mirror is a small round mirror set within an octagonal, red, green, and gold frame inscribed with I-Ching symbols.

It is available in shops throughout the world's Chinatowns. The mirror itself draws negative energy, while the octagonal frame transmutes these harmful energies and renders them harmless. This mirror is traditionally placed at the top of the front door to deflect evil spirits from entering.

Convex Mirrors

Convex mirrors are widely available. They usually have a yellow base with inscribed I-Ching symbols. Convex mirrors are not for hanging indoors, but the exterior of homes, shops, or offices—especially if the front door faces a crossroads, the sharp edges of tall buildings, or a street with traffic rushing in the door's direction. When the convex mirror is placed within the interior of a property, it creates inauspicious conditions. One or more persons within the premises will suffer headaches, ill health, emotional turbulences, insecurity, and scant or dwindling finances. Relationships may also suffer due to misunderstandings and miscommunication.

Gold Fish

An aquarium containing nine goldfish near an entrance will help increase the flow of chi, drawing good fortune and harmony. A picture or scroll of nine gold fish can be used as a substitute. Odd numbers of fish avert evil omens. A reading into the effectiveness of this particular number of gold fish is based on numerology: three times three equals nine, a potent male yang number. This number represents growth and movement. It is best used for generating harmony and prosperity.

Dragon-headed Turtle

The dragon-headed turtle has a baby atop its back and rescues stagnant relationships and persons who are single. This feng shui remedy assists long-lasting one-to-one relationships or attracts new beginnings. The dragon symbolizes protection and good luck. The turtle is synonymous with long life and wisdom for relationships. The baby turtle beckons fresh beginnings. To energize this feng shui cure, secure a red ribbon to the mouth of the dragon-headed turtle and place it in the bedroom. It is recommended that the turtle be placed where it faces the window looking outside after dusk. In the morning, it should be turned to face the interior of the bedroom so that its energy is not exhausted.

Three-legged Toad

The three-legged toad god sits on a pile of gold nuggets and carries a string of six ancient Chinese coins on each side of his body. This is used for drawing success and money luck. To activate the toad god, place it within view of the front door. In the morning, put a coin in the god's mouth to draw prosperity. In the evening, remove the coin and turn him to face the interior. Remember to spend your money wisely or it will diminish.

Clearing Clutter

Traditional Chinese observe an annual springcleaning of homes before Chinese New Year. Apart from its role as tradition and in advancing good hygiene, this was meant to clear old and stale energies to pave the way for New Year blessings.

Moving energy is healthy energy. Stuck energy is like a pool of water left untended to turn murky. Every item we have is connected to us by strands of unseen energy. One who is swamped by clutter is likely to feel drained, lethargic, or easily exhausted. A clearing-out process rejuvenates the soul and uplifts the aura. Clearing clutter is also a therapeutic exercise when performed as a meditation process. While junk is being cleared on the external level, there is a corresponding cleansing of space within the soul.

If the home is cluttered, it is pointless to utilize feng shui enhancement objects, as these would only aggravate problems instead of alleviating them. A home or office in disarray reflects a disorganized mind and scattered soul. This commonly results in unresolve in both physical and material matters. Ridding clutter serves a dual purpose if you donate unwanted items to charity, as this allows others less fortunate to enjoy them while you are being set free of unwanted energies.

The Early Gods of Britain and Wales

by Sharynne MacLeod NicMhacha

The pagan Celts of the Island of Britain worshiped a wide variety of powerful gods and goddesses. Some were invoked for protection, abundance, fertility, and healing, while others were associated with sovereignty, various skills, magical trees or animals, or sacred sites.

To help you develop a connection to these deities in your ritual workings, here are the names and the most important attributes of each.

Alator: "He who nourishes his people"; a tribal god of abundance and protection.

Andraste: Goddess of warfare and victory; she was invoked by the British warrior-queen Boudicca during her revolt against the Romans.

Beltatucadros: "Fair shining one"; a god of war from Cumberland and Westmorland.

Belinus: "Shining one"; a Celtic deity venerated in Britain, Gaul, and northern Italy who may have been associated with the fires of Beltane.

Braciaca: "God of intoxication"; this deity's name is derived from a word for "malt," and he may have been associated with ritualized beverage ceremonies for battle or religion.

Brigantia: "High one"; a powerful and very widely worshiped goddess whose name is similar to the Irish goddess Bridget. She was worshiped by a tribe (the Brigantes), associated with several rivers, and invoked for protection and abundance.

Callirius: "God of the hazel"; a deity of forests, woodlands, and the sacred hazel tree.

Cernunnos: "Horned one"; this widely venerated god was worshiped in Britain and Gaul and is associated with abundance and fertility. His symbols are the stag and ram-headed serpent, and he was invoked for protection and plenty.

Cocidius: "Strong or swift one"; a war god from northern Britain who seems to have also been associated with the wilderness and with protection.

Condatis: "God of the watersmeet"; a deity associated with war, protection, and healing (ideas that are related in Celtic tradition).

Epona: "Divine horse goddess"; this powerful and widely worshiped goddess was associated with horses, abundance, sovereignty, magical birds, and passages to the otherworld.

Genii Cucullati: "Hooded spirits"; this trio of hooded male fertility figures with emphasized phallic attributes often appears in connection with the trio of mother goddesses.

Lugos: The name of this widely venerated god may be derived from a Gaulish word for "raven" or a Celtic word denoting "light." He appears in Welsh myth as Lleu, and is a many-skilled deity associated with protection, healing, abundance, wisdom, and many arts.

Loucetius: "Lightning"; a god of healing waters who was invoked at Aquae Sulis (Bath).

Maponus: "Divine son"; this popular deity, a son of Matrona (the "divine mother"), was associated with poetry and music, the sacred hunt, greenery, and the forest.

Matres: "The mothers"; images of three female divinities, often the same age and associated with symbols of fertility, plenty, and abundance, are found in Romanized Britain.

Nemetona: "Goddess of the sacred grove"; a goddess of healing waters invoked at Bath.

Nodons: "He who bestows wealth" or "cloud maker"; a widely venerated healing deity worshiped at a great temple on the banks of the Severn river, and symbolically represented by the Sun and bodies of water.

Olloudios: "Great tree"; a god of protection and strength, likened to a sacred tree.

Ratis: "Goddess of the fortress"; a powerful female deity who protected the fortress.

Rigonemetis: "King of the sacred grove"; a tribal god worshiped in the third century AD.

Sabrina: Goddess of the Severn River, which runs between modern England and Wales.

Sulis: Patron goddess of the warm healing springs at Aquae Sulis (modern Bath); she was invoked for healing and protection.

Taranis/Tanarus: "The thunderer"; a protective tribal god associated with the sky realm and thunder; his symbols are the wheel, the club or lightning bolt, and the goose (associated with war, strength, protection, and healing).

Toutatis: "God of the tribe"; a god of war and protection.

Verbeia: "She of the cattle"; a goddess of the river Wharfe and of sacred springs.

Vinotanus: "God of vines"; as the name implies, a god of vines and wine, and of woodlands and greenery.

Vitiris: A protective war god sometimes associated with attributes similar to the horned god; he may have been invoked in triple form, and his symbols are the boar and serpent.

In medieval times, elements of British mythology found their way into the storyteller's craft and were preserved in the group of Welsh tales known as the Mabinogi (a word that probably means "a group of tales revolving around divine figures associated with the god Maponus"). While the figure of Mabon only makes an appearance in one of the stories, as a hero of a sacred boar hunt and imprisoned son of Modron, many of these tales focus on the families or relatives of a "divine youth."

Amaethon: "Divine ploughman"; a magician and divine farmer, he taught magic to Gwydion. His theft of a dog and roebuck from the otherworld resulted in the conflict known as *Cad Goddeu* ("The Battle of the Trees"). He is the son of Dôn.

Arawn: One of the rulers of the Welsh otherworld *Annwn* or *Annwfn*; he is depicted as a hunter on a large dappled-gray horse with pale gray garments (white or gray animals are often connected with the otherworld).

Arianrhod: "Silver wheel"; Mother of the bright, skilled god Lleu and the divine figure Dylan who was associated with the sea. Although she appears in an uncomplimentary light in these tales, she was probably originally a powerful, highly revered Moon deity—daughter of Dôn and Beli Mawr and sister of Gwydion.

Beli Mawr: "Beli the great"; a divine ancestor god, consort of Dôn, father of Arianrhod.

Bran: "Raven"; a warrior and leader of people in time of need—often associated with land, migration, and travel. After his legendary death his head lived on for some time until it was buried in London to ward off illness or plague. He is the brother of Manawydan and Branwen.

Branwen: "White or bright raven"; the sister of Bran, associated with the starling. She was married to the Irish king Matholwch.

Cerridwen: This divine sorceress was said to be learned in "the three arts": magic, enchantment, and divination. With her husband Tegid Foel she had an unfortunate son named Morfran ("great crow"), who was also called Afagddu ("utter darkness"). She produced a magical brew to give her son the gifts of wisdom and prophecy. The precious three drops of elixir fell instead on the young lad Gwion Bach, and this transformed him into the seer-poet Taliesin.

Dôn: "Divine ancestress and mother goddess"; her name may be related to the mother Irish goddess Danu. Dôn's children include Arianrhod, Gwydion, Gofannon, Amaethon, and Gilfaethwy.

Gwydion: A divine magician, brother of Arianrhod, and foster-father of Lleu. He plays a prominent role in many of the tales of the Mabinogi.

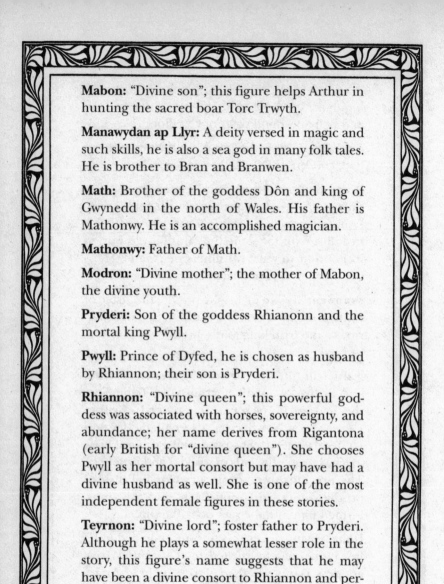

Mabon: "Divine son"; this figure helps Arthur in hunting the sacred boar Torc Trwyth.

Manawydan ap Llyr: A deity versed in magic and such skills, he is also a sea god in many folk tales. He is brother to Bran and Branwen.

Math: Brother of the goddess Dôn and king of Gwynedd in the north of Wales. His father is Mathonwy. He is an accomplished magician.

Mathonwy: Father of Math.

Modron: "Divine mother"; the mother of Mabon, the divine youth.

Pryderi: Son of the goddess Rhianonn and the mortal king Pwyll.

Pwyll: Prince of Dyfed, he is chosen as husband by Rhiannon; their son is Pryderi.

Rhiannon: "Divine queen"; this powerful goddess was associated with horses, sovereignty, and abundance; her name derives from Rigantona (early British for "divine queen"). She chooses Pwyll as her mortal consort but may have had a divine husband as well. She is one of the most independent female figures in these stories.

Teyrnon: "Divine lord"; foster father to Pryderi. Although he plays a somewhat lesser role in the story, this figure's name suggests that he may have been a divine consort to Rhiannon and perhaps even Pryderi's divine father.

The Magic of the Crystal Ball

by Sedwyn

The crystal ball is perhaps the most widely known divination device. It is one of a number of objects (including mirrors, bowls of water, and almost any reflect surface) that can be used for scrying. The mystery and misunderstanding about crystal balls and scrying is also widespread.

Fifth-century Christians believed that "witches and evil spirits" inhabited scrying devices, and they would use them to catch gazers in a hypnotic trance in order to pass devilish messages. Utilizing a crystal ball was strongly discouraged, but by the seventeenth century it was common for German priests to place one on the altar during services. Priests also instructed parishioners in the correct prayers to use when scrying.

Children under the age of twelve were frequently employed to act as "intermediaries with the angels in the stones." Children were used as gazers because they were believed to be pure of spirit and more open to communication than adults.

In England, Queen Elizabeth I consulted on various occasions with Dr. John Dee, a philosopher, alchemist, and mathematician, for advice in governmental matters. A smoky quartz ball that belonged to Dee is now in the British Museum. Edward Kelly teamed up with Dee to interpret angelic communications, which became the basis for the Enochian system of magic. However, the proverbial pendulum eventually swung back, and in 1824 a law was passed in England making the practice of divination punishable by up to three months of hard labor.

Whether or not the church sanctioned the use of scrying devices, they were used and mentioned throughout classic literature. Chaucer's knight in "The Squire's Tale" arrives with a mirror that allows those who look into it to see the "coming shadow of adversity." Shakespeare also uses this device in his plays *Measure for Measure* and *Macbeth*. Writing in the thirteenth century, Roger Bacon's stories mention scrying with a crystal ball that allowed someone to see what was happening in faraway places. Centuries later, several of J. R. R. Tolkien's characters in *Lord of the Rings* use

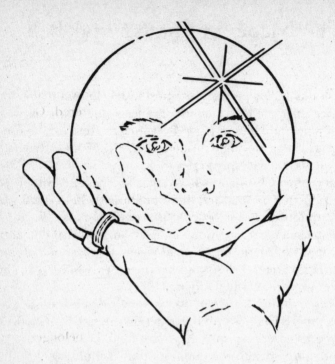

crystal balls called palatirs that allowed them to see and communicate at great distance.

In Victorian England, a form of the crystal ball became popular as the garden gazing ball. This globe of colored glass was intended to reflect the beauty of the surrounding garden and to produce a calm, peaceful state of mind for the gazer.

How a Crystal Ball May Work

In their various natural forms, crystals have been used for healing by many cultures throughout history. People of the past knew that disease may not always originate in the physical body. The "subtle" body, or the aura, may encounter problems or become unbalanced, and this then can manifest into the physical body. A crystal emits vibrations that affect the flow of energy around it, and this can help resolve issues in the subtle body. This is the basis for crystal therapy.

Vibrations surround us all the time, but we are mainly aware of them as sound and light. Vibrations are carried through our bodies by electrical impulses that jump the synapses between the cells. This "electrical wiring" is part of the electromagnetic field that extends outside of our bodies. The vibrations of crystals interact with this electromagnetic field.

As previously mentioned, people believed that crystal balls were inhabited by spiritual beings, but by the early twentieth century, more scientific explanations were being offered. George Kunz, gemologist for Tiffany & Company in the early 1900s, suggested that as one gazes into a crystal ball the optic nerve eventually tires and stops sending visual data to the brain. When this happens, the brain is able to project information. According to Kunz, the gazer believes he or she is receiving information from the crystal, but in fact it is coming from within.

This seems partially plausible. It is also possible that the crystal ball simple helps induce an altered state of consciousness in the gazer. Just as the monotony of rhythmic drumming can produce such a state, perhaps crystals produce a similar effect. Like shamanic journeying and astral projection, one must travel inward in order to reach other realms.

The first time I gazed into a crystal ball, which belonged to a friend, I felt mesmerized and drawn into it. Looking back, I think that a shift in consciousness occurred—something that I had not expected.

Getting Started

There are many types of crystal balls available. Sometimes they are clear as plain glass, or they may be colored, frosted, or with inclusions. Some people feel that interior frost and cracks inhibit energy; others believe they enhance energy. There is no right or wrong choice, because everyone's energy is unique. It is important that the energy of the crystal ball feel comfortable with your energy. As to size, it should fit easily in your hands because sometimes you may want to hold it while gazing. Overall, it is important for your crystal to be comfortable for you, and not too heavy.

Before using it, the crystal ball needs to be cleansed and attuned to the elements. I advise against soaking it (or any crystal) in salt water, because this will leave a salty film on its surface. To consecrate and attune it, begin by passing it through the smoke of burning sage or mugwort or your favorite incense (representing the element of fire). Set the ball on a plate with potting soil (earth), and then place it on a porch or by an open window (air) overnight in the light of the Full Moon (water). As you are doing this, repeat the incantation:

Crystal ball the shape of Luna,
Deep your secrets lie within.
By fire, earth, air, and water,
Now it is time to begin.

When you are ready to use your crystal ball, cast a circle and create sacred space. Sit in a darkened room with a candle (or other light source) behind you, so it is not reflected in the ball. Hold the ball in your hands and relax. You may want to sit in silence or use meditational music or a shamanic drumming CD.

As you sit in meditation before scrying, become aware of the weight of the ball in your hands. This sphere has the shape, energy, and integrity of your sacred circle. See the ball in your mind's eye. Become aware of your energy moving from your heart center and down your arms to the ball. It may help to visualize this as a soft blue light connecting your energy with the energy of your crystal ball.

The crystal ball is a tool to aid in understanding and deepening your spirituality. Bring a question to mind that you need help with, or simply leave you mind open to receive information that you may need. When you are ready, place the crystal ball on your altar and look into it with a soft gaze. Don't expect a clear picture as though you are watching a movie. Images will be subtle and brief, like reflections of clouds moving across the surface of a lake.

Another way to scry with your crystal ball is to combine it with a picture. This can be a card from a tarot deck, an image of a deity with whom you feel a close affinity, or a picture of a place you have visited or would like to visit. Begin your meditation or centering, and have the light source behind you. Place your chosen picture upside down on the altar behind the crystal ball. Viewed through the crystal, the image will appear right side up. Use a soft gaze and watch for subtle alterations within the image.

To keep attuned to your crystal ball, place it on your night table or wherever it will be within sight when you sleep. In this way your subconscious mind and the natural relaxed rhythm of your energy will interact with the energy of the crystal. You may want to coordinate when you place the ball by your bedside with Moon phases or various events in your astrological cycle.

It may take time before you see anything, because you and the crystal ball need to attune to each other. Remember, the information will be subtle. Be patient and you will be rewarded.

Winter Stores Spell

by Laurel Reufner

Here are a few recipes that take advantage of this dark season of spices and roasted things.

Vinaigrette Dressing Roast

1   package basil vinaigrette salad dressing mix

1   cup olive oil

½   cup red wine vinegar

1   four-pound beef roast

Begin by placing the roast in a large and sturdy freezer bag. In a small bowl, whisk together the dressing mix, olive oil, and vinegar to make a marinade. Pour marinade into the freezer bag, and coat the roast. Place the bag in the refrigerator and let it marinate for at least four hours, or more if possible, giving the bag a good shake to recoat the roast on a frequent basis. Bake the roast, with part of the marinade, in a 375°F oven for one to two hours, or until you are certain it is done.

Garlic Roasted Potatoes

My young daughters absolutely love these next two vegetable dishes. They are a nice change from plain vegetables.

4–5   medium baking potatoes

2–3   Tbl. olive oil

1   Tbl. garlic powder

1   tsp. dried basil or rosemary

1   tsp. teaspoon salt

¼–½   tsp. pepper

Wash and peel the potatoes, then cut them into one-inch pieces. Place them in a bowl, and drizzle the olive oil on top. Stir if necessary to make sure all the pieces are evenly coated. In a small bowl, combine the garlic, basil or rosemary, salt, and pepper. Shake the seasoning mixture over the oil-coated potatoes, stirring gently as you go so as to evenly season them. Place the potatoes on a baking sheet in a single layer, and place the sheet in a 350ºF oven for twenty to thirty minutes until they are golden and a fork can be easily poked into one of the larger pieces. For even roasting, give the baking sheet a half-turn about halfway through their cooking time.

Spiced Candied Carrots

1   one-pound bag of baby peeled carrots

1½ Tbl. butter

¼   tsp. ground cinnamon

⅛   tsp. ground nutmeg

Steam the carrots until they are just done. (A fork will easily go into them, but they aren't yet mushy.) Place the carrots into a serving bowl, and put the butter on them to melt. Once the butter is melted, sprinkle on the cinnamon and nutmeg. Gently stir the carrots to coat them with the melted butter and spices. Feel free to adjust the spices to taste.

Pfefferneusse, or Pepper Cookies

These German Christmas cookies take a bit of time to make, but are well worth it. They are a wonderful addition to a cup of hot tea. While not absolutely necessary, try making them about a month in advance so they have time to age.

1   cup sugar

1   cup dark corn syrup

½   cup honey

1   cup butter

2   eggs

5   cups flour

½   tsp. baking soda

1	Tbl. baking powder
½	tsp. black pepper
⅛	tsp. ground cloves
1	tsp. ground nutmeg
1	tsp. ground cinnamon
½	tsp. anise seed (optional)
	Fruit juice (citrus is recommended)

Heat the first four ingredients over low heat until the sugar is dissolved and the butter is melted. Cool the mixture, and add one egg at a time to it, mixing to blend in the first egg fully before adding the next. Sift together the dry ingredients. Gradually add the other ingredients and mix well. Cover and refrigerate overnight.

The next day form the dough into small rolls that are about a half inch in diameter. Wrap and chill the rolls for easier slicing. Remove one roll of dough at a time, leaving the rest in the refrigerator. Using a sharp knife, cut dough into slices that are one-eighth to one-quarter inches thick. Place the pieces on a greased cookie sheet, and, using your finger, place a drop of juice in the center of each cookie. Bake at 375°F for ten to twelve minutes.

How to Write a Spell

by James Kambos

Words have power. All words, whether written or spoken, are alive with the energy we give them. This magical concept was well understood by ancient magicians.

The first primitive alphabets probably originated about 3100 BC in southern Mesopotamia and were developed by the Sumerians. Early alphabets were a combination of words and symbols. These were used primarily to record business and monetary transactions; however, some writings that survived on clay tablets indicate some of these inscriptions were spells and prayers. These were among the earliest written charms. Most experts agree the ancient Egyptians produced one of the most extensive collections of written spells in human history.

In time, possessing any written charms or magical wisdom was dangerous and could lead to charges of black magic, and so the practice of writing down of magical lore declined. Magical knowledge was passed on orally. Only very old Books of Shadows or magical grimoires survived.

Today, a spell or affirmation that you write yourself is powerful, because it allows you to focus on your wish and create a resonant energy. The first step in writing a spell is the same as with a spoken spell: You must have a goal. Once one is clear in your mind you'll be ready to put it on paper. Notice, I did say on paper. A spell that is handwritten is much more powerful than one which is typed. When you write your affirmation by hand your powers of concentration are stronger and energy will flow from your heart and into your power hand. This

energy then streams from your pen and finally takes visual form on the paper. As your spell begins to take physical form on paper, it also starts to manifest itself in the unseen realm of spirit. And at this moment true magic begins.

When you write a spell you are in effect writing a letter to the divine spirit. Keeping this in mind, the materials you use should be of good quality. I suggest the paper have a high cotton content and be pure white. Use a pen you are comfortable with and that contains blue or black ink. The pen and paper you use should be treated as magical tools—do not use them for anything else, and let no one else touch them.

Some magical traditions use red ink, because red is the color of the life force. The choice is yours. If you are artistic, a design relating to your goal is a nice addition. I like to include a simple drawing at the top of the page, depicting the Moon phase I am working with.

Begin your spell-writing when you are sure you won't be disturbed. Your affirmation need not be lengthy. A paragraph or a few well chosen sentences will do. Here is one example of a written spell (for protection during travel).

I, (your name here), *will that my trip be safe and secure in all ways. I will travel to* (your destination) *safely and return home safely. I am protected from all danger. All forms of transportation will be safe and secure. I thank the divine power* (or your personal deity) *for his/her aid. I write this spell for the good of all, and according to the free will of all. So mote it be.*

Once you are finished writing, fold the paper as a letter. Place it in a special drawer or box. You may sprinkle herbs in the drawer that would be appropriate for your desired goal. Tell no one about your spell. A written spell may be kept forever. It may be carried with you, or destroyed in a respectful manner at a designated time, after the spell has worked.

If you work with runes, or some other magical alphabet that you thoroughly understand, you may use it to tap into extra magical power. Writing in a secret alphabet will serve to trigger your psychic powers. But never write a charm in a language you don't know well.

How to Combine the Written Word with the Elements

The masters of written spellcrafting, such as the ancient Egyptians and the whirling dervishes, took the art of spell writing one step further. If needed, the written charm would be combined with one or more of the elements—earth, air, fire, or water. This would complete the spell: For example, if a spell was written to combat an illness the paper with the written spell would be soaked in water, the ink would wash off, and the ill individual would then drink the inky water.

Here is another example. Let's say you wished to rid yourself of a bad habit. You could write your spell during a waning Moon, then soak the paper in salt water and end the ritual by burying the paper and pouring the salt water onto the ground. In this way, you've combined the written charm with the elements of water and earth, where the negativity will be absorbed and purified. An alternative method would be to burn the spell and disperse the ashes to the wind. Here you'd be combining the written word with fire and air to achieve your goal.

Other Factors To Consider

The practice of writing spells may be used by different religious systems. For instance, Pagans may direct a written spell to a specific god or goddess. Christians may petition a saint to aid them.

As is the case in much magical work, timing is crucial. You should try to time your spell-writing with Moon phases and other astrological or seasonal influences. Days of the week can also enhance the power of the written word. Here is a list of the days of the week with planetary and magical associations.

Sunday (the Sun): Health and vitality, general well-being.

Monday (the Moon): Home, family matters, children, women's issues, and magic in general.

Tuesday (Mars): Strength and protection.

Wednesday (Mercury): Communication and travel. A good day to write a spell when you can't decide which other day would be best.

Thursday (Jupiter): Money, wealth, expanding a career or business.

Friday (Venus): Love and friendship; also, home decorating or remodeling.

Saturday (Saturn): Dealing with fears or serious thinking; helping the needy.

If you have your spell planned well in advance, the time of day you write can also add benefits. Magically speaking, the day, like the year, is divided into four parts—morning, noon, sunset, and midnight—each with magical attributes.

Morning: Spells written at this time could include anything dealing with new beginnings—a new job, purchasing a new home, or a new romance.

Noon: This is the solar hour, which deals with health and energy, and spells intended to increase anything; also it is good for expanding a business or adding passion to romance.

Sunset: Twilight spells could deal with spirituality, emotions, or contacting the spiritual realm. Write a spell now to end something, such as a bad habit.

Midnight: The traditional "Witching hour" is a good time to write spells concerned with secrets or occult wisdom. If you aren't sure when to write a spell, midnight is always good.

Spell writing is nearly a lost magical art. If you combine your own ideas with some of those above, you can use the written word to perform powerful magic. Let your imagination go, and customize your spells to suit your individual needs.

Louhi,
Fierce Goddess of the Arctic

by Lily Gardner

Louhi (pronounced "low-hee") has a bad reputation. Books describe her as the evil Witch from the lands north of Finland. But is she? What we know about her comes from the Finnish epic poem, *The Kalevala,* told from the viewpoint of three sorcerer gods. Louhi, as the queen of the shamans, is their chief adversary, which may explain why she is called an evil Witch.

The Kalevala is rich in meaning. It is a metaphor for the Viking invasions from the west, a time when Finland turned from a matrifocal to a patriarchal culture. It is also a story of creation and a lesson in shamanism.

In this story of the shift from a woman-based to a man-based culture, Louhi stands one against three in a contest of wills when the sorcerer brothers invade her land. The three try to make deals with her, but it becomes clear that the "Witch goddess" can not be outwitted, intimidated, or bribed by the gods of the south.

It was understood at the beginning of the epic that the Kalevala brothers were not new to the lands of the north. They journeyed north for knowledge and treasure, just as the shamans journeyed to the realm of the spirit world. The far north was synonymous with the underworld, and Louhi, the crone goddess who ruled the Arctic, defended the gates.

The brothers reached the underworld by crossing a stream that separated the kingdoms of the living and the dead. On the far bank of the stream was a waterfall that turned reality upside down. The ancient Finns believed that the spirit world was the exact opposite of the living world. On the other side of the waterfall stood the iron gate of Louhi, the intersection of the living and the spirit world and the intersection of heaven and earth.

Once inside the gates to the spirit world, two of the Kalevala brothers beheld the Rainbow Maiden. She was Louhi's favorite daughter and more beautiful than any earthly woman. The two sorcerer gods asked for her hand, but she told them bluntly that she preferred the single life, as she said:

> Cold is iron in the winter,
> Thus the lives of married women;
> Maidens living with their mothers
> Are like ripe and ruddy berries;
> Married women, far too many,
> Are like dogs enchained in kennel,
> Rarely do they ask for favors,
> Not to wives are favors given.

To win her heart, one of the gods forged the Sampo, a marvelous mill that ground sackfuls of grain, gold, and salt. Its beautiful cover portrayed the starry heavens. The Sampo is at the heart of *The Kalevala* and symbolizes many things. It is the Finnish version of the cauldron of regeneration. Not coincidentally, it resembles the amanita mushroom, which Siberian shamans consumed to induce the holy visions they sought. It represents the womb and female sexuality. It symbolizes the cosmos.

The brothers gave the Sampo to Louhi in the hopes that she would put in a good word for them with her daughter. She accepted the gift, but allowed her daughter to decide whether or not to wed.

Fearing the brothers might take the Sampo back, Louhi planted it nine fathoms deep in the roots of the Copper Mountain. Meanwhile, the Rainbow Maiden finally decided to wed one of the brothers. They lived happily together for less than a year before she was murdered by a rival sorcerer. The brother, in his

grief, fashioned a new bride of solid gold. When he didn't find the artificial bride satisfactory, he journeyed back to the north to ask Louhi for another daughter. Understandably, she refused.

The brother in a rage coaxed his brothers to join forces with him. They stole the Sampo from Louhi. Such a theft of wisdom is common in myth. It portrays how the father god steals the essence of life, creativity, and inspiration from the female vessel.

The brothers sailed the stream that divides the two worlds. Louhi, turned eagle, swept over the boat and snatched up the Sampo. One of the brothers struck her with his sword and severed the talon that held the magical Sampo. The Sampo broke into pieces and fell in the sea. The lost pieces became the source of wealth for the lands of Kalevala.

In an act of revenge, Louhi kidnapped the Sun and the Moon and held them captive in her Copper Mountain. The world was plunged in darkness. Eventually she was forced to return them. And so we have the Finnish solstice myth.

Louhi, to my thinking, is the true hero of *The Kalevala*, the queen of the north and no-nonsense goddess of magic. Call upon her when you need to assert yourself, when you wish assistance in your magic or when you desire more wisdom. Pray to her when you see the Polestar up in the skies. Honor her at Yule and all through the winter months.

Skadi, Norse Goddess of Winter

by Lily Gardner

Skadi, the patron of Scandinavia, began life as a giant and soon became the goddess of winter. She is bleak and fearsome, but also beautiful and bright as fresh snowfall. Her name means "shadow." She is the dark of the year, but she is also called "wise-bride," and is a giant warrior dressed in white fur and crystal armor.

Why was Skadi admitted into the realm of the gods and made a goddess herself, given the age-old conflict between the gods and giants?

In tales, the gods often ventured into the lands of the giants, or Jotunn, seeking both treasure and knowledge, and often the gods and Jotunn fought. The most famous stories in Norse mythology were the battles between gods and giants. But what we notice when we look at Norse mythology as a whole is that for every battle between the gods and the giants, there is cooperation or intermarriage between the two races. The Norse Pagans knew that to survive in the world, one needed to live in harmony with the forces of nature. Skadi illustrates this balance.

Her Jotunn home was in the castle Thrymheim ("house of uproar"), high in the mountains of the land of the giants. Her father, Thiassi, kidnapped the goddess Idun and her golden apples of youth. Without the golden apples, the gods and goddesses of Aesir quickly aged. Some gods grew spindle-shanked, others paunchy, and many of them lost their teeth.

The mischievous god Loki was made to confess how he had helped Thiassi steal the goddess of youth and was forced by the gods to steal her back. He borrowed

Freyja's hawk-feather cloak and flew to the land of the giants, stealing Idun and flying back. Thiassi, however, gave chase in the shape of a huge eagle. Loki flew into Aesir, Idun held tight in his claw, as Odin, father of the gods, built a huge bonfire within the realm's gates. Thiassi flew into the fire and was consumed by its flames.

When Skadi heard the news of her father's death, she clad herself in crystal armor and strode to the hall of Aesir demanding blood price for her father. The Aesir negotiated with this formidable giant. She agreed not to take a life as payment under two conditions: if the gods could make her laugh, and if she could chose a husband from one of them.

The gods gave Loki the task of jester. He tied the hair from a goat's beard to his testicles, and the tug-of-war that ensued made Skadi laugh.

Her choice of husbands from the gods of Aesir was granted on the condition that she choose blindfolded. Only the feet of the gods were visible to her. The most beautiful feet belonged to Njord, god of the sea, and not to the most beautiful god, Baldur.

The resulting marriage between Skaldi and Njord was an unhappy one. She couldn't rest from the cries of the seagulls in his kingdom and he couldn't rest from the howls of the wolves in her mountainous kingdom. They cohabitated only at the equinoxes when the summer half and the winter half of the year were in balance. This balance of light and dark is the heart of Skadi's legend.

Skadi is the goddess of independent women. Single mothers and women who find themselves in a man's world call upon Skadi for help. If we find ourselves in danger in a winter landscape, we can call on Skadi.

The Key to Your Dreams

by Janina Renée

Library shelves are overflowing with books that recount the fantastic adventures, wonderful insights, creative solutions, and poignant prophecies that other people have culled from their dreams. But suppose your own dreams are very prosaic—always the same old people, places, and situations. They don't seem to tell you anything that you don't already know. Here is an idea that may help open a new dimension to your dream world.

Keep an old skeleton key or clock key by your bedside. Hang it perhaps from your bedpost by a purple ribbon, or keep it in some way close by so you can handle it and contemplate it a few moments before falling asleep.

As you contemplate, picture yourself standing before a long arched door—key in hand. If you're able to achieve a moment of lucidity while you dream, try to recall this image: you, the key, and the door. Picture yourself putting the key in the lock and turning it.

What does this open door reveal? Maybe it is a fancifully decorated room, an enclosed garden, or a staircase leading up or down to someplace else. Let your dream take it from there, with the assurance you'll see something new and worthwhile. Even if the dream doesn't get interesting, you'll still have made some of your own luck. It is widely agreed that "to dream of a key is a good sign."

Midnight Muse: A Spell for Creativity

by Christine Jette

Magical spells are a form of prayer. In them, personal energy is sent outward to the universe with great intention. The energy in spell work is powerful.

When you cast a spell, be sure to let go of expected outcomes. The universe may have something in store for you that is grander than anything you could imagine on your own. Remember, too, that any energy you send outward returns to you three times stronger. You have to be careful always what you ask for. Ethical spell working also requires you to harm none and work for the good of all according to free will.

The following spell is good your job or a project needs a creative boost. Select what you want from the following suggestions and let your intuition guide you.

To Start

Choose the day of the week that best describes your magical intention. Begin your magical spell during the waxing Moon to draw in what you wish to create. The waxing Moon has the power to illuminate your desires. Use the Full Moon to amplify your magical intent and to give your spell workings additional power. *Note:* If you have unresolved issues that may be blocking your creativity, use the waning Moon to remove obstacles first.

Next, choose a candle color based on the following list.

Red for creative passion

Orange to attract success

Yellow for the written word and communication

Purple for spiritual inspiration

White for pure intent

Green for creativity that leads to money

Next, choose a creativity stone. Orange calcite and citrine aid creative flow. Crystal is for clear thinking. Amethyst, holey stone, or jade are for wisdom. Moonstone is for contacting intuition.

Decorate your altar with fresh flowers. Use fresh flowers in the colors of your candles. Red and orange are especially potent.

Choose an incense. Anything spicy or fiery, especially cinnamon, is useful and potent. Sandalwood is good for any purpose.

Choose an herb or oil. Pine, bay leaf, thyme, allspice, cinnamon, peppermint, clover, ginger, orange, and juniper all radiate creative fire. Bay leaf is especially good for writer's block. You may want to tie together an herb bundle with red or orange ribbon, and hang it above your computer or workspace.

Choose a goddess. Athena is good for the written word. The Muses can be applied to various forms of creativity. Diana is good for bold career moves and the courage to start anew.

Choose a talisman. This should be anything that speaks to you of your personal project or creative endeavor: writing, career, art, music, and so on. For example, my writing talisman is a seagull feather that I picked up on a beach in Rhode Island.

Choose a tarot card from the following list to inspire you.

The Ace of Wands for beginning a project

The Magician for the ability to direct energy and create

The Queen of Wands or Empress for creative energy

The Chariot for work as a spiritual endeavor

The Star for inspiration

The Moon for the creative potential of intuition

The Sun for success and passion for your work or project

Casting the Spell

Arrange your altar using the items you have selected. If you feel something is needed that isn't listed, please use it. Likewise, if a suggestion doesn't feel right to you, don't do it. No ritual you do is sacred unless it is sacred to you.

Ground, center, and cast the circle of protection according to your tradition. Recite a blessing, call the quarters, anoint candles with the oil of your choosing, and light the candles and incense.

Invoke your goddess. If you prefer, you can substitute the phrase "creative spirit" for the goddess.

On a piece of construction paper, parchment, or computer paper, write something like this in red ink in your own words:

I call upon (goddess or "creative spirit") *for creative inspiration. Grant me the awareness, ability, and enthusiasm to bring my project to fruition. I ask that this be for the good of all, according to free will, with harm toward none, so must it be.*

When you are done writing, say the words out loud with great intention as you visualize your completed project, just as you imagine it should be. Now pick up the tarot card that most expresses your creative desire. As you visualize your goal, send yourself down into the card and release its specific energy into the universe. Wrap the paper with your words on it around the tarot card. As you hold the perfect vision of your project in your mind's eye, pass the paper and card over the candle flame and recite three times with feeling:

Energy white, energy bright,
Strengthening the spell I cast tonight,
Its equivalent or better I ask of you,
I will do my part and see it through.
My request is pure and made in love,
As it is below, so it is above.

Build energy and release it to the universe to do your bidding, but let go of the need to control outcomes. As always, thank the goddess or creative spirit, dismiss the quarters, extinguish the candles, open the circle, and ground.

Tie the paper in red, green, or orange ribbon, and hang it near your computer or creating place where you will see it every time you work on the project. You can leave the tarot cards on the altar, place them in your work area, or carry a card or two with you during the day to strengthen the connection between you and your creative desire. Repeat the spell whenever you need inspiration.

Believe in the magic of your dreams.

Communing with the Triple Moons

by Edain McCoy

The current year gives extra weight to the old phrase, "once in a blue Moon." If a single solar month contains a second Full Moon, the second Moon is said to be blue. Only one blue Moon can occur in a single solar year, and in some years, may not occur at all. Modern Wiccans often say that four aspects of the self are necessary to embark on any quest: to know, to will, to dare,  and to keep silent. Working with seasonal lunar triads is part of the dare. Self-examination is not easy, and only the honest seeker will discover the wisdom he or she seeks.

That is, the twelve Full Moons of 2005 provide us opportunity to look at our Moon cycles in groupings of seasons. Through these four sets of three Moons, we can see clearly see her rich symbols and the many archetypes of other triads at work—especially the wheel of the year.

The Dedicant's Triad

January 25, February 23, and March 25 are the Full Moons that take us from deep winter to the first days of spring. They appear when the Cailleach, the Celtic crone of winter, rules the land. Yet that same crone is the virgin goddess who gave birth to her son, the Sun, at midwinter.

Connect with her energies by stretching your esbat ritual across the entire cycle of the winter Moons. Stand beneath her full light and inhale the essence of dormancy, the world at rest, protected by the Celtic goddess called the Cailleach, or old woman. Know that somewhere an infant Sun is waiting to emerge.

If possible, go outside and stand beneath the pale silver glow of the Full Moon. Stretch out your arms to embrace and welcome her. You may wish to evoke the power of this first triad by saying:

Ancient Moon, encased in ice,
The Cailleach blue and cold comes thrice;
Allow me to flow along your trail,
Show me the path where will prevails.

These winter Moons can also serve as a focal point for personal life cycle events. During these three Moons take time to meditate, looking back on your period as a dedicant, before you took formal vows of initiation. Connect the winter Moons with the first three months of your studies. Think about what you've learned, how you've grown, and, if necessary, make changes in your practice and personal philosophy. Religion best serves humanity when it remains mutable and allows for change.

If you are a dedicant at this time, use this lunar energy to help you sense the subtle movements of nature and the universe. Ask it to reveal to you what you need to know as you commit to your year and a day of study.

The Initiate's Triad

April 24, May 23, and June 22 make up the second triad of Full Moons. They coincide with the reawakening of the planet in spring. At this time, the Moon is the fertile mother, mating with her god-consort, impregnating the earth (her womb) with the harvest. June 21 is also Midsummer, the point of the Sun's apex.

This period coincides with the role of the new initiate, who is now into a second year of study and has discovered that the learning, the thinking, and the questioning never stop. Paganism is not a path for those who hop from religion to religion.

An appropriate evocation for this triad might be:

The nights grow short, but the Moon rides high,
Still the star of the nighttime sky;
In the Moon of blood the sacred child grows,
Teach me now what I need to know.

Think back to your own initiate period. Compare how your life, thoughts, and actions changed as you continued along your path. If you are now an initiate, spend time under these three Moons meditating on how your life as an initiate differs from that of a dedicant. Ask the deities of the Moon to reveal to you what you need to learn to continue growing.

The Priest's and Priestess's Triad

July 21, August 19, and September 17 take us from the verdancy of summer to the harvest. The deities are aging now. The goddess is giving birth to the abundant yield of the early autumn harvest. As the crops are gathered, each field, one by one, settles into dormancy in preparation for its winter sleep. The goddess is aging, and the sacrifice of the god-consort approaches.

This period corresponds to the priest or priestess part of the wheel of life. Whether or not you use the title, each initiated Wiccan, Witch, or Pagan is a priest or priestess, fully able to merge with and contact the deities without any intermediary.

As the field are plowed under and the days grow shorter, reflect back on this point along your path. Bathe in the light of the harvest Moons and reflect on the harvest, on growth, abundance, and dormancy. Compare these ideas to your time as a priest or priestess, and consider how these autumn Moons have inspired or changed your life. Evoke the energy of the harvest Moons with a greeting such as:

Fertile fields of gold and green,
Harbors the sacred time-between;
Her bounty grows from a single seed,
Show me the mysteries I most need.

Those who are now moving into this phase of their spiritual lives should try to connect to the energy of these three Moons. Ask yourself what harvest and abundance mean in a spiritual sense. At this point you should be able to connect to the lunar cycle with ease and be open to its teachings.

The Elder's Triad

The last lunar triad is October 17, November 15, and December 15. These Full Moons take us back into winter. The god has been sacrificed for the good of the land. The goddess mourns his loss as she prepares, as midwinter's goddess, to birth him anew. Fields lie fallow, and frost dapples the bright orange of autumn pumpkins and squash. The last of the harvest remains to be gathered.

This final triad corresponds with the role of elder, crone, or sage. All of these are terms for Pagans who have either been practicing their faith for a long time or have taken on the tasks of extra study or of mentoring new dedicants.

This is a phase for introspection, a time to reflect on the year you have traveled and to ask for guidance in choosing the direction you want to go in the year to come.

The Moons of the underworld deities contain vast knowledge, as well as the essence of our own shadow selves. It is not easy nor particularly pleasant to come face to face with your true self, and these Moons of the waning year will not withhold their teaching if you feel ready for them.

With age comes wisdom. Allow these three Moons to share their sacred wisdom with you. An example of an evocation to the Moon of this triad might be:

Cold is the night and the short day brings,
The first blue frost from the Cailleach springs,
Let me gather in all the harvest I can hold,
While you share wisdom of ages untold.

Even if becoming an elder, crone, or sage is still far in your future, there is no need for you to shun the darker aspects of this deity. At first the three may appear frightening, even disturbing, but those who dare to allow themselves to be taught by the elder Moons will progress rapidly along in their spiritual quests.

December 30, 2005, the last New Moon of the year, makes a perfect leaping-off point to launch yourself into the cycles of time and life for not only the new lunar year, but for the solar year as well.

To the Grandmother Moon of 2005 we say: "Hail and farewell, and merry must we meet again."

Creating a Witchcraft Circle

by Mavesper Cy Ceridwen

For many beginners in the craft, group practice seems to be a priority. This may stem from a misunderstanding that the craft is like other religions, in which one can join simply by finding a congregation and blending in with the crowd. Witchcraft doesn't work that way. A coven springs from many years of shared experiences by a group of people who build bonds of perfect love and perfect trust.

Creating these bonds isn't easy. But the advantages of group practice include an abundance of energy and a more efficient way to accomplish magical goals. There are also a fair share of problems arising from such factors as a natural clash of egos and shadows. For solitary practitioners who can't find their way into a traditional established coven, forming a witchcraft circle is the best way to start group practice.

Circle bonds are lighter, and its commitments less serious than those of a coven. This does not preclude a spirit of perfect love and perfect trust, but it is not easy. Participant must do their parts in opening up the self to each other, so that all can participate in common growth and movement to the above ideals.

Here's a ritual to launch a witchcraft circle.

Have all invited circle members show up dressed as the element or deity they have chosen to embody. If the group has chosen to work "skyclad," each person can wear symbolic jewelry or carry a symbolic tool.

Space and participants are purified by the four elements. A protective circle is drawn.

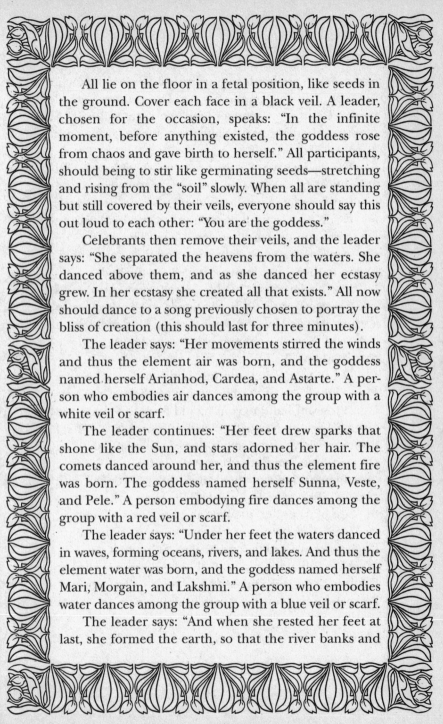

All lie on the floor in a fetal position, like seeds in the ground. Cover each face in a black veil. A leader, chosen for the occasion, speaks: "In the infinite moment, before anything existed, the goddess rose from chaos and gave birth to herself." All participants, should being to stir like germinating seeds—stretching and rising from the "soil" slowly. When all are standing but still covered by their veils, everyone should say this out loud to each other: "You are the goddess."

Celebrants then remove their veils, and the leader says: "She separated the heavens from the waters. She danced above them, and as she danced her ecstasy grew. In her ecstasy she created all that exists." All now should dance to a song previously chosen to portray the bliss of creation (this should last for three minutes).

The leader says: "Her movements stirred the winds and thus the element air was born, and the goddess named herself Arianhod, Cardea, and Astarte." A person who embodies air dances among the group with a white veil or scarf.

The leader continues: "Her feet drew sparks that shone like the Sun, and stars adorned her hair. The comets danced around her, and thus the element fire was born. The goddess named herself Sunna, Veste, and Pele." A person embodying fire dances among the group with a red veil or scarf.

The leader says: "Under her feet the waters danced in waves, forming oceans, rivers, and lakes. And thus the element water was born, and the goddess named herself Mari, Morgain, and Lakshmi." A person who embodies water dances among the group with a blue veil or scarf.

The leader says: "And when she rested her feet at last, she formed the earth, so that the river banks and ocean shores are her feet, the fertile fields her stomach, the mountains her ample breasts. The goddess named herself Ceridwen, Demeter, and the corn maiden." A person embodying earth dances among the group with a green veil or scarf.

The leader says: "She became that which is, was, and always will be, born from her own sacred dance and from infinite joy. From here elements—air, fire, water, and earth—she created her consort to give her love and company, and to share her dominion." The dancers tie their veils or scarves in one knot, and they dance holding on to the center knot, saying: "I am the god."

The leader says: "In this sacred moment, in this space between the worlds, what once was has been once again created. May the knot we tied this night be a source of nourishment and balance, and keep us in joy, trust, and love."

The leader raises the left hand and touches the open right hand of the person next to her or him, saying: "From my hand to your hand I form this circle and give my word that I shall act with love and trust. This I promise freely. The circle is done." All respond: "The circle is done," and then repeat the oath.

When all have pledged, the leader covers all with green and silver veils, saying: "This circle will serve, to the best of its power, the lady and her son and consort. Guide us, support us, protect us, keep us, energize us, teach us, transform us, and heal us. So mote it be."

All meditate on and feel the power of Mother Earth's green veil and Mother Moon's silver shroud. Feast and enjoy your new path of sharing.

African Divination:
The Hakata Oracle

by Stephanie Rose Bird

Across the African continent, divination enables people to understand the present and predict the future. This article focuses on *hakata,* an ancient oracle barely understood outside of its home in southern Africa.

Hakata are tablets similar to the dice referred to in different languages as *akata, ditaola,* or, simply, bones. To understand how to use the hakata oracle, it is important to understand the groups of people who use them. The spiritual practices, beliefs, mythic stories, folklore, and cultural outlook of the Shona people and the geography of their lands shape and informs our ability to consult the hakata oracle.

African Oracles

Various oracles akin to hakata exist in southern African cultures in the language groups stemming from Bantu, called ChiShona. These diverse people include Kalanga, Karanga, Zezuru, Ndau, Korekore, and Manyika people. The majority of ChiShonas reside within Zimbabwe though they also live in parts of northwest Mozambique, South Africa, Malawi, Botswana, and Zambia.

Storytelling and art-making customs are the markers that define Shona culture, so it is natural that the hakata oracle combines various of these forms. One unique example of Shona oral tradition that is a guiding force to hakata divination is *tsumo-shumo*, or "proverbs." Tsumo-shumo lends a greater philosophical complexity to hakata divination sessions and provides a delicious middle ground, as the stories are explored by both diviner and the person who has requested the reading.

Oracles bridge the gap between mundane and magical existence. Words, gestures, sounds, and artifacts remove the separations created by conventional ideas of time and space. The hakata oracle exists within the context of southern African culture, and it reflects the Shona outlook on the world. In particular, most problems are viewed with a kind of moral complexity within the Shona framework. This is where Shona cosmology diverges from Christian or Muslim good-versus-evil absolutism, which otherwise influences the belief system fairly strongly. The beauty of hakata lies in the acceptance that there are no definitive answers to difficult questions.

Hakata's Mythic Heritage

The hakata oracle is anchored by the cosmology of people who continue to live close to nature and in accord with her cycles and weather phenomena such as rain, crop yield, and safety from dangerous animals. Shona mythology differs greatly from Western mythology. For example, let us consider the story of Ditaola. Ditaola is a mythic hero who killed a monster called Kammapa. Kammapa's appetite was so voracious that he ate all of humanity but for one woman, Ditaola's mother. As the last woman on earth she gave birth to a son, and he came into the world adorned with charms around his neck. He was named Ditaola, which means diviner or seer in the Sotho language (and which is another name for hakata). The hakata oracle is a tool with a divine and mythic heritage.

The diviner or a mentor usually creates the hakata oracle by hand. Four small rectangular tablets are inscribed with a series of four standardized signs that reflect the Shona's social, cultural, and spiritual practices. To begin the divination, the diviner shakes the hakata and then casts them hard onto the ground. This very act reiterates the Shona's long-term connection with the earth. The cast lots fall into configurations that reveal a message believed to be directed by ancestral and spiritual forces. The diviner interprets falls of the cast lots in terms of their relationship to all concerned.

Duality is a concept of great cultural significance to the ChiShona and other sub-Saharian Africans. The hakata oracle incorporates duality and opposition as well as mythology and folklore. The complex interaction of opposing forces is clear to observe within the Hakata tablets whose very names and personal attributes suggest polarity.

Makakata Symbolism

To use makakata (which is the plural form of hakata), you must be able to identify each hakata individually by visual observation. Understanding the physical traits of each hakata equips the diviner and recipient of the reading with layers of meaning useful in deciphering difficult questions. A great deal of emphasis is placed on hakata with carved sides facing up; however, as you will see in the following samples, those that face down add further meaning to the reading.

Tokwadzima (senior male; elder authority figure): This hakata represents controlled strength, assertiveness, confidence, judicious decision-making, and wisdom. It suggests a connection to the ancestors, authority figures, and elders. The crocodile, a significant symbol in myth and in the lives of the Shona people, is the symbolic representative of Tokwadzima.

Kwami (senior female): This hakata is a nurturing, caregiving protectress. Kwami represents maternal instinct and deep insight. She symbolizes community togetherness and the village mentality. Kwami's hakata contains an interlaced double-knot motif suggestive of a snake, the symbol of the continuity of life.

Chirume (junior male): This hakata is the young male relative, or uncle, figure. Chirume's presence suggests youthful enthusiasm, boundless energy, and sometimes anger or quick decisions. Impulsiveness, the warrior's call to action, and naïve idealism are all connected to Chirume. The junior male is represented in the hakata as two parallel bands of lozenges suggestive of tribal warrior markings and the skin of a crocodile.

Nokwara (junior female): This hakata is the passive aunt or sister figure. Nokwara embodies flexibility and willingness to compromise. She is known to comply with the wishes of the others and suggests a gentle response and cooperation instead of confrontation or independence. Nokwara's symbol is a single interlaced band.

Sample Shona Oracle Sessions
Reading One

The diviner throws the makakata, and says, in the Karanga dialect: *Rutokwadzima ane ngwena.* ("Two Tokwadzima, or male elders, have the crocodile.")

This proverb is spoken when the tokwadzima and kwami hakata carvings are faceup, and the nokwara and chirume are facedown.

The diviners continues with the reading: Elder figures are wise yet often they lack the flexibility of the youth in the community. Elders have broad vision, deep insight, strength, and a strong connection to the ancestors; they are formidable, especially when a senior male and female are paired, as indicated by this fall. Elder wisdom is incompatible for those who are impulsive or who enjoy taking risks.

This fall warns that it may be very difficult to accomplish your goals. So you need to stay strong and keep your spirits up. Perseverance is required. Salute your ancestors, and pay attention to the advice they send through dreams or intuitive feelings. Listen to the advice of older relatives, suggestions from your teacher, boss, or other influential figures.

In this reading, both nokwara and chirume are facing down. Invoke nokwara and chirume for what they offer: creativity, enthusiasm, and the energy to move forward. The vigor and bravery of chirume could help achieve your goal. The gentle approach that uses diplomacy and compromise as suggested by nokwara could help you win a difficult competition.

The diviner suggests further actions: Continue to toss and read the makakata to develop a full picture of what is entailed to meet your goal and shed light on the situation.

Reading Two

The diviner throws the makakata, and says, in the Karanga dialect: *Ngwena ino mwana.* ("Crocodile has a child.")

This is a very fortuitous fall because tokwadzima and nokwara are facing upward. African wisdom favors the pairing of opposing forces, and this fall contains two opposing forces: both male against female and young against old. Good things occur when youthful energy and innovation is tempered by elder wisdom.

This fall indicates new opportunities and prospects—whether in areas of romance, travel, employment, or a move to a new location. All will most likely have a positive outcome. The energy needed to carry out challenging endeavors is present and represented by nokwara. Tokwadzima represents the insights and judicious qualities of authority figures and the ancestors.

The fact that chirume and kwami are facedown accentuates the probability of success. At times, chirume is warrior-like and too ready to use forceful tactics or express strong opinions. Kwami can represent overprotectiveness that borders of meddling and interference. Kwami is community-orientated, and she tends not to support individualistic actions or selfish decisions.

The diviner suggests further actions: Initial indications from this fall are good. The client should meet with success in the venture questioned. He or she should still trust his or her instincts and intuitive feelings regarding the question, as the venture lacks the protection that either chirume or kwami could provide. A few more tosses of makakata should paint a complete picture as to how to proceed.

In Conclusion

The dualities at the heart of the hakata oracle are apparent in each of these two readings. Senior tablets represent depth, coolness, proper custom, insight, community, and feeble weakness.

Each characteristic is observed in elders in African society. The junior tablets represent vitality and energy—the jubilance that leads to folly or that provides healing. The junior tablets and senior tablets represent qualities observed in members of the community.

Clearly, the ideal reading and the ideal member of society is closer to the center—not too old or young in spirit or actions. With the hakata oracle, an outcome that represents symmetry is most desirable, as it represents the mystical coolness and balance that are revered by many Africans.

Practical Psychic Protection

by Ellen Dugan

Here is a topic that winds up magic users and psychics alike: psychic protection. For the life of me, I do not understand why folks tie themselves up into a knot over this very normal and practical idea. For those of you who have natural psychic abilities, such as clairvoyance or psychometry, learning how to shield yourself is a necessary thing. A natural and untrained psychic is like a sponge. You soak up vibrations from people, places, and objects, and often end up feeling overwhelmed, angry, sad, or depressed from the constant input. A principle of psychic protection is learning to turn off psychic impressions for your own sake.

If you are a magical practitioner, learning psychic protection is a useful thing. It will help you to shield yourself from negativity, keep your aura clear, and sustain your magic and mental health. It will also protect you from any magical dabbler who is drawn to you and has decided that you were the one to listen to all their imagined problems

Now, before you start to hyperventilate wondering if it is safe for you to venture outside of your homes without proper psychic protection, relax. I sincerely doubt that psychic vampires are lurking and waiting to pounce on you. Below are just some everyday scenarios and ways to handle them with practical psychic protection.

Practical Protection for the Sensitive

Some people are very sensitive to psychic impressions. They may or may not be clairvoyant or empathic, but they are sensitive to the energies around them.

These folks might try experimenting with a bit of color or crystal magic to keep themselves grounded at all times. This means wearing colors in deep greens and blues for healing, or black to ward off negativity. Turquoise, in particular, is a cheerful, dynamic, and very healing color. Deep, dark-purple bolsters self-confidence and strengthens shields. Gold is better than silver, as silver jewelry is receptive to psychic impressions, and gold is more projective—protecting and guarding health.

With crystals, sensitives tend to be drawn toward moonstone jewelry set in silver. Here is a tip, if you are easily overwhelmed by other people's emotions, then lay off the moonstones. Try carrying a small piece of obsidian, jet, or turquoise.

For subtle, herbal aromatherapy remedies, ladies you can try using lilac- or lavender-scented soaps and perfumes. These are cleansing and keep negativity at bay. Also, guys should try sandalwood, bay, or pine fragrances. Any of these scents will increase your protection and keep you from picking up on other people's emotional garbage.

The Psychic Vampire

Psychic vampirism is much less dramatic than folks imagine. A psychic vampire is, at worst, an energy leech. They try to attach themselves to you and drain away your enthusiasm, good mood, and energy. Signs to watch for: a person who constantly has to touch you or wants a long hug, whether or not it's appropriate. And this scenario doesn't just apply to a woman trying to extricate herself from a guy's overexuberant hug. Men in social situations can be victims of a female psychic vampire as well.

How do you know for sure when you've encountered a psychic vampire? Well, any physical contact will make you vaguely uncomfortable, perhaps a bit sick to your stomach. Your mind races considering options for escaping such a person.

Rest easy, you have a couple of choices for how to deal with the offender. (No, none of these involves a sharpened wooden stake or a rope of garlic.)

Escape route one: Make up an excuse to avoid close contact. Say: "I have a cold," or "I have a sunburn on my back," or "I pulled a muscle," whatever. Move back and fold your arms across your chest—this will close down your energy chakras across your chest and solar plexus, both huge sources of emotional energy. Psychic vampires in particular feed off your energy, so close down those chakras and put your game face on. Look the offenders square in the eye and smile. It confuses them and breaks the link.

Escape route two: Move back and distance yourself. Stand up if they are sitting, or sit down if they are standing. Put a table between the two of you if you are both seated. Put your hands in your lap, well away from theirs, and cross your feet and put your toes on the floor so you can stay grounded.

Escape route three: Send the offender a mental push. (No, this is not manipulative; it's defensive.) Concentrate on the image of him or her backing away, then remove yourself from the situation as quickly as you can.

Escape route four: This is really obvious, but don't let them touch you. Say simply: "I am not comfortable with that," and step back. Most psychic vampires have to touch you to drain you—so don't let them.

The "Haunted" House

Often the first question I hear when folks find out that I am both a Witch and a clairvoyant is "What do I do to rid my house of the spirits that haunt it?" My answer: If you think there is an unwelcome presence in your home, then it's time to clean house. I do not recommend attempting a séance or to communicate with the ghost. Instead, I advocate blessing the house with incense or sweet grass, salt water, and candle light. With salt water draw stars or equal-armed crosses on every door, mirror, and window in the house. Announce: "I bid all energies not in alignment with myself to be gone."

Typically what you are sensing is leftover emotional energy in the home. If you are sensitive to older homes and vibrations, then keep yourself grounded by carrying hematite in your pocket or wearing amethyst jewelry Both are protective and calming.

Set out clusters of crystals in your house, and perform a cleansing regularly just after a Full Moon. Another idea is to fill the house with laughter and love. A home filled with friendship, laughter, and happiness is hard to drag down with old negative energy.

The Best Protection

In the end, the best sort of psychic protection is a great sense of humor. If you can laugh at yourself and the ridiculous things in your life, then you are already several steps ahead of the game. When confronted with someone you believe is a psychic vampire, try to picturing them in a cheesy, Halloween-costume black cape. Now imagine this person trying to walk up to you, but instead tripping on the cloak's hem. You'll be so busy snickering to yourself that the vampire won't have time to cause you any problems. When confronted with difficult people or unpleasant circumstances and psychic environments, take a deep breath, put up your shields, and smile. It works like a charm.

Pine Tree Lore

by James Kambos

I grew up surrounded by the beauty of nature in the Appalachian foothills of southern Ohio. These hills are like no other place. Here, the soft sweet air of May is made even sweeter by the perfume of the flowering black locust trees. In June, the frothy white flowers of wild honeysuckle spill over rocks and old fence posts. But what I remember most is being lulled to sleep by the tangy pine-scented air that drifted down the hillsides and through my bedroom window on dewy summer nights. My boyhood home stood safe and secure beneath a stand of white pines. Even then I was fascinated by their quiet year-round beauty, and how their evergreen branches stretched like sheltering arms overhead.

The Ancient Pine Tree

Pine trees are truly the dignified Ancient Ones of the forest. The fact that most pines are evergreen has meant they have been consider among the most magical of trees throughout the ages.

Figures vary on how old pine trees are. Some naturalists say pine trees have grown on Earth for at least fifty million years. Others estimate the figure could be closer to one hundred million years. What we do know for certain is that when first woman and first man looked out across the landscape, they saw pines that were already ancient. To understand fully how the evergreens became associated with magic, we have to imagine what our ancient ancestors must have felt when they experienced winter's approach for the first time.

The deciduous trees that were lush and full of life earlier in the year took on the brilliant colors of autumn. Then, frost crept into the forests, and the hours of daylight diminished. As the sky turned the color of pewter, icy winds and rains stripped the remaining leaves from the trees, leaving them black and naked. Pine trees, however, still stood tall and majestic, their branches still covered with the green color of life.

It is no wonder the world's early people looked upon the pines as guardians of the earth's mysteries. To our ancestors, the evergreens symbolized life's eternal forces, and hinted that our planet had a never-ending cycle of seasons that would sustain us for all time.

As the frosts deepened and the snows fell, the pines remained green, their branches undisturbed as they wore snowy winter coats of white. We owe the pines our reverence, for in their way they helped the human race survive. As the pine branches hung heavy with snow, they offered some degree of protection from the brutal forces of winter. No doubt, many early wanderers found some measure of safety and comfort as they camped beneath a grove of pines.

As the seasons turned and spring brought the green of new foliage to the earth, early people honored the evergreens by making them a symbol of life's continuity and of hope. Because of the evergreen beauty of pine trees, they were used in folk magic to represent strength, fertility, endurance, good fortune, and prosperity. Eventually, pine trees also came to be used in purification, health, and protection rituals.

Pine trees grow throughout the Northern Hemisphere and are the largest group of cone-bearing trees. At least thirty-five varieties can be found in the United States—including spruce, fir, hemlock, and white pine. Their wide growing range makes it easy to incorporate pines into magical rituals. Since pines are also classified as herbs, many parts of the tree can be used as powerful ingredients for spell casting.

The Magical Uses of Pine Trees

Many of us think of using evergreens only as part of Yule and Christmas celebrations, but their magical uses extend well beyond the Yule season. Here are some ways to use pine to enhance your magic year-round.

To ensure a bountiful spring, as part of your Ostara ritual, take a small pine branch and place it in a flowing stream or river. Give thanks for the returning season of light.

For fertility, use a fir branch to represent a maypole during Beltane. Also, include three pine branches in a sacred bundle, along with branches of oak and hawthorn, and burn this in your Beltane fire. This will ensure strength and the fulfillment of wishes.

During spring, to welcome the Green Man place branches of pine near your door, on fences, at garden gates, or in barns.

In late summer, make a swag of pine and goldenrod to ensure good health for the coming winter.

Include pine cones in fertility spells for an extra boost of power.

To remove negativity, place two small pine branches in the form of a cross before a ritual fire. Bless them and then place them in the flames.

To purify your home during the winter, mix a pinch each of ginger and allspice with a drop of olive oil in a quarter cup of water. Anoint the tips of a small pine branch with this mixture, and sprinkle the mixture about your home. Begin by facing east and move in a clockwise direction. Pay special attention to the windows, doors, and fireplaces.

At Yule, pine wreaths are among the most ancient and potent forms of pine magic. Pine represents life, and the round shape of the wreath symbolizes eternity. Decorate the wreath with natural materials, and include a few small glass ornaments to repel the evil eye.

The centerpiece of the Yule season is the Christmas tree. The holiday tree represents the Tree of Life. The lights symbolize the stars of heaven and the star at the top of many trees represents the divine spirit. When you decorate your tree include some ornaments shaped like fruits and vegetables, especially pickles, apples, berries, nuts, and corn dollies. These serve to remind us of the coming growing season and the bounty that lies ahead. A popcorn garland is also a nice touch. As a side-note, if you are fortunate enough to own any antique German glass ornaments, cherish them, as they were among the first ever made. These should be treated as family heirlooms.

As you can see, the magical lore concerning pine trees is rich and varied. The magicians of long ago used pine trees to power their spells in many ways, especially spells for youth and longevity. One such spell follows. It was written by the late author Valerie Worth, and is from her book, *The Crone's Book of Charms and Spells* (Llewellyn, 1971), which I consider a classic.

A Charm for Eternal Youth

Go to a grove of pines, when the Moon is new, and in the earth beneath their boughs inscribe a circle, as wide as you are tall. Lie down within it, your arms extended to meet the circle's rim, and say these words:

> *The ancient pine*
> *Is evergreen*
> *The crescent Moon*
> *May never wane*
> *The circle bound*
> *Ever round*
> *And so my life*
> *As light and leaf.*

Pluck the needles from a green pine branch, take them home, and wind them tightly round about with a hair from your head and a long green thread. Keep this charm beside your bed, so that you may dream of eternity. Each night before you sleep, repeat the words that have conjured youth from the enchanted grove. Ever after, you should wear some token of green—jade, emerald, or other stone, ornament, or article of clothing—in honor of this fair spell now threaded through your life.

In Conclusion

Pine trees have much to teach us, for they have witnessed many ages. But the most important lesson we can learn from these evergreen trees is that winter—both the winter season and the winter we sometimes feel in our hearts—does not last forever

Purifying Your Senses to Tap into the Highest You

by Janina Renée

In many of the world's spiritual traditions, the desire to purify one's mind and heart is supported by symbolic efforts to "purify the senses."

This is a discipline achieved by cultivating good thoughts, words, and deeds, by guarding one's sense-doors to avoid taking in the negative, and by diligently working to purge oneself of undesirable tendencies. However, ritual activities can also help reinforce mental striving in the effort to achieve a purity.

The Sense of Hearing

Let's start with the sense of hearing. A Zen Buddhist ritual involves striking a bell, which represents the voice of the Bodhisattva of Compassion, urging us to purify our sense of hearing. At the same time, the sixth-century Syrian author Jacob of Serugh's "Homily on the Blessed Virgin Mary" says, "Let us purify our hearing for her pure account." And an Islamic *fatwa* advises, ". . . purify your hearing faculty from listening to backbiting, for both the speaker and the listener are deemed sinners."

The act of purifying one's hearing has two applications: closing your ears to unwholesome communications (such as gossip, hate talk, and the like), and opening them to good and inspiring words and speech and to sacred music and chants.

After an evening of listening to Chinese chants, the sounds can so ring in one's aural memory that even well into the next day, it is difficult for impure or petty thoughts to wedge themselves into the brain. Spending time away from the noisy world, especially in the solitude of nature, also helps clear your mental state and attunes your inner ears to finer messages.

Going back to the sound of the bell: Bells have long been reputed to have a protective quality, scaring away demons and purifying the atmosphere. Whenever you hear a bell, you can say a blessing, such as, "As this pure sound resonates and clears the air about it, so may I purify my hearing," or simply, "I purify my hearing." When going forth, you might want to pause and cup your ears in case any bell sounds are to be heard in your vicinity, then say the blessing. You can increase your chances of hearing a bell by hanging some high quality wind chimes near by.

Also, when you've heard some very disturbing talk or news, you can clear your head by ringing a bell and letting the sounds reverberate inside your ears. You can achieve a similar effect by holding a seashell to your ears. According to ayurveda, India's ancient tradition of health maintenance, some symbolic actions for purifying hearing include dabbing a small amount of sesame oil or almond oil in one's ears.

Incidentally, I believe that attempting to purify hearing can lead to a greater intuitive connection to others, because we can listen with sincerity and better hear what they are saying, and what sort of needs they are expressing, without filtering their words through our preconceptions.

As with the hearing, we can also attempt to purify our other senses and their respective sensory organs.

The Sense of Sight

For edifying vision, it is good to keep sacred images about you. Whenever you lay your eyes upon some new inspirational sight, you could say, "As this sacred image fills my eyes with joy and light, so may my mind be cleared and purified." Natural vistas can have a soul-cleansing effect, too, so when you are gazing at an expanse of bright blue sky, green field and forest, or a serene landscape that is blanketed in snow, you can say a similar blessing.

You might also think about the physical benefits of good visuals. As Emerson has pointed out: "The health of the eye seems to demand a horizon."

Consider other symbolic gestures. Some people like to wash their eyes with an herbal rinse. Some meditate on the colors blue, indigo, or purple for purifying vision, as well as on gemstones in those colors, such as amethyst or lapis lazuli (which also stimulate the ajna chakra). Also, some people do regular simple visualization exercises, such as imaging one's eyes of mind filled with glowing light.

The Sense of Smell

Deep breathing exercises are important to yoga, Taoist practices, and others traditional practices that advocate the intake of fresh air as important to purification. As you exhale, think about letting go of stale thoughts and attitudes. Whenever you have the opportunity to inhale some pleasant or purifying incense or other fragrance, do so.

Whenever you encounter particularly spiritually uplifting scents such as sandalwood, juniper, cedar, frankincense, bay, and myrrh, you could say, "As this fragrance penetrates my senses, so may my mind be cleared, so may my thoughts be purified." Although it sounds trite, stopping to smell the flowers will also help clear your senses.

Ayurvedic practitioners often rub a little sesame oil in the nostrils to clear the passages. As Dr. John Peterson advises, after applying the oil, "Pinch and release your nostrils rapidly while inhaling sharply." Breathing exercises are another traditional method of purification, and taking deep breaths in clean fresh air is very stimulating.

By the way, it has been said that good spirits avoid people with gross thoughts, words, and actions because those kinds of human emanations actually stink up the spiritual atmosphere around them. On the other hand, people with good thoughts, words, and actions emit a pleasing fragrance that is diffused through the astral realms and attracts beneficent spirits, as well as good things in general.

The Sense of Taste

Many Buddhist and Shinto traditions require purifying the mouth before prayer. In Japan, shrines and temples often provide fountains and ladles for people to rinse their mouths (and hands) before worshipping. Praying and chanting are also a way of clearing negativity and priming the mind and mouth for truthful and beneficial speech.

Cleansing your mouth can be part of your daily ablutions. For example, when rinsing your mouth or brushing your teeth and tongue, you can mentally invoke a blessing, saying to yourself, "As

I clean my mouth, so may I purify my voice. As I clean my mouth, so may I purify my speech. My voice and speech are clear and pleasing."

Ayurvedic practice recommends rinsing and gargling with warm water, herbal tea or water in which medicinal herbs have been soaked, or sesame oil. (One doesn't swallow the sesame oil afterward; it is spat out and then the mouth is rerinsed with warm water, as this helps clear phlegm.)

If, on occasion, you accidentally say something foolish or hurtful, you could rinse your mouth afterward as a way of reinforcing your awareness of the need always to cultivate more skillful speech.

Practices that promote general bodily purification include fasting or ingestion of special foods, drink, and medicine such as fruit, juices, or teas known to have detoxifying or antibiotic qualities. As a blessing while you practice these purifying techniques, you could say or think, "As I ingest this [substance], savoring its unique flavor, so may it benefit my entire body."

A substance does not have to taste good for you to savor its taste. You can, with practice, train yourself to appreciate the tastes of bitter herbs, tea, medicinals, and such without actually having to like them.

The Sense of Touch

Ritual forms of washing and bathing are, of course, integral to many spiritual and healing traditions. When a full bath is impractical, some simply concentrate on the face, hands, or feet. Any time that you are washing or bathing, you could say or think, "As I cleanse my body, so may I cleanse my spirit."

Many ayurvedic practitioners give themselves a morning massage with scented oils (even adding a few drops to the hair), as this promotes the circulation that expels impurities and stimulates energy flow. Whenever you are out in the elements, you can also revel in the wind and rain, imaging them blowing or washing through you.

Regarding the idea of touch, you might also think about how you can "touch" others in a wholly pure and healing way, through caring gestures.

Purifying the Body and Spirit

Although it is not these ritual actions in and of themselves that effect a state of purity, their enactment renews our pledge of commitment to mental discipline and reminds us of the need to guard our senses. This vigilance includes minimizing contact with people, places, and entertainments where you are likely to see, hear, read about, and otherwise experience things that do not uplift or improve you.

At the same time, make a point of knowing where wholesome and inspiring experiences are to be found. Ultimately, many traditions hold that these forms of physical and symbolic purification develop the psychic senses and make us more receptive to positive spiritual influences.

Articles for Spring

Spring in Ancient Rome

by Sorita Loock

In the ancient world, the coming of spring heralded a joyful time. Nowhere was this more clear than in the spring goddess celebrations of ancient Rome. Throughout April the Romans held a number of festivals celebrating different goddesses associated with the Earth and with growth.

April began the Roman New Year with the festival of Venus and Fortuna on the first day of the month. Married women would wash the statues of Venus from head to toe—hanging golden necklaces around the necks of the Venus statues, and offering roses and other flowers to her. Venus was the most celebrated of goddesses and was always ready to help with love relationships if she was asked.

Women would also honor Fortuna, entering her temple naked and making offerings of incense as they asked for beauty, fame, and fortune. Today we all at least occasionally ask for Fortuna's help—though we may call her Lady Luck. When we call, Fortuna may bless us but also remind us to help others less fortunate and so practice what we preach.

Invocation to Fortuna

Approach, strong and abundant goddess—
Fortuna, thou wide wandering and unconquerable
queen—
We give endless praise to thee.
We ask that you bless us with abundance
In your benevolence.

Wise you tread the land
Spreading fortune by your hand.

Three days later on April 4, the Megalesia began—a weeklong celebration of the Magna Mater (Great Mother) who gave birth to the gods. Statues were carried through the streets in carts pulled by oxen. Fresh flowers were scattered, and there was much music and celebration. It was a week of processions and games, culminating in a horse race to win the prize of the first palm branch.

The Roman poet Ovid recorded that the Romans gave honor to their parents and to the Magna Mater, whom they considered the mother of all. She is the great goddess described in modern Wiccan and Pagan writings. She may be called for any pagan or Wiccan ceremony.

Invocation to the Magna Mater

O mother of the gods,
From whom all flows,
You sit at the center of the world
And approach in your lion-drawn chariot.
Great queen,
We praise and honor thee—
Without whom we would not be.
Bless our rites and bring delight to our souls

On April 12, Cerealia, the weeklong festival of the earth goddess Ceres, began. People wore white robes in Ceres' honor, made offerings of incense, salt, and spelt, and celebrated with games.

The festival of Tellus Mater (Earth Mother) was celebrated on April 15. It was organized by the Vestal Virgins and celebrated both in the city and outside the walls in the country. Ceres reminds us of the benefits of preparation and planning, of sowing the seed for future harvest. We can honor Ceres by baking spelt bread for her and offering it along with salt and incense.

Invocation to Ceres

Lovely and delightful Ceres,
You are the nurse of peace.
You gave to men the seeds to harvest nature's bounty.
Your venerable nature brings bliss and desire.
Come goddess, in your snake-drawn chariot,
Rejoicing in summer's increase,
And bring health and concord to us here now.

April 21 brought the festival of Palilia, in honor of the goddess Pales, who watched over shepherds and their animals. This festival was important as it was during this time that Romulus founded Rome. People leapt fires and were sprinkled with water from a laurel bough. Offerings of milk, millet, and millet cakes were made to the goddess to protect the herd from disease and predators. Sulphur, pine, and laurel were burned to bless and purify the sheep.

Whenever we are out in nature and want to connect more with it, Pales beckons us to meet her. A simple shrine made of pine cones, stones, and leaves can show our praise to Pales.

Invocation to Pales

O kindly Pales,
We ask that you favor us when we travel the countryside.

We ask that you guard the flocks and springs and groves.
We honor you with sweet-smelling pine and laurel
And ask that you keep hunger and poverty far away.
Ancient Lady, may we increase in your care.

Two days later on April 23 came the Vinalia, a festival to Venus as goddess of gardens and vineyards. Offerings of myrtle, mint, rushes, and roses were made to her along with incense and prayers for beauty and charm.

All of us can benefit from the goddess of love's attention. At this time we ask Venus for her help and blessings on our gardens, which are as much a part of nature as any forest or glade.

Invocation to Venus

Beautiful goddess,
For thee the checkered earth pours forth its lovely flowers;
For thee the ocean expanses smile
And the sky gleams with light.
Gracious Venus,
You alone can bring peace to the hearts of men and women.
I ask that you grant beauty to my words and deeds
And bring sweet love to the heart of all that live—
That all may meet and unite after their kind,
And sing your praises

The final festival of April was the Floralia, beginning on April 28 and running for five days. During these days, games were held for Flora—the goddess of flowers and the flower of youth—and prayers made for ripening of fruit.

Men and animals were decked with flowers, especially roses, and women wore bright dresses.

The games were a time of unrestrained merriment—with many theatrical performances and lewd farces. Flora reminds us of the natural beauty that surrounds us and invigorates us.

Invocation to Flora

Beautiful goddess of the flowers,
Gracious Flora,
We sing your praises and honor your fruitfulness.
Help us to grow and fulfill our dreams,
As we dance with the quickening of spring
Feeling your energy flow through our veins.
Lovely Flora, we call to you at this your time.

For modern Pagans these festivals embody the fertility of the earth, and the earthy aspects of the bountiful goddess. The Romans deities were very particular in their offerings, and offerings to them should be appropriate whenever possible. By making the effort to burn their preferred scents and offer their preferred foods, we show the gods that we are open to their ways and seek to learn from their timeless wisdom.

The ancient Roman festivals also remind us that the although the gods were particularly worshiped at festival time, all times were perfect for god worship.

We do not need to limit ourselves to celebrating eight sabbats, but we can honor and celebrate our gods always, thanking them for their blessings and gifts, and asking for even more.

Basic Shamanic Tools and Practices

by S. Y. Zenith

In many indigenous cultures, the shaman is considered both "doctor" and priest. Some regard shamans to be heretical, while others believe that individuals are chosen by the higher forces to become shamans.

Although shamanic practices may vary in different countries and cultures, there are many basic similarities in most systems. As a rule, shamanism is a religious perspective that venerates nature. The guardian spirits and other spirit-helpers acquired by a shaman serve as important sources of spiritual powers.

Guardian spirits are known to manifest in animal forms such as wolves, bears, birds, fish, reptiles, and even as human. The shaman usually ventures on a night-long solitary outdoor vision quest to find and connecting with guardian spirits, tutelary spirits, totemic animals, or spirit familiars. Once the connection with spirit allies is made, the allies protect the shaman from illness, hostile spirits, and other evil forces.

When modern medicine can't provide remedies or explain an illness, the shaman is consulted. During healing, if his or her diagnosis ascertains that the patient suffers from soul loss the shaman descends to the lower world to retrieve the soul of a patient. In some cases, the shaman finds the guardian spirit of the patient and then escorts it back to the body of the sufferer so that he or she may regain good health. During exorcism rites, the shaman will banish disease-causing spirits with invocations and cajoling.

The main duties of a shaman are to cure illness, accompany the souls of the deceased into the otherworld, and protect the tribe or clan and its livestock from malevolent forces. Drumming, chanting, dancing, fasting, vision quests, and the acquiring of totemic spirits are essential components of shamanism.

Basic Shamanic Tools

Shamans around the world possess traditional or individually devised tools for their work. The shamans of indigenous cultures don traditional costumes and complete their ensemble with drums, rattles, mirrors, and other implements. One shaman may use plain but comfortable clothing for shamanic work while another may prefer an elaborate outfit. The adornment of the costume depends largely on the individual shaman. The following are some common shamanic tools.

Drums

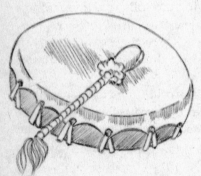 The drum is generally a one-sided, hand-held instrument used for accompanying ceremonial singing and dancing. It may be shaped as an oval, or it may be round with wires strung in strategic positions and holding metal pendants. Some pendants serve as spirit arrows to direct against enemies.

Mirrors

Shamanic mirrors are usually made of metals such as silver, brass, bronze, iron, or nephrite, and are not necessarily shiny and clear. They are useful as visualization tools. Small silver mirrors are especially useful in healing rituals for absorbing baneful intrusions and drawing out diseases from the body. Some mirrors are attached to the shaman's costume with one usually positioned over the chest. The mirror absorbs both visible and invisible energies in all frequencies and serves as a protective armor.

Staves

A staff represents a horses that the shaman rides during spirit journeys to other realms. It is sometimes adorned with conical shells that jingle as the shaman dances. In ritual, the staff is used for purposes such as controlling and banishing evil spirits.

Fans

In areas such as inner Mongolia and Siberia, shamans use a special ritual fan called the *dalbuur* for healing ceremonies. It is usually made from feathers or horsehair.

Whisks

A whisk composed of a bunch of twigs may be used for sprinkling holy liquids on objects, places, and persons. Energized wooden spoons are used in place of the fan or whisk.

General Cleansing, Purifying, and Divination

Use a simple visualization ritual for reestablishing inner equilibrium when you feel out of sync. Sit in front of the altar and close your eyes. Visualize being gently drenched and cleansed by a waterfall cascading into a pool before you. See your spirit body stepping into the pool to be purified by the waters. Drink the water and allow it to penetrate your entire being to restore balance. Say thanks to the water spirits open your eyes.

Another common purification method uses fumigation. Light a smudge stick of sage or a smudge bundle in a heat-proof container. Place it on a tiled or cement floor. Walk around the smoke, and waft yourself in the incense to purify and cleanse the auras.

A smudge stick of sage, juniper, or thyme may be passed around the body three times in the morning to strengthen spiritual protection. Smudging may also be done for loved ones and treasured objects. When spending time within your sacred space or in front of an altar, you can call upon the assistance of one or more spirit-helpers to empower liquids for protective, healing, and other purposes.

As an offering to the spirit-helper, fill a cup or bowl with mineral water or vodka and throw it in the air. Meditate for a few minutes, and attune yourself with the spirit-helper's powers. Ask that your breath be energized, and when ready blow three times into the container of liquid to infuse it with the power of the spirit-helper. Thank the spirit-helper. The empowered fluid may be poured on the right palm, whereupon a sip may be taken before rubbing the rest over the crown of the head and in the middle of the forehead.

Quartz Crystals

Traditionally, most shamans consider crystals given to them by another shaman or found serendipitously to be the most powerful. In modern times, crystals are often purchased and cleansed before use. For shamanic work, it is essential to obtain a pure, clear quartz crystal without chips or irregularities within. Preferably, the points should be clear and sharp with facets equal in shape and size.

Shamans believe that quartz crystals are more sentient than most other rocks and excellent for enhancing visionary powers and serving as energy-transfer devices. Some shamans hold a piece of quartz crystal to the forehead to assist in clarifying insight about a person or event in a distant location.

Crystals are usually found among the contents of a shaman's medicine pouch. They are employed in healing rituals when a guardian spirit's healing energy is being transferred to a diseased part of a patient's body.

Chopstick Divination

There are various divination methods in shamanism. One of the most simple is the Mongolian method of using a chopstick. This method is employed for questions about lost objects, a person you haven't seen for a long time, business matters, and travel.

To perform the chopstick divination, it is essential to know the exact locations of the four directions. Take a chopstick, stand it on one end, and watch it fall. When the chopstick falls, observe the direction the tip points, as this indicates the answer. In interpreting, use your intuition. Some shamans prefer to form their interpretations based on the four directions, but these may have different symbolic meanings to different people. Some simply take the left direction to mean "negative" and the right to signify "positive," in situations where "no" or "yes" answers are required.

Egg and Mirror Divination

Another method of divination uses an egg and a mirror. Place the egg on a mirror and watch the direction it rolls to. When the egg comes to a halt, the direction where the top points designates the location where an activity should be conducted or where a lost object may be located.

Sunset Rejuvenation Ritual

This ritual revives energies spent during the day and rejuvenates the soul. It also helps those with inner discord to find inner peace.

During twilight hours, go to the altar and light some sage or juniper in a smudge pot. Sit in front of the altar, and for a few minutes wave the smoke from the smudge pot over your face, chest, body, and limbs. Meditate on the energy-giving forces of the heavens and nurturing vibrations of the earth. Feel the body relaxing and surrendering to the universal flow instead of pushing against it. Light four small candles and place them the four directions on the altar. Call to the spirits for blessings and guidance. Open your heart to feelings of harmony with nature, people, and the spirit world. Visualize a positive and better future. Upon completion of the ritual, say a word of sincere thanks to the spirits of the four directions and your personal guardian spirits.

The Wishing Tree of Prince Edward County

by Dallas Jennifer Cobb

Once upon a time a magical maple tree grew near West Lake, in Prince Edward County, Eastern Ontario, Canada. At the time, it was said to be the largest maple tree in the world, and the last great maple east of the Rocky Mountains.

An easily recognized landmark, the tree was a meeting place for the Native people of the area. Elders and leaders met under the tree while the tribe gathered nearby preparing food and making temporary camp. The children and youth would play close to tree, gathering small bits of bark from the ground and tossing them up into the tree. If the bark caught on a branch or in a nook, then the thrower of the bark was granted a wish— hence the tree's name: the Wishing Tree.

Mohawk and Algonquin peoples met in the shade and shelter of the magical tree. They traded crafts, tools, horses, and food. Seasonally the tribes gathered for feasts and pow-wows, giving thanks for their abundance and creating opportunities for young people to meet mates. Throughout North America, the Wishing Tree was renowned in many Native communities as the site of gatherings and celebrations. Tribes also resolved conflicts, negotiated territory, and formed trade agreements at the tree. It is said that in the sixteenth century the Wishing Tree was where local Mohawks negotiated their joining with the Iroquois League.

In the eighteenth century, when European settlers came to the area they, too, discovered the Wishing Tree and met there with Native leaders to trade and negotiate land rights. As the population grew, the path to the tree was widened to accommodate horseback travelers and a larger volume of visitors.

In the later 1700s, a wave of United Empire Loyalists, fleeing the American Revolution, settled in Prince Edward County. Crossing Lake Ontario, they landed in the area. They stayed because they enjoyed the fertile lands and the island's isolation.

The increased settler population brought change to the area. Native communities moved away into hunting lands that were still fertile and abundant. The settlers built permanent homes and buildings. Increased population also brought increased travel along the path where the Wishing Tree stood. When a road was built to accommodate wagon travel, it was constructed around the tree.

Like the Native inhabitants, the settlers also regarded the Wishing Tree as a sacred place, a place of peace. Many families traveled to it for family picnics and outings. It was popular with young lovers who would go to sit quietly under its lush branches and wish on true love. Almost everyone who came would gather bark, throw it into the tree, and if it stuck make a wish.

In the late 1800s, the girth of the Wishing Tree was measured at over eighteen feet. It was documented to be over 160 feet in height, and then estimated to be roughly 670 years old. The Wishing Tree had witnessed many changes: the gathering of Native peoples, the arrival of the European settlers, the arrival of the Empire Loyalists, and the gradual departure of the Native peoples. As the residents of the area changed, the Wishing Tree remained—a place of peace and magic.

In 1925, the Wishing Tree was hit by lightning. Local residents trimmed off the damaged branches and limbs in an attempt to save the tree. At this time, the age of the tree was then confirmed to be more than 700 years. In 1953, the Wishing Tree finally died. It was cut to the ground leaving only a massive stump. With the trunk exposed, the growth circles of the tree were counted—confirming its age to be 731 years. But after living and working magic for so many years in Prince Edward county, the Wishing Tree did not just die and fade away. In fact, it was reincarnated in Wellington, Ontario. Town residents and parents were involved in rehabilitating an decrepit old playground in the town park. Rather than purchase shiny plastic playground equipment, the community members wanted something else.

Relying on the commitment of more than two hundred volunteers, the playground's design was considered. Dreams and wishes were sketched out and mulled over. Slowly a theme emerged—the historical roots of Prince Edward County.

Researching local history, the story of the Wishing Tree was rediscovered and incorporated into the theme of the playground. Designers quickly realized the tree was symbolic of many inhabitants of the area, their wishes and dreams, and the peace they continually negotiated. The mythology and history surrounding the Wishing Tree was thrilling and paralleled the energies that propelled the community-based park project. All of the characteristics of the Wishing Tree—time and space for conflict resolution, a place of shelter, a center for peace, and a magical spot for wishing—would be brought into the playground through the reincarnation of the Wishing Tree.

In May 2003, seven hundred volunteers worked for six days, through rain and shine every day, to build the park. At the center of the park stood a magnificent maple. Approximately 270 years old, its branches spread wide over what became the play area. The tree stood at the center of everything, destined to become a place of gathering, sitting, communing, and peace and unity.

Dubbed the Wishing Tree, the grand maple tree in Wellington has become renowned again for its magic. With their playground now in full operation, local children know that the magic of the Wishing Tree is real. Each day, they search the ground for bits of bark, ready to throw them into the branches of the Wishing Tree in order to make some more wishes. Clearly there is lots more magic to come in this community.

Greek Wicca

by Olivia O'Meir

Greek Wicca is a tradition combining ancient Greek culture, myths, religion, and beliefs with Wiccan ones. As with other Wiccan traditions, Greek Wiccan practices vary by individual. In this article, I seek to offer my views on Greek Wiccan beliefs, deities, and holidays.

Greek Wicca Beliefs

Greek Wicca has a creation story, which comes from Hesiod's *Theogony*, his account of the origin and genealogy of the gods. Hesiod tells us Chaos was first, appearing out of nothing. From Chaos came five deities: Earth, Night, Tartarus (part of the Greek underworld), Eros (the personification of attraction), and Erebus (a dark place associated with the underworld.) These gods and goddesses gave birth to other gods.

Greek Wicca contains an understanding of the afterlife. After death, the deceased go to the underworld, or Hades, where the gods Hades and Persephone rule. The underworld in Greek myth is found either beneath the earth or beyond the ocean toward the west. In Greek Wicca, it is a place of rest before rebirth.

Two concepts in the Greek Wicca tradition are "know thyself" and "nothing in excess." These are the wise words written above the Oracle at Delphi. The first concept asks a person to be completely honest with one's self, to look in the mirror and face the Mt. Olympus and the Hades within. The second relates to moderation and mental, physical, and spiritual balance. These are, of course, difficult to obtain and sustain, but they are something to strive for.

"Self-responsibility" is another tenet of Greek Wicca. We are faced with choices everyday. Self-responsibility reminds us not to blame others for our choices and mistakes.

Greek Wicca also follows the Wiccan Rede: "An' it harm none, do what thou wilt." This is observed out of respect for the divine in others and ourselves. Spell work plays a large role in Greek Wicca, especially as a tool to communicate with the divine. The true purpose of Greek Wicca is to connect with the divine in and around us. Save for this idea and for the Rede, there is no restriction on how spell work can be used.

Deities

Greek Wicca sees the God and Goddess in ourselves and in the world around us. Greek Wicca acknowledges and respects duality and equality. The original twelve Olympians (listed below) contained an equal number of gods and goddesses— six of each. When Dionysus took Hestia's place the list was put out of balance, though Dionysus is a god that can relate to either gender.

In Greek Wicca, the gods and goddesses are not thought to be perfect. They can be immoral and often make mistakes. They have human qualities, and we can read their stories and learn from their mistakes.

The twelve Olympians include: Zeus, Hera, Aphrodite, Ares, Poseidon, Demeter, Apollo, Artemis, Hephaestus, Athena, Hermes, and Hestia (later replaced by Dionysus).

In Greek Wicca, other deities can be worshiped. For example, many worship Hades, Pan, Hecate, Gaia, Hestia, Orpheus, Aesculapius, as well as demigods and heroes. Hercules is often worshiped as a god of strength and transcendence.

Greek Wicca encourages its followers to take on a patron deity. Each of the Greek heroes has a god or goddess as a patron. There are several ways to find a patron god—including divination, dreams, or meditation. There are many deities. Everyone can find a god or goddess to connect to.

Holy Days

The Greek Wiccan observes the esbats and sabbats, as they attune us to the divine and the rhythms of nature. In addition, a Greek Wiccan will celebrate major festivals related to their patron, such as the Thesmophoria (October 11–13) in honor of Demeter, and so on.

The esbats are celebrated at the New and Full Moons. These are times to work magic. The New Moon is a time of endings, change, and intuition. The Full Moon brings ideas and projects to fruition.

The sabbats are the seasonal rites of Greek Wicca. They are a time for celebration and festivity. Greek Wicca observes the eight Sabbats as Spring Equinox, May Day, Summer Solstice, Lammas, Fall Equinox, All Hallow's Eve, Winter Solstice, and Candlemas.

During the Spring Equinox day and night are equal. From here until the Fall Equinox, the days grow longer. The lesser Elusian mysteries are celebrated at this time, as Persephone returns from Hades to visit her mother Demeter. She is again Kore, the maiden goddess of spring. The Spring Equinox also marks the start of the new year. Planting and cleaning are activities for this sabbat.

May Day brings fertility and sexuality. The flowers are coming into full bloom. The weather is getting warmer. It is a time of love, and the God and Goddess celebrate their union.

Summer Solstice celebrates the fullness of summer and the Goddess in her royal glory. The day is longer than the night. Enjoy it with a party or by spending time in nature.

Lammas is the first-harvest festival. It is a time to cull fruits and herbs. While still celebrating summer, it marks a turning toward fall and winter. It is the time of the father.

Autumn Equinox brings the greater Elusian mysteries. Kore becomes Persephone and returns to her throne and to her husband Hades. It is a time of thanksgiving for the harvest. Now, the nights begin to grow longer and the days fade.

All Hallow's Eve is a time to honor ancestors and loved ones. The veil between the worlds is thinnest now. Activities relating to magic and divination are enhanced.

The Winter Solstice signals the longest night and the rebirth of the God. The light begins to return, and activities that focus inward are highlighted now.

Candlemas is a time when life begins to stir anew. Spring is coming. It is a time of healing, initiations, and worship of the divine twins, Apollo and Artemis. Apollo represents physical healing, and Artemis represents spiritual healing.

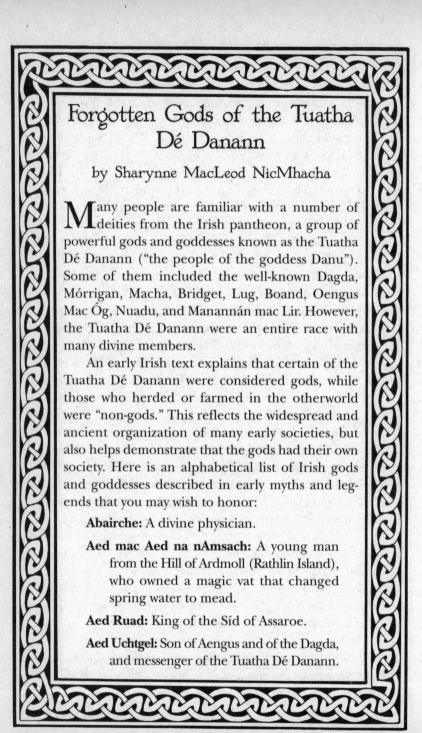

Forgotten Gods of the Tuatha Dé Danann

by Sharynne MacLeod NicMhacha

Many people are familiar with a number of deities from the Irish pantheon, a group of powerful gods and goddesses known as the Tuatha Dé Danann ("the people of the goddess Danu"). Some of them included the well-known Dagda, Mórrigan, Macha, Bridget, Lug, Boand, Oengus Mac Óg, Nuadu, and Manannán mac Lir. However, the Tuatha Dé Danann were an entire race with many divine members.

An early Irish text explains that certain of the Tuatha Dé Danann were considered gods, while those who herded or farmed in the otherworld were "non-gods." This reflects the widespread and ancient organization of many early societies, but also helps demonstrate that the gods had their own society. Here is an alphabetical list of Irish gods and goddesses described in early myths and legends that you may wish to honor:

Abairche: A divine physician.

Aed mac Aed na nAmsach: A young man from the Hill of Ardmoll (Rathlin Island), who owned a magic vat that changed spring water to mead.

Aed Ruad: King of the Síd of Assaroe.

Aed Uchtgel: Son of Aengus and of the Dagda, and messenger of the Tuatha Dé Danann.

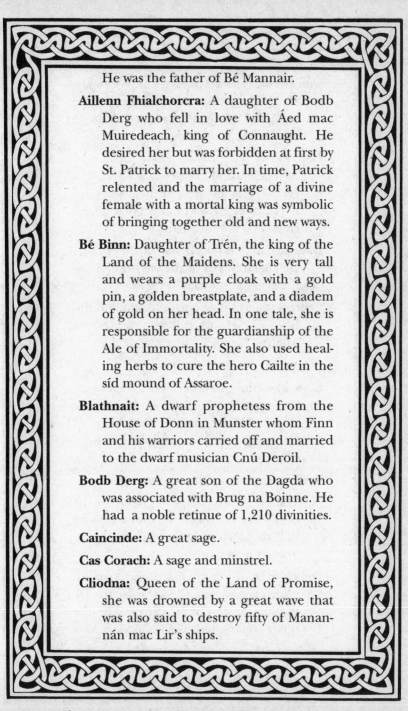

He was the father of Bé Mannair.

Aillenn Fhialchorcra: A daughter of Bodb Derg who fell in love with Áed mac Muiredeach, king of Connaught. He desired her but was forbidden at first by St. Patrick to marry her. In time, Patrick relented and the marriage of a divine female with a mortal king was symbolic of bringing together old and new ways.

Bé Binn: Daughter of Trén, the king of the Land of the Maidens. She is very tall and wears a purple cloak with a gold pin, a golden breastplate, and a diadem of gold on her head. In one tale, she is responsible for the guardianship of the Ale of Immortality. She also used healing herbs to cure the hero Cailte in the síd mound of Assaroe.

Blathnait: A dwarf prophetess from the House of Donn in Munster whom Finn and his warriors carried off and married to the dwarf musician Cnú Deroil.

Bodb Derg: A great son of the Dagda who was associated with Brug na Boinne. He had a noble retinue of 1,210 divinities.

Caincinde: A great sage.

Cas Corach: A sage and minstrel.

Cliodna: Queen of the Land of Promise, she was drowned by a great wave that was also said to destroy fifty of Manannán mac Lir's ships.

Cnú Deroil: A dwarf musician who was part of Finn's retinue. His music was so beautiful that jealous musicians drove him out of Slievenamon.

Dairenn: A daughter of Bodb Derg who desired to be Finn's only wife for one year. When he refused her, she gave him a silver goblet of mead that intoxicated and confused him.

Díangalach: A noble Druid of the Tuatha Dé Danann. His death was one of the three greatest losses to them.

Echtga: Daughter of Núadu Argatlám who is associated with the mountain Slieve Aughty.

Etain: Sister of Bodb Derg.

Étain Fholtfinn: Daughter of Aed Uchtgel. She was the swiftest of her people, the favorite of her father, and lover of Oscar, son of Oisín. She died of grief when he died.

Ferdoman: A son of Bodb Derg.

Fer Tuinne: A musician who played for the people of the Brug. His music could lull to sleep warriors in battle or women in childbirth.

Fethnaid: Daughter of Fidach, and a superb musician and delight to the Tuatha Dé Danann. Her death was one of the three greatest losses of the gods.

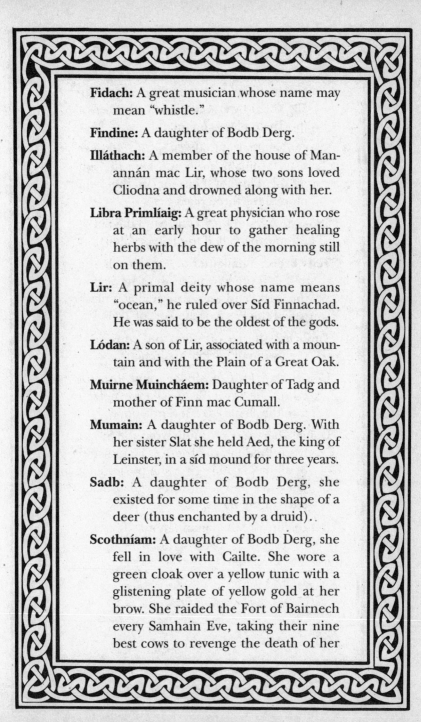

Fidach: A great musician whose name may mean "whistle."

Findine: A daughter of Bodb Derg.

Illáthach: A member of the house of Manannán mac Lir, whose two sons loved Cliodna and drowned along with her.

Libra Primlíaig: A great physician who rose at an early hour to gather healing herbs with the dew of the morning still on them.

Lir: A primal deity whose name means "ocean," he ruled over Síd Finnachad. He was said to be the oldest of the gods.

Lódan: A son of Lir, associated with a mountain and with the Plain of a Great Oak.

Muirne Muincháem: Daughter of Tadg and mother of Finn mac Cumall.

Mumain: A daughter of Bodb Derg. With her sister Slat she held Aed, the king of Leinster, in a síd mound for three years.

Sadb: A daughter of Bodb Derg, she existed for some time in the shape of a deer (thus enchanted by a druid).

Scothníam: A daughter of Bodb Derg, she fell in love with Cailte. She wore a green cloak over a yellow tunic with a glistening plate of yellow gold at her brow. She raided the Fort of Bairnech every Samhain Eve, taking their nine best cows to revenge the death of her father and grandfather. She was eventually killed by Cas Corach, a member of the Tuatha Dé Danann

Slat: A daughter of Bodb Derg. She and her sister Mumain lured and kept the son of the king of Leinster in their síd mound for three years.

Tadg Mór: A son of Núadu, from the Síd of Almu (now called the Hill of Allen).

Teite Brecc: A daughter of Ragamnach, she and 150 other women went to play in the waves and were drowned at a place called the Wave of the Fort of Téite.

Tudhcha: Mother of Aillén and consort of the divine physician Abairche.

Uaine: Daughter of Modarn and lover of Finn. She was able to change herself into the shape of different animals.

Úaine: Daughter of Buide from the Síd of Dorn Buide in the south. The minstrel of all of Tír Tairngire, she possessed a flock of otherworld birds which made enchanting music.

Uchtdelb: Wife of Manannán mac Lir.

Flower Essences for Magical Transformation

by Jonathan Keyes

For millennia, plants have been used to provide food, shelter, clothing, and medicine. If you've ever been uplifted by the scent of an plant such as lavender, jasmine, or lemon balm, then you also know the ability of herbs to shift moods and help us relax and enjoy life. This ability of flowers to generate emotional transformation is at the core of flower essence therapy.

In 1930, an English homeopath by the name of Edward Bach developed a method for healing deep emotional and spiritual complexes through the use of flower essences. Bach felt that flowers carried a subtle yet dramatic ability to address detrimental emotional patterns and help people release them at their root. In Bach's view, flowers carry very simple messages that are undisturbed and pure in their resonance. He felt that by aligning ourselves with the vibration of flowers, human beings could transform and alleviate the pain and discomfort they were feeling.

Bach initially came up with a group of thirty-eight flowers he felt addressed the main human emotional problems. Since Bach's time, numerous other people have worked to develop hundreds of other essences that address specific emotional concerns.

Flower essences are very simple and easy to make. Anyone with access to some good water, a plain glass bowl, some brandy, and some tincture bottles can make them. The trick to making a flower essence is knowing what flower you want to work with and then developing a relationship with that particular flower and plant. Intention and good relationship is everything in this process, the tools and methods are only secondary. Once you have decided on the flower, learn everything about it—where it lives and what other plants it likes to hang out with. Does it like Sun or shade? Dampness or dryness? Examine how it expresses itself and moves with the Sun. If you can, take a nap or daydream with your eyes closed near the plant to receive messages about its properties.

When you are ready, go outside a few hours after the Sun has come out so the flower is not too wilted by the heat. Fill a clean, clear glass container with about eight ounces of purified water. Take a short while to meditate with your chosen flowers, stating state your intention to use its essence for healing. It is key to ask the flower for its assistance in this work—usually flowers are delighted to be part of a healing flower essence, but there have been times when I have gotten the distinct message not to pick certain flowers.

After you have meditated with the flowers for a short spell, gather the most perfect flower heads just below where they meet the stem, and place them gently on the surface of the water. Fill the top of the container with flowers, then leave the bowl of water in the sunshine for about four hours. You will notice about that time that the flowers are slowly starting to wilt and their essence has been delivered to the water. At this point you may pour the water into an eight-ounce amber bottle (available at health food stores). This is known as the mother essence.

From the mother essence, you can then make stock bottles of essence. Add four drops of the mother essence to a one-ounce tincture bottle filled with brandy. From these stock bottles, you can then make the dosage bottles that you will use when you need to take a remedy. To make a dosage bottle, simply take two drops from a stock bottle and place it in a new one-ounce tincture bottle. add a teaspoon of brandy, and then fill up the rest with good water. In this final step, you can add two drops of a number of different flower essence stocks to make a mixed remedy, though I would recommend against using more than five flowers at a time.

I often advise starting a healing regimen with flower essences on a New Moon and planning for it to last two weeks (until the Full Moon) or four weeks (until the next New Moon). At that point, I would reevaluate and see if you need to continue or if a change has taken place. When taking a flower essence, a normal dose is four drops twice a day. Sometimes you may find the need to take doses more frequently (in acute cases of emotional trauma), or less if the flower essence seems especially strong.

There are many flower essences. I can only discuss a few. I prefer to work with flowers that grow in the Pacific Northwest. I encourage you to experiment with flowers in your native region. Here is a list of some flower essences and their properties. These essences can be found in most health food stores and are made by either the Flower Essence Society (FES) or by Bach remedies.

Agrimony (FES, Bach): This essence is helpful for those who have a tortured inner mental and emotional state. They may appear outwardly happy but tend to feel bound up and tight inside with many plaguing worries. Agrimony helps to release repressed emotions and transform inner pain into true inner peace.

Angelica (FES): For those who feel cut off and disconnected, especially from the spiritual realm, angelica helps to bring a sense of greater protection from the unseen energetic and spiritual world around us.

Black-eyed susan (FES, Bach): This essence helps us to release deeply held emotional intensity, body memories, and trauma from childhood or past lives. It transforms negative energy that is trapped inside.

Blackberry (FES): This essence translates our intentions into actual manifestations. It is helpful for those who have difficulty motivating themselves.

Bleeding heart (FES): For people who are broken-hearted by the loss of loved one, this essence helps us to protect and nourish our heart centers.

Borage (FES): For those with a heavy heart who need to be uplifted to experience greater buoyancy in life.

Chamomile (FES): This essence helps those with changeable, up-and-down moods and who are often anxious and tense in their stomach or solar plexus region.

Dandelion (FES): This essence is helpful for those who tend to have an excessive zest for life. It helps people relax, reflect, and stay centered.

Goldenrod (FES): This essence is helpful for those who are too stuck in conforming to the conventions and social norms established by parents or society. It helps one have a stable sense of one's own individuality.

Mugwort (FES): Mugwort helps us access the psychic realm and brings greater understanding through our dreams. It also helps to soothe nightmares, insomnia, and hysteria.

Mullein (FES): I call this essence the grandfather. It helps us remain solid, erect, and surefooted while still maintaining a gentle, relaxed "grandfatherly" quality.

Oak (FES, Bach): This essence is for those who have the weight of the world on their shoulders. It is helpful for the workaholic type who just can't relax.

Oregon grape (FES): This essence is for those who tend to feel anxious and paranoid. It helps to relieve tension and come to greater openness and good will.

Sunflower (FES): This essence is helpful for those who tend to be bashful, shy, and unsure of themselves. It helps this type to feel confident and radiant.

Willow (FES, Bach): This essence helps those who are rigid and unyielding to adapt and flow. It is useful for those who hold on to old pain and resentments.

Yarrow (FES): This essence helps those who tend to be too open and vulnerable to the emotions of others. It helps bring greater protectiveness to the aura so that one does not "bleed" out vital energy and vitality.

Rescue Remedy or Five-Flower Formula: These formulas combine essences to help relieve tension, anxiety, and anguish that is acute and intense. They help one to relax and gain a greater sense of ease and tranquility.

Mujaji, Rain Goddess in the Flesh

by Stephanie Rose Bird

To most of us, goddesses seem mythic, divine—often outside of the realm of mere mortals. In parts of southern Africa, it is believed that certain rain goddesses come down to earth and inhabit the bodies of queens. This article explores the concept of sacred leadership in southern Africa, focusing on Mujaji, the goddess whose lineage continues to the present day.

My engagement with the rain queens of the Mujaji line focuses on positive aspects. I pay tribute to the notion of rain giver as fertility goddess who ensures harvest and the blossoming of creativity. This article shares personal engagement with Mujaji. Inspirational recipes, rituals, and invocations useful in conjuring the spirits of rain are shared for use in your magical work as well.

A Snapshot of Southern Africa

Mujaji is associated with the Shona, people from southern Africa who speak the Bantu-based languages called ChiShona. The majority of ChiShona speakers reside within Zimbabwe, but a few live in South Africa, Malawi, Botswana, and Zambia. Shona people are an ethnicity defined by language rather than geography.

Most contemporary Western societies observe a separation between mythic figures and political leaders. In *A Dictionary of African Mythology: Mythmaker as Storyteller,* author Harold Scheub paints a vivid portrait of sacred leadership as it relates to the Shona. He describes how the monarchy of the Karanga people split after passionate disagreements.

The leaders of the Karanga, called Mambo ("Chiefs"), could not get along. Each son of Mambo Monomotapa decided to create his own empire. One son, Mambo Maulwi, set up his capital in Zimbabwe. He didn't need to rule by force but had supernatural powers that controlled rain. He was looked upon as a god on earth, or sacred leader. Maulwi gave birth to a daughter, Dzugudini.

Dzugudini had a son named Makaphimo, but she wouldn't name the father (who is believed to have been a Mambo) so she was made to suffer. Eventually, Dzugudini and her baby were forced to leave the village. She headed south and eventually founded Lovedu. Dzugudini died in Nareni, and her son Makaphimo died in Khumeloni.

Mahasha, brother to Makaphimo, was a great farmer, and another of Dzugudini's sons, Mudiga, had control over lions. Muhale, Makaphimo's son, ruled Khumeloni along with two other brothers Mahasha and Mudiga. There were several other leaders from this line—Pheduli, Khiali, and Mugede. Mujaji, called "transformer of the clouds" *(khifidola-maru-a-daja)*, is believed to be both daughter and stepsister of Mugede.

The Making of a Legend: Mujaji's Origins

Mujaji, goddess of fertility, sustenance, cycles, and life itself hails from the distinctive line of rainmakers that began with Mambo Monomotapa. Mujaji I, the goddess who came to live on earth, first appeared around 1800. Mugede fathered Mujaji II as well, so this rain queen was both daughter and stepsister to Mujaji I, and so it has gone for many generations. Mujaji's exploits are legendary. Many leaders through the ages have appealed to Mujaji I for rain. During numerous African wars, Mujaji's reputation saved her people.

Mujaji is immortal and inaccessible. She is at the center of life, as only she possesses the power to create rain, change seasons, or inflict society with droughts or floods. If she is angry, there is no rain, and this leads to horrendous droughts. Constant care, respect, and vigilance to her honor are required to assure her assistance. Mujaji's contemporary descendants have no military power, but still yield spiritual influence within their community because of their ability to conjure rain.

The Importance of Water to Life

In the book *After God Is Dibla: Igbo Cosmology, Healing, Divination and Sacred Science in Nigeria* (Karnak House, 1999), author John Anenechukuri Umeh gives a rare glimpse into the magical uses of the water by West Africa's Igbo people. Umeh describes *igba ogogo mmili*, or "dancing waters"—a ritual involving an excitedly playful washing of one's body during a rain shower. *Mmili uji osisi*, meanwhile, is water gathered from natural bowls, depressions, or holes in trees. *Mmili akwukwo osisi* is water gathered by plant and tree leaves.

Try some of the Igbo methods of interacting with the rain when you feel that your ideas are stale and lack creativity. To do your own igba ogogo mmili bath, take a wash outdoors during a rain shower—in the nude if possible. Try gathering water from inside burls and other depressions in the surfaces of trees.

Rainwater is easy to collect on the ground as well. Collection from a rural environment or at the very least away from excessive traffic is best. Simply place multiple containers outside during a rain storm. Fresh rainwater is best, but you can store rainwater for a few days if necessary.

Lightning water is collected during a thunder storm. It is believed to bring dramatic changes to situations and an air of spontaneity or even capriciousness. Lightning water is associated with Yoruban angelic forces and the orishas Shango and Oya.

Use rainwater to bless your besom before spiritual cleansings and clearings, or during the creation of a circle.

Use rainwater to charge or renew crystals, rocks, and minerals. Once they are cleansed, clear the stones again with moonlight. Record the sounds of rain or a thunderstorm. Play this during rites or ceremonies involving new beginnings, to generate ideas, to relax, or to meditate.

Fire and water work together beautifully to inspire projects, spark creativity, and contact the muses. Bring a floating candleholder outdoors on an evening of heavy rains during the New or waning Moon. Leave this out overnight in a safe location. Go outside at dusk the next evening wearing all white. Focus on your intentions, then place three small lit white or pink floating flower candles inside a bowl of rainwater (using your dominant hand).

Face west and recite as you continue to focus on the floating candles:

As rain comes from the sky,
Show me reasons to try;
Drops of rain, fresh as morning dew, cleanse and renew.
Sweet Mujaji, make everything in my sight
Bright, fresh, and sparkling like you.

Recite this three times with building intensity. Gaze at the fire as you visualize a successful transformation. Use some of the rainwater on your fingers to snuff each candle. Lift your hands high in the air, and as the smoke is released, chant:

So it is written, so it will be done!

Gently blow the smoke so that it will carry your messages forward. Remember to look forward to rain, and to welcome it and use it in your magical workings. Thank the Mujaji goddesses of the rain daily for the gifts they bestow on the earth.

Healing Water

by Sheri Richerson

From the beginning of time man has known that water has healing properties. However, today many people think of water only as a something to quench thirst, to bathe in, or to put out fires. Water is one of the most important substances in the physical reality.

In recent years, scientists have proven that water carries energetic imprints. Water that is prayed over, blessed, or programmed with thoughts of love will form beautiful crystalline shapes. Water that is subjected to negative thoughts or vibrations will form nasty, chaotic-looking shapes. When you take into consideration that the human body is comprised of roughly 80 percent water, you can begin to understand its importance to us. Water is an interactive medium that is used by all living creatures. Water stores life and shares information with all living creatures.

In nature, water maintains its healthfulness by moving along in various vortexes. Hydrotherapy is based upon using water's natural movement. This can be as simple as a warm bath, or it can be as involved as water gardening. The sound of moving water can help relieve stress and reach a higher state of awareness. This has been proven to ease pain in injured athletes, arthritis patients, and people with diabetes. Moving water helps some who suffer with chronic pain to receive therapeutic benefits inexpensively.

Small water gardens can be made from galvanized metal tubs, flower pots, a plastic container, wading pools, feeding troughs, or any other item that will hold water. In this way, it is possible to have your own healing water garden right in your own yard.

If you decide to create an outdoor pond, or even a waterfall, pick a site that you feel comfortable relaxing in. The location of the water feature will play an important role in the amount of healing your receive. For many, having the Sun sparkling on the water is a big attraction, but a shaded pond can be refreshing as well. Shaded ponds tend to lend a feeling of lush coolness to a garden. Keep in mind that the amount of light present in the water molecules will determine the purity and balance of the water. Well-lit water creates balanced consciousness and health.

Adding a waterfall to your pond can be quite easy. Many kits come pre-made, and all you have to do is assemble them and add the water. Waterfalls lend their own magic and charm to a garden. Feng shui experts suggest that moving water should be placed in front of your home. They also say that having a body of water near the house is a good thing. Fences are discouraged because they are said to block chi. However, you may add boundaries or an open type of garden gate or some fragrant, climbing vines or roses. If you have room for a circular garden, try adding a fountain to attract birds and other wildlife.

If you cannot have an outdoor water garden, there is always the option of an indoor water garden. Many manufacturers make pre-assembled indoor water garden kits. These can include waterfalls and fountains that are smaller than those typically used in an outdoor setting and are self-contained. You are only limited by the amount of space you have available.

Regardless of where you choose to place your water garden, indoors or out, be sure to make it both natural and pleasing. It should be a place where you can relax and forget the day's worries. Its soothing sounds will help to create a sanctuary for healing.

Remember, too, to drink enough water yourself during the day. Water is an important part of a healthy lifestyle both inside and outside.

The Magical Penny

by Cerridwen Iris Shea

Though always in danger of being discontinued, the penny will endure because of its strong history and its constant magical potential. The first pennies struck in 1787 were made of 100 percent copper. By 1982, the rising cost of copper forced the U.S. Mint to change to a mixture of copper and zinc. Pennies retain their copper color and connection to Venus. Indian head cents were first minted in 1859, but discontinued in 1909 when the Lincoln cent replaced it. The steel cent was produced between December 12, 1942, and December 18, 1946, to aid in war efforts. In 1959, the Lincoln Memorial was placed on the reverse side of the Lincoln portrait, giving us the current form of the coin.

Pennies are thought lucky. The penny loafer brings prosperity, because it is a shoe that holds cash. If you come across an original Indian head cent, or a steel cent, you might want to think about selling it to a collector. You can also use pennies for magical purposes.

Pennies have dates stamped on them. Let's say you want change in your life: You can create a spell for change using pennies whose years add up to the number 5 (1967 is an example: $1 + 9 + 6 + 7 = 23$; $2 + 3 = 5$). Below is a quick cheat sheet for numbers and some of their meanings. Spend some time studying numerology in depth and it will only enhance penny magic.

1—Self, fame, reputation

2—Partnership, love, marriage

3—Creativity, friendship, celebration

4—Family, building for the future

5—Change, travel

6—Career, life path

7—Skill, knowledge, wisdom

8—Prosperity, abundance, infinity

9—Health, spirituality

0—Beginnings and endings

Pennies with your birth year are powerful. As you sort through the pennies in your purses and your pockets, put these aside and add them to penny spells to make them more personal. Pennies from the current year help with magic in the present.

As for types of spells to use pennies in, love and money are the most obvious. For a love spell, take a penny with your birth year and a penny from the current year. Take two dried rosebuds. Dab everything with rose oil and put it in a red felt bag. Remember not to fixate on a specific individual, or you cross the line into manipulative magic. You want to draw the best partner possible to you, and that may not be the person for whom you currently pine.

A money spell would be to take a penny from the year of your birth, a penny from the current year, a whole nutmeg, a whole clove, and a lodestone. Dab them with clove or patchouli oil and place in a green felt bag.

For prosperity in the home, place a penny at each corner of your property and one under your doormat. If you live in an apartment, put a penny on the inside of each of the four corners of the apartment, and one under the doormat.

Washing with a penny wrapped in a washcloth on Beltane brings good fortune. A penny in your wallet ensures your wallet is never empty. Holding a shiny penny when tired can help with flagging energy.

I usually have pennies in my pocket or the bottom of my purse. When I come across a sacred site, or when I'm walking and find the gift of a special stone, shell, or tree branch, I leave pennies in thanks. A colleague of mine places the offering of a penny in the bottom of each jar candle she prepares.

Pennies can be given as spontaneous charms or turned into jewelry, amulets, or talismans. Play with your pennies and find your own ways to incorporate them into your magical life.

A Family Imbolc Ritual

by Twilight Bard

Picture yourself a farmer in northern Europe hundreds of years ago. In the depth of winter, the fields are frozen and your food stores are running frighteningly low. Firewood stocks are quickly depleting. You watch helplessly as your children, pale from lack of sunlight and growing thinner by the week, wake up each morning crying from limbs numbed by the chill, and go to bed at night complaining of rumbling stomachs. Each day is a struggle for your family's survival against hunger and cold.

Then something begins to change. Slowly, the days grow noticeably longer. The Sun, like an old friend, comes back to melt the frost that envelopes the land. The season of lambing comes abruptly, bringing a new, much needed food source: milk. Suddenly optimistic that your family will make it through the winter, you begin preparations for the new growing season.

The story above describes the spirit behind Imbolc (literally "ewe's milk"). No longer as dependent upon the land for survival as our Pagan ancestors, we now celebrate this holiday on February 2 as a time of renewal and purification. Following is a simple ritual that even a family with young children can celebrate together.

Imbolc Ritual

Gather your family around a small, glowing lamp just after dusk, and turn off every other light in the house. If your family keeps to a more formal tradition, you can cast a circle, call quarters, and invoke gods and goddesses here, but it is not necessary. Have on hand a cup of milk (it can be animal, soy, or rice, depending upon your preference) and a broom (preferably a ritual broom decorated with red ribbons).

If your children are willing to sit and listen to a story, tell them a seasonal, age-appropriate tale. Or, you can simply tell the story of the season as described above. After the story, say:

> *We celebrate Imbolc tonight,*
> *And welcome the feast of waxing light!*

Hold up the cup of milk and say:

> *In the shortest days and darkest nights,*
> *There always remains a spark of light.*
> *Father Sky and Mother Earth,*
> *Provide for all with life's rebirth.*

Take a sip of the milk, and pass the cup around for everyone to have a taste. Say:

> *Now the light is lengthening days,*
> *Let us brighten our home, and set each lamp ablaze.*
> *To the dark and the winter we bid goodbye,*
> *as the Sun comes back to brighten our lives!*

Encourage the children to turn on every light in your house. Try to have at least one light in every room. Let them get excited and race about to perform the task. When they meet back in the ritual area, cheer for the light's return. Hold up the broomstick and say:

> *Farewell to the winter! Farewell to the cold!*
> *In with the new, out with the old!*
> *Greetings to the light, bright and warm,*
> *Goodbye to the dark! Negative energy be gone!*

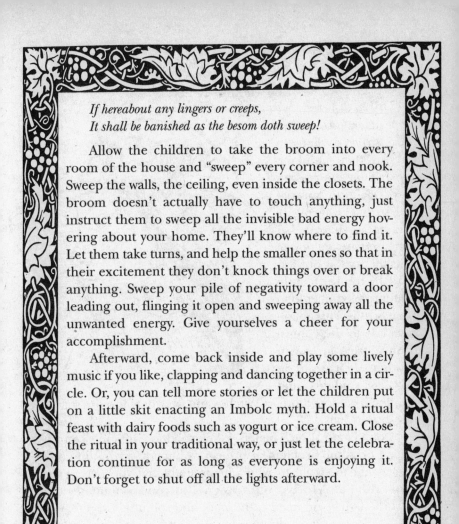

If hereabout any lingers or creeps,
It shall be banished as the besom doth sweep!

Allow the children to take the broom into every room of the house and "sweep" every corner and nook. Sweep the walls, the ceiling, even inside the closets. The broom doesn't actually have to touch anything, just instruct them to sweep all the invisible bad energy hovering about your home. They'll know where to find it. Let them take turns, and help the smaller ones so that in their excitement they don't knock things over or break anything. Sweep your pile of negativity toward a door leading out, flinging it open and sweeping away all the unwanted energy. Give yourselves a cheer for your accomplishment.

Afterward, come back inside and play some lively music if you like, clapping and dancing together in a circle. Or, you can tell more stories or let the children put on a little skit enacting an Imbolc myth. Hold a ritual feast with dairy foods such as yogurt or ice cream. Close the ritual in your traditional way, or just let the celebration continue for as long as everyone is enjoying it. Don't forget to shut off all the lights afterward.

The Thinking Cap

by Janina Renée

Teachers sometimes instruct students to put on their thinking caps. This expression may relate to an old belief that wearing a pyramidal shaped hat increased mental power. This theory was put forward by the thirteenth-century philosopher John Duns Scotus. This notion gave rise to the conical "dunce" caps once worn to stimulate learning in problem students, and  it influenced depictions of Witches and wizards who wore shamefully pointy hats.

Don't laugh at such beliefs. When you have difficulty concentrating on some problem or project, you might try putting on a special hat to signal to your unconscious that you need extra inspiration and focus, and to signal to your roommates and coworkers that you need extra space and solitude. Despite what Mr. Scotus says, your thinking cap doesn't have to be pointed—any hat will do once you designate it as such, though you might want to choose something whimsical, such as a wizard's hat left over from Halloween party, a velvet Tudor cap from the Renaissance Faire, or a big floppy fedora.

To add extra thought-magic, you can decorate your hat with pins, beads, flowers, feathers, or embroidered designs that symbolize your interests and aspirations. Alternatively, if you have a jacket or cape with a spacious hood, you could put it on, pulling the hood down over your face as a way of shutting out distractions.

Chinese Creation Myths

by Julianna Yau

Every culture and religion has its own collection of creation myths—whether it be several different myths or many variations of a primary myth. These are not usually labeled as "myths" by the culture or religion to which they belong, because the word is often attached to the idea of falseness. However, the myths may also indicate any traditional story or tale that is meant to explain or help understand certain mysteries, regardless of its credibility. Within this article, I'll be referring to myths of the latter sort.

A creation myth is one of the more important kind of myths, because it serves to explain some important questions: How did things come into being? Why are we here? And so on. The various origin questions people ask are often addressed in multiple stories—some myths will explain only the creation of the world, others explain only the creation of humans, and others still explain some combination of the things that exist.

Creation myths are not merely stories told for the satisfaction of a child's curiosity—they may also reveal to an attentive reader or listener the underlying philosophies of the culture or religion to which the myth belongs. Also, because myths generally original through oral traditions, myths can be variable—and sometimes reflect the personal ideas and beliefs of whomever was telling the myth.

Before modern science, creation myths were what persons used to explain how everything came to be. Currently, many people may wonder how these myths could be thought the truth, but myths are not meant to tell literal truths. The truths are hidden in the symbols and images used in the stories. Many traditional creation myths involve a god or goddess, and sometimes more than one. The deity may be a deity of creation, or a deity who was or is involved in more than creation. There may also be a specific deity for the creation of different things—the universe, the world, vegetation, animals, and humans.

In China, for example, there are many creation myths. Some of these myths deal specifically with the creation of humans, and others with all of existence. Versions of these myths vary, depending on the historical time frame and the geographic location. Also, as the Chinese culture spreads across a large expanse of land, there are often entirely different myths originating from different regions.

One of the recognized creation myths of China is one found in the writings of the Taoist writer Chuang-Tzu. The creation myth recorded by Chuang-Tzu tells of how the emperor of the Northern Sea (who was named Hu, from the word for "hasty") and the emperor of the Southern Sea (who was named Shu, from the word for "heedless") were involved with the creation of the world and of humans. These two emperors often met at the land of the center, which also had its own emperor (who was named Hun-Tun, or "chaos"). Hun-Tun was a unique being, because he lacked any orifices for seeing, hearing, eating, or breathing.

Because Hun-Tun was hospitable to Hu and Shu, Hu and Shu decided to repay Hun-Tun's kindness by giving him the necessary orifices so that he may see, hear, eat, and breathe. Hu and Shu gave Hun-Tun one orifice each day. Unfortunately for Hun-Tun, on the seventh day after receiving his final orifice, he died. Still, it was Hun-Tun's death that gave birth to the world.

This creation myth gives way to several interpretations, but also leaves some important questions unanswered. For example: Where did the emperors originate? And exactly how did Hun-Tun's death cause the world to come into being? Still, there is likely something crucial to learn in the fact that the world formed out of the god's efforts to create orifices.

A more popular character of Chinese creation myths is Pían Ku (sometimes spelled Phan-Ku), or the first being. Pían Ku is featured in several well-known creation myths, many of which are remarkably different. In these stories, the narratives begin with the concept that in the beginning, there was nothing. From this nothingness, the narratives continue, came something. In one of the myths, the nothing becomes a cosmic egg from which Pían Ku is born. This concept of a cosmic egg is not unique to Chinese mythology and actually appears in the myths of many different cultures (such as India).

In another story, the nothing becomes a something that divides into a female part and a male part (often correlated with yin and yang). From these parts develop the "lesser parts," which work together to create Pían Ku. What follows Pían Ku's creation is the creation of the world and its inhabitants.

In yet another creation myth, Pían Ku is the divine creator. He was said to have created the entire world with a set of tools—the exact types vary depending on the telling; sometimes they may be axes, and other times they are a hammer and chisel. Stories describe how he chiseled the mountains out of the sky. Many times, Pían Ku has for companions the Tortoise, Phoenix, and Dragon of the Chinese pantheon. In most versions of the myth, the celestial bodies (i.e., the Sun, Moon, and stars) existed before Pían Ku began creating the world.

An different creation myth tells of the destruction of Pían Ku, an event necessary so that the world and its inhabitants could be created. This concept of the creation of a primeval being for the creation of the world is similar to the myth involving the emperors of the Northern Sea, the Southern Sea, and the center. However, this Pían Ku story is specific regarding how things came into being. It explains that all of Pían Ku became the world as we know it: His flesh became the soil. His bones became the rocks. His blood became the rivers and oceans. His hair became vegetation. His breath became the wind. His voice became the thunder. His teeth became metals. His sweat became the rain. His tears became the dew. His right eye became the Moon, and his left eye became the Sun.

Perhaps the most disturbing part of this myth is that it tells of fleas or vermin that had infested Pían Ku's body before his death—these were what became humans. Obviously, the originator of this myth did not think too kindly of humans.

One more creation myth, specific to the creation of humans, may be of a more familiar tone. In this myth, Pían Ku created humans after shaping the world with his tools. Using clay, Pían Ku modeled many human figures, and left the models to dry in the sunlight. During the drying process, dark clouds appeared, and Pían Ku worked quickly to relocate all of the models into a shelter before a storm began. However, he was unable to relocate all of the models before the storm began, and some of the models were damaged in the storm. This, the myth explains, is why there are some persons who are physically handicapped. After all of the models dried, Pían Ku infused them with yin and yang. The ones infused with yin became women, and the ones infused with yang became men.

Creation myths are plentiful, and provide wonderful insights into a culture's beliefs. Although we don't have to believe the stories literally, the myths can still be entertaining for children and any adult who is willing to take the myth with a grain of salt. Creation myths are a great starting point for persons who want to learn about the mythology of different cultures, because these myths are a good place to begin understanding where a culture is coming from.

Holy Book Magic

by Diana Rajchel

My friend Shahzad worried when I began appearing at work with dark circles under my eyes. "What's wrong?" he asked.

"I'm having nightmares," I replied

"But you told me you don't have nightmares."

I sighed and told him the truth: "Yes, I rarely experience anxiety-based dream states, but these weren't my dreams. I'm having other people's nightmares."

As I dropped him off at his apartment that night, he turned to me and said, "Sleep well."

I winced. "I'll try."

Then he said: "You won't have any dreams tonight."

He was right. That night, I did not dream.

Help from Holy Books

Later I discovered what had happened. That night while I slept, Shahzad read a verse in Arabic and stated my name at the end. The magic Shahzad used did not care that I am Pagan. Shahzad simply cared that I needed sleep.

A few months later Shahzad told me about his own problems with nightmares and how he knew to help me. After he suffered a series of Armegeddon-like nightmares, his mother read a verse from the Koran over him, banishing his dreams so her then-fifteen-year-old son could sleep. Shahzad claims that since then, when he sleeps, he does not dream.

While frowned upon by Muslim scholars, what Shahzad and his mother did comes from a common foundation of folk practice among Pakistani Muslims. Readings of Koran verse may be prescribed almost like medicine for anything from illness to court cases. Muslims return to the Koran not only for guidance, but as the key to cures for common travails of life.

The Koran stands on the shelf with the Bible and the Torah as a foundation text for biblio-faith-generated magic. Ceremonial magicians and Voudon practitioners use holy books often for either inspiration or for direct use in ritual. Voudon spells often require a petitioner to read a Psalm from the Bible. Ceremonial magicians may read Psalms, call upon Archangels, and petition Christ (depending upon the magician's philosophy).

Some Magical Theory

Holy books work magically because the large number of people who place faith in the books empower the texts. Examples abound in pop culture of the belief that the Bible acts as a charm against evil. In films like *The Exorcist* and in books like Stephen King's *The Stand,* the "good book" is seen as powerful. What people believe collectively can empower an object without specific individual manipulation. Collective cultural belief empowers the texts. The very words printed in the books resonate. Whenever someone sincerely enacts a ritual or prayer from a holy book, that person "feeds into" the resonation. Because of the constant feeding from true believers, practitioners who do not share the beliefs that the books expound can still tap the energy and use them with only slightly less success as they borrow the "charge."

Alternatively, reading from a holy book can contribute to the altered mental state needed to enact successful magic. A Pagan or atheist ceremonial magician may benefit from reading Abrahamic verse as a means to occupy the conscious mind while enacting a ritual that requires a subconscious response. The powerful imagery used in the Bible can provoke a stream of images in the mind that assists the visualization necessary in magical workings.

Traditions

In many of her magic texts, Ann Riva recommends a Psalm recitation for every prayer petition. Catholic priests assign specific prayers for protection, fertility, and purification. Islamic folk-prayers are read or written from the Koran for healing, blessing, and material assistance. One form of Qabala commits itself entirely to the analysis of scripture in the Torah, seeking hidden messages from God to later extrapolate into magical practice. Some practitioners go so far as to justify the use of biblio-based magic by quoting from the books themselves.

Psalms

Many Western biblio-magic practitioners, such as adherents of Santeria and Voudon, frequently use Psalms in their ritual workings. Biblical Psalms were believed to be the prayers of King David. Those who use them believe his words render results in their own personal battles—ranging from court cases to difficult neighbors. One simple spell for mental stability suggested by Anna Riva is to light a white candle and recite this Psalm:

> They that trust in the Lord shall be as mount Zion, which cannot be removed, but abideth for ever. As the mountains are round about Jerusalem, so the Lord is round about his people from henceforth even forever. For the rod of the wicked shall not rest upon the lot of the righteous; lest the righteous put forth their hands unto iniquity. Do good, O Lord, unto those that be good, and to them that are upright in their hearts. As for such as turn aside unto their crooked ways, the Lord shall lead them forth with the workers of iniquity: but peace shall be upon Israel.   —Psalms 125: 1–5

Koran Verse

Muslim magicians practice from the premise that King Solomon created white magic while Satan (Shaitan) created black. Islamic magicians seek to attain union with Allah while controlling elemental forces in their immediate environment—such as djinn, beings that live in a parallel dimension to their mortal counterparts and who practice Islam in that dimension. Some Islamic magic practices require complicated operations that strongly resemble Western ceremonial magic. The Koran contains prayers of protection and celebration that assist in these ceremonial workings. Practical prayers such as the one used on Shahzad have been absorbed into folk culture, often without the approval of mullahs.

A common *sura* (verse) used for protection titled "The Day-break" can be spoken as a prayer or worn as a talisman:

I seek refuge in the Lord of the Daybreak. From the evil of that which He created. From the evil of the darkness when it is intense. And from the evil of malignant witchcraft. And from the evil of the envier when he envieth.

Bibliomancy

While any book can serve as a divination tool, bibliomancy practitioners most commonly use holy books. All a person needs to do

is hold the book for a moment with a question in mind, and open a page and read the first few lines the eye catches. The possibilities for holy books and magic extend far beyond the Abrahamic religious traditions, particularly if operating on a flexible definition of "holy book." The Norse Eddas offers a strong resource for inspiration and sacred observance, as do the Hindu Vedas or Greek epic poetry. So long as the source has an emphasis on the relationship between humans and divinity and comes from a strongly supported tradition, it can carry the metaphysical charge or the subconscious link needed for effective magical practice.

In order to work with holy books in magic authentically and so gain the maximum results, a person should take care to avoid reinterpreting the verse to fit his or her own belief patterns. The reasons for this extend beyond academic purism—in reality, the texts have enough belief invested in them as they are, and to attempt magic by rephrasing the words to fit personal beliefs is like trying to swim up current on the Mississippi River on a very bad day.

Like many aspects of the occult, working with holy books in magic is not for everyone. If you feel a need to adjust the prayer to your beliefs, you may find more success with other types of magic.

Salt of the Earth

by Elizabeth Barrette

Salt, sodium chloride, is essential to human life. From the beginning of time, we have held it sacred, drawing it out of its hiding places to use in everything from spell craft to cooking.

I encourage you to take a look, for just a moment, at some of the interesting and mystical aspects of this amazing substance.

The History of Salt

One of humanity's early discoveries was that salt can preserve food. This made an already desirable resource all the more useful, though on the whole salt was difficult to obtain—it was rare, hard to mine, and consequently expensive.

Most often, people hacked out of the earth in mines formed from ancient dried ocean beds. They could also boil water from salty springs until only the salt remained, or set seawater to evaporate in large shallow pools. Without a ready source of salt, many of our ancestors had to rely on eating meat or salty plants to get the necessary nutrient sodium.

So precious was salt that the Romans actually paid their soldiers in the substance. A good soldier was "worth his salt," and from this practice we get our modern word "salary," which means something like "salt wages." Abyssinians also used salt as currency. The Arabs had an expression, "There is salt between us," to acknowledge the sacred or to seal honorable agreements. Salt traders often came under attack because of their precious cargo. More recently, Mahatma Gandhi began India's movement for peaceful independence by marching with his followers to Dandi, where he set about producing salt—an activity reserved to the government.

Still, too much of a good thing turns bad. Armies sometimes scattered salt on fields to render them barren, giving rise to the phrase "salt the earth behind them"—meaning to deny resources to an enemy by destroying them. Sailors knew that drinking salt water could kill. Of course, today we also know that too much salt in the diet can ruin our health.

Salt Correspondences

Ruled by the planet Earth, salt also represents the element earth. It holds a secondary connection to water, because seawater is briny. For this reason, many Pagans prefer to use sea salt for magical use, though rock salt has a more solid, earthy sense to it. Pure, distilled salt sometimes stands for the divine.

In alchemy, the symbol for salt is the same as that for water: a circle crossed by a horizontal line, representing the flat horizon of the sea dividing the world. Regarding the body, salt corresponds to the blood and to the womb. Its energy is receptive and feminine.

The rituals of many deities around the world include the application of salt. The Egyptians consecrated altars with a sprinkling of salt. Priests of Osiris lit festival lamps filled with oil and salt. Sumerians made offerings of salt to their sea goddess Tiamat—one of whose epithets is "dragon of the bitter waters." The Greeks and Romans added salt to their sacrifices, dedicating the substance to Poseidon, Neptune, and Aphrodite. In Finland, people say that the sky god Ukko created salt by dropping a spark of divine fire into the sea. The Aztecs worshiped a salt goddess called Huixtocihuatl.

Salt's Magical Uses

If you could choose just one mystical item to have on hand always, make it salt. This substance has an almost infinite range of magical and spiritual applications. The most common include banishing, grounding, hex-breaking, luck, money, protection, and purification. The matter of consecration we have already covered above. Salt can also serve as a replacement for blood if you want to adapt an old spell for contemporary use. It can even be dyed, or mixed with colored ingredients, to create a more specific, color-based energy.

For banishment, salt repels all manner of hostile energy and entities. If something nasty bothers you, throw a pinch of salt at it. Add some salt to banishing incense, powders, or washes for extra kick. This also works to discourage gremlins from snitching socks out of the washer or dryer. Heavy-duty hauntings and other such problems can be handled by scrubbing yourself with salt. With a bit of advance preparation, you can also obtain a salt bomb to plunk in your bath as a more elegant and  enjoyable solution to this problem. To keep unwanted visitors from returning soon, spill salt on the doorstep as they leave.

For grounding, keep salt in a dish on your altar or carry it in a small pouch. Eating salt is not only good for grounding, it helps shut down psychic awareness and to refocus your attention on the physical realm. Conversely, avoid eating salt if you wish to practice and enhance your magical abilities.

For hex-breaking, burn salt to thwart all manner of curses or ill wishes. Bathing in saltwater or seawater also works for this. One interesting variant for burning is "black salt," variously described as salt mixed with black pepper or charcoal. This is thought especially effective for dispelling jinxes.

Throw salt after a fisherman, or over the side of the boat, to ensure an abundant catch. Tossing a pinch of salt over your left shoulder brings general good fortune. Dress the ground with a bit of salt before beginning any construction project.

For money, tie pouches of salt to a wreath hung on your door. Add some to foods cooked with the intent of attracting wealth, such as rice or round golden cornbread cakes. Put rock salt in money-attracting talismans. Never allow your household to run out of salt, which implies running out of money.

For protection, sprinkle salt across the threshold to prevent malignant entities from entering your home. Add salt to comfort foods for extra protective value. Eat a pinch when a severe storm threatens, or before embarking on a journey. Salt lain to rest with the dead represents the immortal spirit and grants peace in the afterlife. Hung on to a baby's crib, salt grants protection from malicious spirits, and it plays a key role in naming ceremonies around the world. In Latin America, a blend of ingredients called "rattlesnake salt" protects homes and businesses. Use salt to trace a circle around yourself before beginning a major spell. You can also carry a pouch of salt with you for general protection.

For purification, place magical stones in a dish of salt for a week. Add salt or a bath bomb to tub water, and soak in it to remove illness and bad moods. This is especially popular in Afro-Caribbean traditions. Sprinkle salt in a new home before moving in, to erase any negative energy left by the previous residents.

In Conclusion

Salt is one of the oldest and most important substances employed in ritual, and it remains an essential part of contemporary Pagan practice. We use it on our altars, in our spells, in our kitchens, and in our bathrooms. It brings security and good fortune. As an offering, it pleases the gods and goddesses.

Always keep it handy—and don't take that with a grain of salt.

Eostra and the Ancient New Year

by Sorita Loock

The new year was celebrated at Spring Equinox by the earliest great civilizations—the Babylonians and Sumerians. The Sumerians called their new year the "festival of the sowing of barley," and they planted their crops for the year to come at this time. The Babylonians called their Spring Equinox festival simply the "beginning of the year."

Babylonian New Year

The Babylonians celebrated their new year with great rituals. Their great creation epic, "Enuma Anu Enlil," was recited twice. In the story, actors and actresses ritually reenacted the conflict of Marduk, the ruler of the gods, with Tiamat, a dragon of chaos from whose body the world was created. After Tiamat was slain and lay dead in the mountain, she was restored to life through the chanting of the second part of the epic.

The Babylonian king would undergo a ritual humiliation, stripping off all his finery and asking for forgiveness from the gods for all his wrong choices and bad deeds. He represented the people and so was praying on behalf of all of them. To do this, he had to be dressed as one of them.

After this, processions of statues of the gods would flow through the cities, and there would be a week of chaotic festivals that represented the creation of the universe out of chaos. Masters and servants would reverse roles, and the king be replaced by a mock king. At the end of the week all returned to normal. And the people had faith that their celebration had ensured the continuation of the bond between the gods, the earth, and mankind.

Sumerian New Year Traditions

The Sumerians celebrated the new year as the time when their goddess Inanna returned from the underworld. With her return, the land could again grow fertile, a theme which recurs in the later Greek myth of Demeter and Persephone.

Invocation to Inanna for the Spring Equinox

We spend the day in plenty, assembling with great joy,
And hail Inanna with the praises of the gods and all mankind.
Holy priestess! Created with the heavens and earth!
Inanna, first daughter of the Moon, lady of the evening star,
Mighty, majestic, radiant, beautiful, and youthful,
You who gave the gifts of the gods to mankind—
We sing your praises as you rise in the skies.
Bless us with your wisdom, you who are the joy of all.

Greek New Year Traditions

In ancient Greece, the Spring Equinox was marked by the festival of Artemis Elaphêbolos ("the deer-shooting"). Stag-shaped cakes called *elaphoi* were made from dough, honey, and sesame seeds and offered to Artemis to curry her blessing for a plentiful hunt. These cakes make an ideal offering for modern Pagan celebrations, honoring the Moon goddess and the Horned God in a single cake.

Invocation to Artemis

Fierce maiden huntress, beautiful Artemis,
You dwell on the woody hills, surrounded by your sacred hounds.

Chaste and virtuous lady, unconquerable queen,
We honor you and sing your praises to the Moon.
Grant us skill, courage, and good health,
And that we may know your wiles and stealth

Roman New Year Traditions

The Romans also celebrated Spring Equinox as a time of new beginnings, honoring Minerva and Mars. Mars was originally a vegetation god and so gives his name to March, the month of the equinox. Minerva was honored as patron of crafts and the arts, and artisans were exhorted to pray for her favor in order to increase their skills. No bloodshed was permitted on Minerva's birthday, March 19, which began a five-day celebration.

Invocation to Minerva

Illustrious Minerva, sprung from the head of Jove,
We honor your wisdom and might.
O thou who art the purger of evils, all victorious queen,
Bless us with knowledge that we may rejoice in your skills
And follow your ineffable flame of inspiration.

On the second of the five days of Minerva, the Romans included a festival called the Pelusia, a celebration of the Egyptian Isis who had been adopted and beloved of the Roman people. This festival was fundamental in the Egyptian calendar, as it secured the annual inundation of the Nile, an event vital to the fertility of Egypt.

Old Europe's New Year

In Europe, the goddess Eostra was celebrated at the equinox, Eostra's symbols are the hare and the egg, and they are combined in her myth. The story tells of how Eostra came upon a lapwing that was nearly frozen and close to death. To heal the bird, Eostra turned it into a hare. However, the hare was confused and still laid eggs.

Invocation to Eostra

Beautiful goddess of the dawn, shine forth your light upon us
That we may sing of your wisdom and love.

Blessed by your fertility like your companion the hare,
Eostra, where you walk, rainbows are formed
And blossom grow by the light you bring.
We praise you and honor you as you herald the spring.

March is also the time of the "mad March hare," when hares were said to box. Hares were associated with Witches, who were believed to be able to shape-shift into them. Hares were also thought able to take away misfortunes. Try visualizing a hare, and think about all the things you wish to be rid of, like ill health or poverty, and then sing this modern version of an old charm:

Hare spirit, swift as lightning,
These afflictions need affrightening.
Lady bright and lord of might,
Send them from me, give them flight.
Now they do reside in you.
Run, run, hare spirit, till fall of dew.

Eggs have long been seen as a symbol of fertility, rebirth, and new life. The yoke symbolizes the returning Sun, and the egg white the nurturing power of the Goddess. At this time of the light and dark in equal balance, chickens also begin to lay more eggs, stimulated by the light. As such, eggs are the perfect symbol for the coming of spring. This fact was surely recognized by our ancestors who made this association between the egg and the equinox.

In more recent times Eostra's hare and eggs have become popularized into the Easter bunny and chocolate eggs. The goddess' name was also borrowed, but changed into Easter, which remains one of the most significant Christian festivals and maintains the theme of rebirth.

At the Spring Equinox, Pagans celebrate the return of the Maiden Goddess from the dark realms of winter. Her return is seen in the rebirth of nature, visible in emerging flowers, blossoming trees, and other beauty. The equinox is a time of beauty and growth and a time to honor the gods and yourself as you move through the wheel of the year.

Dance to the Goddess

by Olivia O'Meir

There are as many ways to worship the Goddess as there are goddesses. Ritual is one popular way, but she can also be honored through the arts—in painting, sculpture, music, and dance. Out of all the arts, dance stands out because of the intensity of its physical activity.

Dance is a type of prayer that involves the mind, body, and spirit. A repetitive motion can create a meditative and ecstatic experience, much as with chanting or drumming. Dancing is a way to build up energy that can be released and sent to the Goddess. It is also a way to honor the body and the body's sexuality. By honoring ourselves in dance, we honor the Goddess.

In modern Paganism, the Goddess is most often viewed as having three aspects: maiden, mother, and crone. These aspects relate to the stages and aspects of a woman's life.

The Maiden

The maiden is viewed as a young girl. She is unmarried and unattached to a partner. She is independent, like the goddesses Artemis and Kore. Maiden-dancing goddesses represent the power of seduction and sexuality. They can also be related to celebration and to release. Such goddesses include the Maenads, the Apsaras, the Muses, Bast, Uzume, and Venus.

The Maenads are the followers of Dionysus. During their dancing they become wild, expressing the repressed side of themselves. They celebrate and honor the twice-born god with their moves.

The Apsaras are Hindu goddesses. Their collective name means "moving in the water," and they are called so because of their seductive and sensual dances. They have also been called "daughters of pleasure," "lightning princesses," and the "cloud damsels." In some sources, the Apsaras are considered nature spirits or fairies. They are singers and dancers, known for having many lovers—men and gods alike.

The next set of goddesses are the Muses. The nine sisters serve as inspiration for artists and writers. Each Muse represents a different area of the arts. Terpsichore ("lover of dance") is the Muse of dance and choral singing. She is often depicted in art as dancing with a lyre and plectrum, an instrument used for plucking stringed instruments such as the lyre.

The Japanese goddess Uzume is well-known for her sensual and sexy dancing. She is a lusty goddess who wears flimsy garments that she sheds during her dancing for the entertainment of the gods. Her outrageous dancing made Amaterasu, the Sun goddess, leave the cave she was hiding in. This act restored sunlight and warmth to the world. Her followers are called *nuru* and *yuta* and still practice forms of shamanism.

The Mother

The mother represents the maturation of the maiden into full womanhood. She is fertile and active. The mother represents growth and creation. She is associated with goddesses like Brighid, Isis, and Hera. Mother-dancing goddesses represent manifestation and creation. They can also represent fertility, family, and birth.

Xochiquetzal is a goddess of dancing, song, and other arts. She has many faces and is depicted as a love and Moon goddess, a fairy queen, and a Madonna-like figure. Xochiquetzal became mother of humanity after a great flood destroyed the last world. Xochiquetzal lives on a high mountain, accompanied by musicians and female dancers.

Hathor is the mother of the gods and queen of heaven. She is the winged cow who gave birth to the universe. She has many forms: a lioness, a cow, a woman, and a tree. In addition, she is the guardian of women and all female animals. She is a patron of pleasure: music, art, touch, and dancing. The priestesses in Hathor's temples danced and played music to worship her.

The Crone

The crone is a woman in her later years. She is the wisdom of life and is associated with life's mysteries. Hecate, Kali, and the Morrigan are well-known crones. The dancing crone represents death, banishing, and destruction—all of which are vital to the circle of life: birth, death, and rebirth.

The most famous dancing crone is the Hindu triple goddess Kali Ma. Kali is a creator, preserver, and destroyer. She has a dance that banishes all the negativity in the universe. It is believed Kali danced the world into creation and she will dance to end it.

After killing some demons, Kali Ma became drunk on their blood and started to dance. Her dance became more wild and ecstatic. Eventually, her dancing would end the world. The god Shiva, realizing this, threw himself under her feet. Kali stopped when she looked down and saw Shiva and realized she was killing him. Shiva's sacrifice stopped her for awhile, but the time will come when Kali will begin to dance again and bring this world to an end.

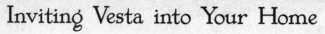

Inviting Vesta into Your Home

by Twilight Bard

Does the daily bump and grind of household chores get you down? Do you count dust bunnies among your household pets? Are forming an intimate relationship with the pizza delivery guy? If household chores have been lower on your busy priority list than you like, it's time to invite some goddess energy into your home.

Vesta is the Roman goddess of the hearth, and the hearth is the heart of the home. She was worshiped by Romans at home and in her temple where her sacred fires were tended to by the Vestal Virgins. Keeping a shrine and calling to Vesta before performing domestic duties will inspire you to focus your efforts.

Start by setting more mundane goals for yourself. The goal can be to tackle one specific task (organizing a closet, preparing lunches, scrubbing the toilet) or to hit the dust and clutter head-on for a only specified amount of time. You would be surprised how you are willing to throw yourself into your work when you know you can stop in thirty minutes. And as with exercise or meditation, if you stick to your cleaning regime daily, things will improve over time.

To employ Vesta's aid, keep a simple shrine on your hearth. This may be a traditional fireplace or a modern stove or even the top of your microwave. A red candle, censer, and a small bowl will do nicely. When the time comes for mundane chores like cleaning or cooking, take a moment to center yourself before Vesta's shrine. Light the candle, and burn some cinnamon incense for energy or lavender for harmony. Place an offering of kitchen herbs to Vesta in the bowl, and say these or similar words.

Lovely Vesta of grand old Rome,
Goddess of the hearth and home,

You who keep the homefires burning
For all the feasts as the wheel is turning,
Of my own free will, you I serve
And give praise that you deserve.
Lady Vesta, in your name
I do light this sacred flame;
Please accept this humble token
As a symbol of my eternal devotion.
Dearest Virgin of purest light,
Bless our home both day and night
With love, peace, health, safety,
Happiness, order, and prosperity.
For these blessings I do beseech thee,
If it is your will, so mote it be!

Envision Vesta's energy descending upon you with the clarity and strength to complete the tasks at hand, then open the windows to let in natural light and fresh air. Turn on some music and get to it. As you work, notice the energies of Vesta empowering you.

A Witch's Secrets for Extending Your Youth

by Magenta Griffith

People say I look much younger than I am. When I was eighteen, this bugged me. I hated being asked, "Why aren't you in school?" and so on. Now, it pleases me to no end to be asked when my fortieth birthday will be when it's years behind me. And when people ask, "How can you look so much younger than you are?" I smile and say, "Magic." But it's the kind of magic that takes years and years to practice—in fact, it's a lifelong pursuit.

If you are young, I describe below how to stay young. If you're older, this article will help you extend the youth you have left.

Tips for Staying Young

Don't Smoke

This is the one herb that everyone should stay away from. Not just because it has been associated with more kinds of cancers than there are pickles in a jar, but also smoking causes *wrinkles*. That's right, the leathery faces of certain cigarette ad icons are not just age—they are one result of smoking. So if you are smoking to look older, then you're on track.

If you already smoke, stop. There are plenty of programs that will help. Set a goal, taper off, and then throw away the coffin nails. If you find you crave the act of smoking, try rolling a mixture of mint and comfrey leaves in cigarette paper, and smoke that. There will be no nicotine, but taste is akin to a menthol cigarette. The first three weeks after you stop smoking will be the hardest; after that, no sweat.

Drink Water

Speaking of sweat, you should drink lots of water, both in summer and winter. It doesn't have to be eight glasses a day, but many of us don't get enough water. During the summer, I keep a quart jar or two of water in the fridge. I usually put a handful of mint leaves in it to give it a bit of flavor. Herb teas count, but black tea and coffee don't. And there are so many lovely herb teas. Try blending your own. Go to any store that sells herbs in bulk, buy whatever smells good and is meant for culinary use, and experiment.

Sleep

Always get plenty of sleep. A little chamomile tea before bed will help relax you and can be drunk every night. Warm milk is another great way to get to sleep. If you don't like the taste of milk, try adding a little honey and cinnamon. If you add chocolate, you will be defeating the purpose of getting to sleep, because chocolate is a stimulant. If you have a lot of trouble sleeping, occasional use of valerian, either in a capsule or as a tea, will help you get your eight hours. Valerian tastes awful though; if you are using it as a tea, I suggest you mix it with mint or other strong-flavored herbs. It can  be helpful to use valerian for a few nights to establish or reestablish a healthy sleep cycle; it's safe to use for about a week at a time.

Watch What You Consume

To stay young, you want to keep your weight stable. It's better to be a few pounds overweight than going up and down. So eat a healthy diet. Of course, that's easy to say, but hard to accomplish in our busy lives. Try your best to use common sense. Vegetables and fruits in reasonable quantities are healthy. Lots of fats, oils, and grease are not. You need protein, but how much seems to vary from person to person. Whole grains are better for you than refined starches. Vitamin pills will not replace a healthy diet, but they will help fill in the gaps.

If a healthy, low-salt, low-fat diet seems bland, use herbs and spices to add taste. Cayenne is the most extreme spice you can add. Dill helps perk up most vegetables. Basil goes well with tomatoes. There's no need for a fattening salad dressing—just blend vinegar and a little olive or walnut oil with your choice of dill, chervil, or tarragon. Remember fresh ground pepper. It perks up anything.

If you crave sweets, try spices instead. Use low-fat milk, flavored with cinnamon and nutmeg and served hot or cold, as a more healthy treat. I also sprinkle spices on low-fat cottage cheese and use it as dessert.

Brush and floss your teeth after every meal, if you can. At least once a day, give your mouth a thorough cleaning, including scraping your tongue. You can brush your teeth with a mixture of baking soda and salt, and use a fluoride mouthwash, or you can use any commercial toothpaste with fluoride. Rinse your mouth with hydrogen peroxide, then rinse with plain water. Get your teeth cleaned professionally twice a year, and have cavities filled promptly. Putting off dental work only makes the problem worse. False teeth are expensive and never look as good as your own.

Skin Tips

I hate to say it, but to stay young you simply have to avoid direct sunlight as much as possible. Wear a hat when you are out, especially if you will be in the Sun for any length of time. Use moisturizer with sunscreen every day. This means you, too, guys. Wear sunglasses to prevent squinting, which causes the wrinkles around your eyes that will seem to age you. The skin under your eyes is some of the most delicate skin on your body. Protect yourself.

Of course, you do need some exposure to the Sun every day, in order for your body to make vitamin D. Also, exposure to natural light during the winter helps combat seasonal affective disorder and the general winter blahs many of us get. So don't avoid the Sun totally.

To keep your skin from drying out, avoid excess bathing, and avoid soap. A quick shower two or three times a week is adequate, unless your work or play get you very dirty or sweaty. Even so, consider rinsing without soap, or use a mild non-soap, non-detergent cleanser. Soap and detergents cause your skin to age faster. If your skin is oily, use a face mask made of equal amounts of oatmeal and warm water. Spread this on your face, avoiding your eyes, and sit quietly until it dries. Then gently wash it off. Use make-up only minimally. As you get older, your skin dries out, faster in some climates than others. As your skin dries, you need to work to it keep moist and supple. If you must dye your hair, use the herb henna. This has been used for thousands of years to produce wonderful reddish tints, and also make hair stronger. The chemicals in permanents and straighteners are not good for your hair or your health. Find styles to make the most of the hair you have, instead of trying to make it look like something else.

Be Active, Baby

Regular exercise is important to staying young. You simply have to stay moving to keep from aging. Dancing is great exercise, as long as it does not involve loud music (which destroys your hearing), late hours (remember, you need your sleep), and smoky rooms. Yoga is good for retaining flexibility throughout your life. Weight-bearing exercise is important to build bones. Find what you like to do—walking, yoga, swimming, biking—and continue to do it on a regular basis for the rest of your life.

Gardening is terrific exercise, and growing your own herbs means you can use them in your diet. Also, there is nothing quite as relaxing and rejuvenating as the miracle of watching a plant grow from seed into a full sized item ready to harvest.

Meditate on a regular basis. This activity helps to keep your blood pressure normal and relaxes your muscles, so you don't get those worry lines in your forehead. Meditation can be a simple as sitting in a chair for five minutes and counting backward from ten to one, over and over. I commute by bus, and so I can meditate on the ride to work most mornings. If you have to drive, maybe you can take time on your morning coffee break to go somewhere quiet for a few minutes.

When you drive or ride in a car, wear your seat belts, and if you ride a motorcycle, always wear a helmet and other protective gear. (Nothing will age you more than a horrible injury.) If you participate in sports, wear the proper protective equipment—helmets, shin guards, pads. Know your sport, and learn what to do to keep yourself safe.

Have good sex, but be picky in your choice of partner or partners. Sexually transmitted diseases are not going to go away anytime soon, so educate yourself and protect yourself. Married people—anyone in a long-term relationship—live longer than singles on average, but you need to be with the right person. No one deserves domestic violence or abuse.

Stay connected to friends and family. People who have many friends and strong connections to their families live longer and are happier. If you are on bad terms with your biological family and it can't be helped, work on building your network of friends. Get involved in the community around you.

Last Tips for the Youth-Minded

For an extra edge on keeping young, practice magic. To do this, simply work on visualizing yourself as the age you wish to be. Start by picturing yourself as you are, but with the imperfections slowly fading away. Feel those blemishes and pimples fade, feel your hair grow the way you want it to, feel yourself healthy and strong. Hold the image, and work with it.

If you are still quite young, don't be in too much of a hurry to get older—it will happen. If you're a bit older, be realistic in what you want to be. Remember a time when you felt healthy and young, and feel your connection with that time. Feel those wrinkles fading, those aches receding.

Above all else, the magic will work itself if you avoid worry and stress and practice moderation in all things (including moderation). If you occasionally have fried food, or wear make-up, or skip exercising, that's okay. If you aren't having fun, there's no point in living longer. Just be sure not to overdo any of these things.

Magical Names

by Raven Kaldera and Tannin Schwarzstein

Taking on a new name is often a new magical dabbler's first contact with the art of mythical pathworking. This art consists of finding the cosmic "grooves" in the universe that have been created through the power of human belief, and using that groove to "slide" toward a particular destination. Using mythic symbols and words of power for magical work are classic examples of this kind of pathworking.

On a practical level, we all live myths, and therefore we constantly slide along these grooves, though we usually aren't aware of it. Becoming conscious of these patterns is a hard enough. Deliberately adding new mythic patterns that you don't fully understand—such as ritually taking on a new name—can make your life even more complicated.

There is great benefit and self-empowerment in naming yourself. It can inaugurate a new phase of your life, or help you move toward a new goal. In a very real sense, it is an act of self-enchantment. However, you need to be careful that your enchantment achieves the goal you intend.

A New Name Is a Map

If you've been floundering in regard to your life's path, a new name can open a new and clear course before you. It's like being given a map and a compass, with the road marked in bright red paint, ready to follow. This can be useful for people who are wanting to go somewhere important, but do not know where to start.

It can be tricky, of course. If all your friends are used to calling you Steve, they may have trouble remembering that you are now going by Perseus. At the same time, if new people can't seem to remember your new name or automatically associate it with you, perhaps there's something more appropriate.

There are three primary sources for magical names. One is the names that originate from the old tales about gods and heroes. The second is the list of creatures and items that humans have taken for totem symbols throughout the ages, and the last is the phenomenon of "combination" names, which are words strung together in order to paint an image about a particular trait.

People who take on the names of deities often don't realize that this is tantamount to giving yourself to that deity as a servant, tool, or avatar. If you take on the name Thor, it means that all the roads that lie beyond in your life belong to him. Taking on the name of a deity or mythic figure is an almost guaranteed way to be sure that you will be enacting some part of their myth for the rest of your life, or for at least as long as you bear that magical name.

Therefore, think carefully before you choose such a name. For example, choosing the name Lilith can give you strength and courage, and the ability to defy social pressure. It will also mean that the experience of alienation will be a recurring theme throughout your life. Involvement in codependent relationships will generally result in break-up and abandonment, because the Lilith pattern forces separation at the first hint of possible subservience. If this all sounds like a good idea to you—if the struggles inherent in the name are ones you're gladly willing to take on—then go ahead, but do it with your eyes open.

This also applies to taking on the names of the magical tools, pets, or servants of these beings. For example, taking on the name of Sleipnir—Odhinn's eight-legged horse—is akin to giving yourself to this god to be his tool and servant. You'll spend the rest of your time under that name either being used by him or fighting being used by him. Also, remember that heroes frequently have divine patrons, and taking on their names means that you get that patron as well—even if the hero in question has an ambivalent or adversarial relationship with that deity. Examples are Cuchulain, who was chosen by the Morrigan but never fully accepted the ramifications of that choice (and died young in part due to that refusal), and Hercules, whose original Greek name was Heracles, for "glory of Hera," and who was driven to feats of awe and terror by her alternating approval and rage.

Keep in mind also that if you take on the name of a mythic figure who has a particular partner or consort, you may draw into your life a person who has those qualities. (Doing this deliberately makes a really great love spell, but pay attention to the whole myth, especially if it has an unhappy ending.) Isis may get her Osiris, but then she will lose him. She may rebuild him from the parts she can find, but he—and their marriage—will never be the same again. Similarly, if terrible things happen to the loved ones of the mythic figure that you identify with, this pattern can cause trouble for the very real people in your life who get inadvertently cast in those parts.

Taking on the name of a totem animal or object will also give you the qualities of the creature that you honor in this way. Make sure that you choose this kind of a name on the basis of traits that actually reflect your personality, or you'll find yourself forced into an unfamiliar skin. There is some argument as to whether this sort of name brings on the idealized, mythical qualities of the animal, or the actual traits that it bears in nature. In our experience, both are true, but the real-world qualities may not be apparent until you're locked into that creature's pattern. For example, Wolf (an all-too-popular name) is associated with macho warriorship in our culture. Certainly, as wolves are a predator species the name of Wolf can give strength, agility, courage, and cunning. However, in the real world, wolves are a highly hierarchical and pack-oriented species. A lone wolf is permanently unhappy, often ill or defective, and sometimes unpredictable or rabid. No wolf is happy or healthy unless they are part of a pack and know their place in it. To be a Wolf is constantly to be seeking a place for yourself in a pack and to be worried continually your place and status. If you're not comfortable with that side of Wolf, don't choose it as a name.

With mythical creatures, we don't have an Audubon manual to turn to in order to find out about their inherent qualities, so things can get slippery. They do, however, have inherent qualities that may or may not be described fully in any individual myth. For example, if you want to name yourself Dragon (or some variant thereof), read everything you can about dragons in every culture. Although European dragons vary from oriental ones, they do have some properties in common—they are huge, reclusive loners that often have a vengeful streak, and they are compelled either to guard or to hoard something (and the line between the two can be pretty fuzzy). Part and parcel with being the keeper of some kind of treasure is vigilance, but this can also mutate into paranoia. Your best bet for finding out about the shadow qualities of Dragon is to talk to actual human beings who have borne that name in some form for an extended period of time—perhaps a bare minimum of five years. They will be able to give you insights as to the subtle ramifications of this path. Remember, however: Asking people why they chose or were given their name is a way of seeing inside their personal path. If they willingly reveal that information, take it as a gift of trust. If they don't wish to discuss it, respect their privacy.

Taking on the name of a sacred object is equally fraught with difficulty and responsibility. If it is an object that is used as a tool—such as Crystal or Sword—you can expect to find yourself being used by the cosmos as a walking avatar of that purpose. This is fine if you're comfortable with a path of such service—sincere service is among the most honorable of paths—but if you didn't expect it, it can feel very restrictive. Keep in mind also that taking on these names in a different language has the same effect. It doesn't matter if you're Dragon, Drachen, Draco, or Lung, the results are the same.

"Combination" names—such as Wolfsong, Treeheart, or Moonblade—are very popular because the combinations seem so infinite, and they give the illusion that you are designing your own unique name. However, all words have occult meanings, and there are millennia of connotations behind every word and word combination. When you take on a name, you take on not only the meaning that you attribute to the word, but also other people's associations, including the associations of our ancestors. To assume that you can use a word of power in absolute isolation is foolish. For example, some deities have attributes and honorifics added on to the end of their names to indicate a certain function. If your combination name is the accidental English translation of that attribute, you may become an unknowing channel of that god.

The literal meaning of the words may also catch up with you. Wolfsong refers to the howling of a wolf, and it may draw other wolf-types to you, or make people feel vaguely uneasy at your very presence—just as a wolfsong tends to cause a primal fear reaction in humans. Treeheart refers to the elemental spirit of a tree, and carries with it all the implications of having a driving need to protect the forest and its inhabitants. It can also refer to the quality of heartwood as being beautiful and vulnerable. Moonblade may sound elfin and fanciful, but it refers to the curved sickle wielded by the lunar crone goddess, and to take this name is to become her tool of reaping and winnowing. It can also imply being bound to the defense of lunar values—home, children, women, and the cycle of life.

Of course, if your magical name was given to you by your patron deity and you had little choice in the matter, you will have to accept that this is a life lesson from the powers that be. If it's a myth that doesn't bode well for your loved ones, you have two choices. First, you can isolate yourself and work that myth hard and strong until you've learned everything you can from it—at which point you respectfully ask the gods to set you free from it and give you another name. Or, alternatively, if it's clear that this is a lifetime commitment with no chance for release, you can only work to inform your loved ones about it, try to keep them clear of its sucking vortex, and cultivate other myths on the side that will protect and nourish your relationships. This may mean taking on a second name and learning how to change hats when necessary. This takes practice but can be quite effective.

We hope that as you take on this magical step of investing yourself with a new name, you'll do your homework and research before harnessing yourself to a cart that you didn't consciously choose. Ideally, a new name should be a source of mindfulness on your magical path, awakening you to a new perspective. Every time someone speaks your magical name, it should be a source of constant empowerment for you, regardless of whether it is a friend or a detractor. Naming is one of the ultimate human gifts: We have the power to name things. Use this power well.

A Water-Drinking Exercise

by Janina Renée

Although our bodies are about 80 percent water, for many of us, a failure to take in sufficient amounts of liquid (exacerbated by a preference for dehydrating stimulants like coffee and cola) can lead to major health complaints.

A large number of Americans suffer from fatigue, but little do they suspect that their problem may be due to improper hydration. Similarly, lack of water is the culprit in many cases of migraines and other headaches, angina, constipation, indigestion, colitis, diabetes, cholesterol, asthma, high blood pressure, and obesity.

Because hydration is so important to our basic cell structure and function, dehydration is even a prime cause of aging. As Dr. Alexis Carrell (the Nobel Prize winner for physiology and medicine) has observed: "The human cell is immortal. It is only the fluid surrounding it that degenerates. If you replenish this fluid at regular intervals, and give the cells what they require for nutrition—the pulsation of life can go on forever." This makes sense, as cellular life reproduces the ancient ocean environment.

Nature writer Loren Eiseley has explained that drifting cell masses of the early ocean lived in a "nutrient solution," but life's emergence onto land "forced the cells to bring the sea shore with them, to elaborate in their own bodies the very miniature of that all embracing sea from which they came."

This knowledge can help us appreciate what a good thing we are doing for our bodies whenever we drink water and other wholesome fluids. Sometime when you are enjoying a cool refreshing glass of something, you might try a visualization exercise to boost that liquid's revitalizing powers. Just speak the following affirmation.

As I take in this fluid sustenance,
The restorative power of elemental water
Flows through my being.
Its liquid circulates throughout my body.
It penetrates and rehydrates my every cell,
As it carries nutrients,
Rejuvenates my tissues,
Boosts my energy,
Enhances healing,
And refreshes me completely.

Although science provides us with no photographic images of the cell-hydrating process, you can use your imagination to picture how it can work. Perhaps simply visualize rivers of fluid circulating through all parts of your body, replenishing every cell, and rejuvenating every iota of protoplasm.

Spring's Promise

by Laurel Reufner

This yummy spring bread recipe came from my friend Marianne's family. Start by preparing your favorite dough from scratch, or by defrosting store-bought bread dough. Roll it into a small oval, and tuck a raw, unbroken egg into the center of the oval, covering it and holding it in place with a lattice of dough.

To be extra creative and Pagan, Marianne's mother would make rabbit shapes out of the dough, placing the egg in the rabbit's tummy. If you don't feel as creative, or don't like baked eggs, simply shape the dough into ovals, much like soda bread, and bake.

Almanac Section

Calendar

Time Changes

Lunar Phases

Moon Signs

Full Moons

Sabbats

World Holidays

Incense of the Day

Color of the Day

Almanac Listings

In these listings you will find the date, day, lunar phase, Moon sign, color and incense for the day, and festivals from around the world.

The Date

The date is used in numerological calculations that govern magical rites.

The Day

Each day is ruled by a planet that possesses specific magical influences:

MONDAY (MOON): Peace, sleep, healing, compassion, friends, psychic awareness, purification, and fertility.

TUESDAY (MARS): Passion, sex, courage, aggression, and protection.

WEDNESDAY (MERCURY): The conscious mind, study, travel, divination, and wisdom.

THURSDAY (JUPITER): Expansion, money, prosperity, and generosity.

FRIDAY (VENUS): Love, friendship, reconciliation, and beauty.

SATURDAY (SATURN): Longevity, exorcism, endings, homes, and houses.

SUNDAY (SUN): Healing, spirituality, success, strength, and protection.

The Lunar Phase

The lunar phase is important in determining the best times for magic.

THE WAXING MOON (from the New Moon to the Full) is the ideal time for magic to draw things toward you.

THE FULL MOON is the time of greatest power.

THE WANING MOON (from the Full Moon to the New) is a time for study, meditation, and little magical work (except magic designed to banish harmful energies).

The Moon's Sign

The Moon continuously "moves" through the zodiac, from Aries to Pisces. Each sign possesses its own significance.

ARIES: Good for starting things, but lacks staying power. Things occur rapidly, but quickly pass. People tend to be argumentatitve and assertive.

TAURUS: Things begun now last the longest, tend to increase in value, and become hard to alter. Brings out appreciation for beauty and sensory experience.

GEMINI: Things begun now are easily changed by outside influence. Time for shortcuts, communication, games, and fun.

CANCER: Stimulates emotional rapport between people. Pinpoints need, supports growth and nurturance. Tends to domestic concerns.

LEO: Draws emphasis to the self, to central ideas or institutions, away from connections with others and emotional needs. People tend to be melodramatic.

VIRGO: Favors accomplishment of details and commands from higher up. Focuses on health, hygiene, and daily schedules.

LIBRA: Favors cooperation, social activities, beautification of surroundings, balance, and partnership.

SCORPIO: Increases awareness of psychic power. Precipitates psychic crises and ends connections thoroughly. People tend to brood and become secretive.

SAGITTARIUS: Encourages flights of imagination and confidence. This is an adventurous, philosophical, and athletic Moon sign. Favors expansion and growth.

CAPRICORN: Develops strong structure. Focus on traditions, responsibilities, and obligations. A good time to set boundaries and rules.

AQUARIUS: Rebellious energy. Time to break habits and make abrupt change. Personal freedom and individuality is the focus.

PISCES: The focus is on dreaming, nostalgia, intuition, and psychic impressions. A good time for spiritual or philanthropic activities.

Color and Incense

The color and incense for the day are based on information from *Personal Alchemy* by Amber Wolfe, and relate to the planet that rules each day. This information can be taken into consideration along with other factors when planning works of magic or when blending magic into mundane life. Please note that the incense selections are not hard-and-fast. If you can not find or do not like the incense listed for the day, choose a similar scent that appeals to you.

Festivals and Holidays

Festivals are listed throughout the year. The exact dates of many of these ancient festivals are difficult to determine; prevailing data has been used.

Time Changes

The times and dates of all astrological phenomena in this almanac are based on **Eastern Standard Time (EST)**. If you live outside of EST, you will need to make the following changes:

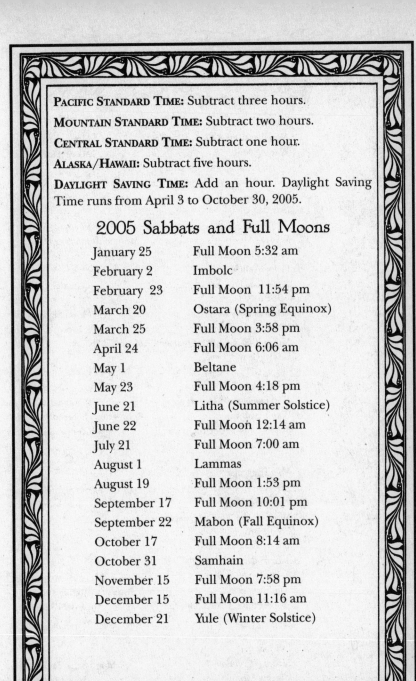

PACIFIC STANDARD TIME: Subtract three hours.

MOUNTAIN STANDARD TIME: Subtract two hours.

CENTRAL STANDARD TIME: Subtract one hour.

ALASKA/HAWAII: Subtract five hours.

DAYLIGHT SAVING TIME: Add an hour. Daylight Saving Time runs from April 3 to October 30, 2005.

2005 Sabbats and Full Moons

January 25	Full Moon 5:32 am
February 2	Imbolc
February 23	Full Moon 11:54 pm
March 20	Ostara (Spring Equinox)
March 25	Full Moon 3:58 pm
April 24	Full Moon 6:06 am
May 1	Beltane
May 23	Full Moon 4:18 pm
June 21	Litha (Summer Solstice)
June 22	Full Moon 12:14 am
July 21	Full Moon 7:00 am
August 1	Lammas
August 19	Full Moon 1:53 pm
September 17	Full Moon 10:01 pm
September 22	Mabon (Fall Equinox)
October 17	Full Moon 8:14 am
October 31	Samhain
November 15	Full Moon 7:58 pm
December 15	Full Moon 11:16 am
December 21	Yule (Winter Solstice)

Capricorn ♑

1 Saturday
New Year's Day • Kwanzaa ends
Waning Moon
Moon Phase: Third Quarter
Color: Black
Moon Sign: Virgo
Incense: Lavender

2 Sunday
First Writing (Japanese)
Waning Moon
Moon Phase: Third Quarter
Color: Yellow
Moon Sign: Virgo
Moon enters Libra 11:19 am
Incense: Poplar

☽ Monday
St. Genevieve's Day
Waning Moon
Moon Phase: Fourth Quarter 12:46 pm
Color: Gray
Moon Sign: Libra
Incense: Maple

4 Tuesday
Frost Fairs on the Thames
Waning Moon
Moon Phase: Fourth Quarter
Color: Red
Moon Sign: Libra
Moon enters Scorpio 7:00 pm
Incense: Gardenia

5 Wednesday
Epiphany Eve
Waning Moon
Moon Phase: Fourth Quarter
Color: Brown
Moon Sign: Scorpio
Incense: Cedar

6 Thursday
Epiphany
Waning Moon
Moon Phase: Fourth Quarter
Color: Green
Moon Sign: Scorpio
Moon enters Sagittarius 10:44 pm
Incense: Evergreen

7 Friday
Rizdvo (Ukrainian)
Waning Moon
Moon Phase: Fourth Quarter
Color: White
Moon Sign: Sagittarius
Incense: Ginger

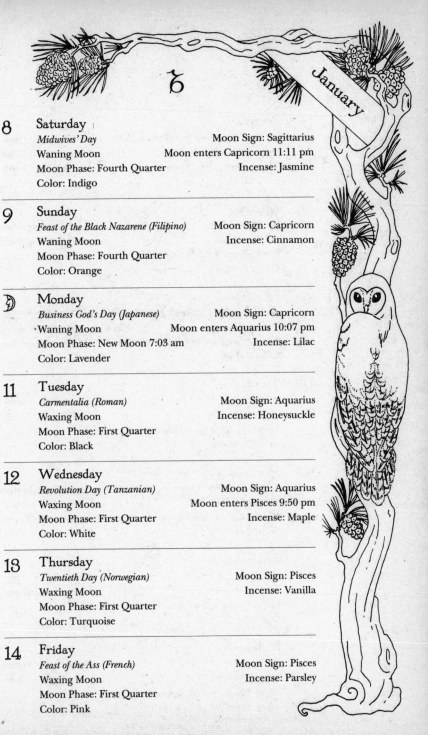

8 Saturday
Midwives' Day
Waning Moon
Moon Phase: Fourth Quarter
Color: Indigo

Moon Sign: Sagittarius
Moon enters Capricorn 11:11 pm
Incense: Jasmine

9 Sunday
Feast of the Black Nazarene (Filipino)
Waning Moon
Moon Phase: Fourth Quarter
Color: Orange

Moon Sign: Capricorn
Incense: Cinnamon

Monday
Business God's Day (Japanese)
Waning Moon
Moon Phase: New Moon 7:03 am
Color: Lavender

Moon Sign: Capricorn
Moon enters Aquarius 10:07 pm
Incense: Lilac

11 Tuesday
Carmentalia (Roman)
Waxing Moon
Moon Phase: First Quarter
Color: Black

Moon Sign: Aquarius
Incense: Honeysuckle

12 Wednesday
Revolution Day (Tanzanian)
Waxing Moon
Moon Phase: First Quarter
Color: White

Moon Sign: Aquarius
Moon enters Pisces 9:50 pm
Incense: Maple

13 Thursday
Twentieth Day (Norwegian)
Waxing Moon
Moon Phase: First Quarter
Color: Turquoise

Moon Sign: Pisces
Incense: Vanilla

14 Friday
Feast of the Ass (French)
Waxing Moon
Moon Phase: First Quarter
Color: Pink

Moon Sign: Pisces
Incense: Parsley

Capricorn ♑

15 Saturday
Martin Luther King, Jr.'s Birthday (actual) — Moon Sign: Pisces
Waxing Moon — Moon enters Aries 12:27 am
Moon Phase: First Quarter — Incense: Violet
Color: Gray

16 Sunday
Apprentices' Day — Moon Sign: Aries
Waxing Moon — Incense: Sage
Moon Phase: First Quarter
Color: Gold

☽ Monday
Birthday of Martin Luther King, Jr. (observed) — Moon Sign: Aries
Waxing Moon — Moon enters Taurus 7:06 am
Moon Phase: Second Quarter 1:57 am — Incense: Coriander
Color: White

18 Tuesday
Assumption Day — Moon Sign: Taurus
Waxing Moon — Incense: Poplar
Moon Phase: Second Quarter
Color: Maroon

19 Wednesday
Kitchen God Feast (Chinese) — Moon Sign: Taurus
Waxing Moon — Moon enters Gemini 5:24 pm
Moon Phase: Second Quarter — Sun enters Aquarius 6:22 pm
Color: Yellow — Incense: Pine

20 Thursday
Inauguration Day — Moon Sign: Gemini
Waxing Moon — Incense: Sandalwood
Moon Phase: Second Quarter
Color: Purple

21 Friday
St. Agnes Day — Moon Sign: Gemini
Waxing Moon — Incense: Rose
Moon Phase: Second Quarter
Color: Rose

178

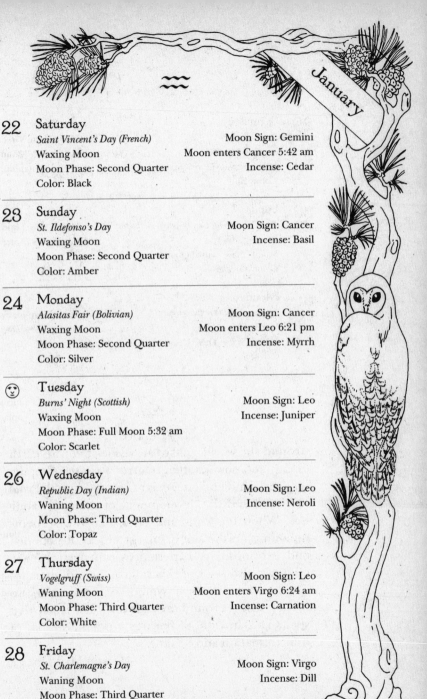

22   Saturday
Saint Vincent's Day (French)   Moon Sign: Gemini
Waxing Moon   Moon enters Cancer 5:42 am
Moon Phase: Second Quarter   Incense: Cedar
Color: Black

23   Sunday
St. Ildefonso's Day   Moon Sign: Cancer
Waxing Moon   Incense: Basil
Moon Phase: Second Quarter
Color: Amber

24   Monday
Alasitas Fair (Bolivian)   Moon Sign: Cancer
Waxing Moon   Moon enters Leo 6:21 pm
Moon Phase: Second Quarter   Incense: Myrrh
Color: Silver

☻   Tuesday
Burns' Night (Scottish)   Moon Sign: Leo
Waxing Moon   Incense: Juniper
Moon Phase: Full Moon 5:32 am
Color: Scarlet

26   Wednesday
Republic Day (Indian)   Moon Sign: Leo
Waning Moon   Incense: Neroli
Moon Phase: Third Quarter
Color: Topaz

27   Thursday
Vogelgruff (Swiss)   Moon Sign: Leo
Waning Moon   Moon enters Virgo 6:24 am
Moon Phase: Third Quarter   Incense: Carnation
Color: White

28   Friday
St. Charlemagne's Day   Moon Sign: Virgo
Waning Moon   Incense: Dill
Moon Phase: Third Quarter
Color: Coral

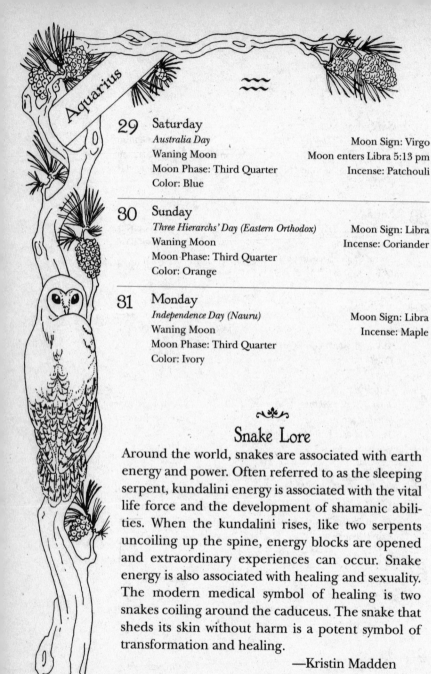

Aquarius

≈≈

29 Saturday

Australia Day
Waning Moon
Moon Phase: Third Quarter
Color: Blue

Moon Sign: Virgo
Moon enters Libra 5:13 pm
Incense: Patchouli

30 Sunday

Three Hierarchs' Day (Eastern Orthodox)
Waning Moon
Moon Phase: Third Quarter
Color: Orange

Moon Sign: Libra
Incense: Coriander

31 Monday

Independence Day (Nauru)
Waning Moon
Moon Phase: Third Quarter
Color: Ivory

Moon Sign: Libra
Incense: Maple

Snake Lore

Around the world, snakes are associated with earth energy and power. Often referred to as the sleeping serpent, kundalini energy is associated with the vital life force and the development of shamanic abilities. When the kundalini rises, like two serpents uncoiling up the spine, energy blocks are opened and extraordinary experiences can occur. Snake energy is also associated with healing and sexuality. The modern medical symbol of healing is two snakes coiling around the caduceus. The snake that sheds its skin without harm is a potent symbol of transformation and healing.

—Kristin Madden

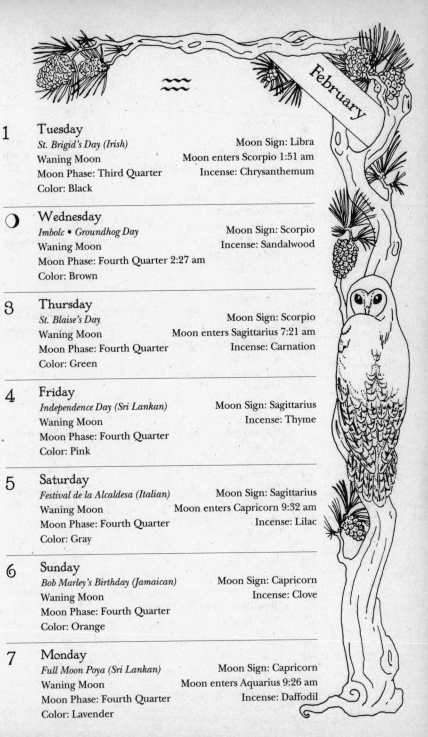

≋

February

1   Tuesday
St. Brigid's Day (Irish)   Moon Sign: Libra
Waning Moon   Moon enters Scorpio 1:51 am
Moon Phase: Third Quarter   Incense: Chrysanthemum
Color: Black

☽   Wednesday
Imbolc • Groundhog Day   Moon Sign: Scorpio
Waning Moon   Incense: Sandalwood
Moon Phase: Fourth Quarter 2:27 am
Color: Brown

3   Thursday
St. Blaise's Day   Moon Sign: Scorpio
Waning Moon   Moon enters Sagittarius 7:21 am
Moon Phase: Fourth Quarter   Incense: Carnation
Color: Green

4   Friday
Independence Day (Sri Lankan)   Moon Sign: Sagittarius
Waning Moon   Incense: Thyme
Moon Phase: Fourth Quarter
Color: Pink

5   Saturday
Festival de la Alcaldesa (Italian)   Moon Sign: Sagittarius
Waning Moon   Moon enters Capricorn 9:32 am
Moon Phase: Fourth Quarter   Incense: Lilac
Color: Gray

6   Sunday
Bob Marley's Birthday (Jamaican)   Moon Sign: Capricorn
Waning Moon   Incense: Clove
Moon Phase: Fourth Quarter
Color: Orange

7   Monday
Full Moon Poya (Sri Lankan)   Moon Sign: Capricorn
Waning Moon   Moon enters Aquarius 9:26 am
Moon Phase: Fourth Quarter   Incense: Daffodil
Color: Lavender

Aquarius

≈≈

Tuesday
Mardi Gras
Waning Moon
Moon Phase: New Moon 5:28 pm
Color: Maroon

Moon Sign: Aquarius
Incense: Evergreen

9 **Wednesday**
Chinese New Year (rooster) • *Ash Wednesday*
Waxing Moon
Moon Phase: First Quarter
Color: Yellow

Moon Sign: Aquarius
Moon enters Pisces 8:59 am
Incense: Coriander

10 **Thursday**
Islamic New Year
Waxing Moon
Moon Phase: First Quarter
Color: White

Moon Sign: Pisces
Incense: Geranium

11 **Friday**
Foundation Day (Japanese)
Waxing Moon
Moon Phase: First Quarter
Color: Rose

Moon Sign: Pisces
Moon enters Aries 10:21 am
Incense: Sandalwood

12 **Saturday**
Lincoln's Birthday (actual)
Waxing Moon
Moon Phase: First Quarter
Color: Brown

Moon Sign: Aries
Incense: Juniper

13 **Sunday**
Parentalia (Roman)
Waxing Moon
Moon Phase: First Quarter
Color: Gold

Moon Sign: Aries
Moon enters Taurus 3:18 pm
Incense: Poplar

14 **Monday**
Valentine's Day
Waxing Moon
Moon Phase: First Quarter
Color: Silver

Moon Sign: Taurus
Incense: Rose

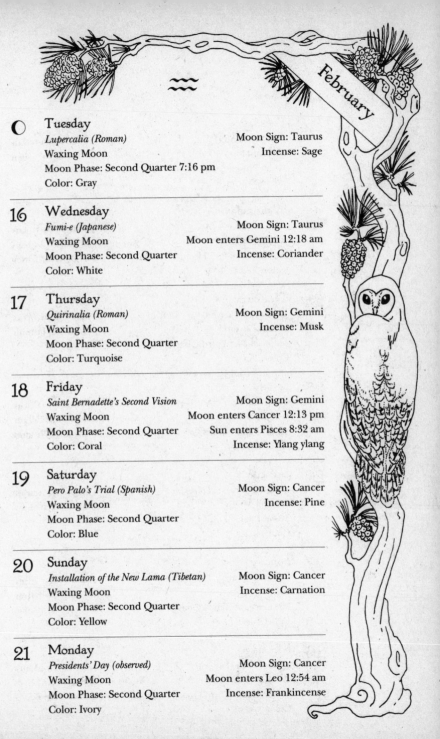

≈≈≈

February

○ Tuesday
Lupercalia (Roman)
Waxing Moon
Moon Phase: Second Quarter 7:16 pm
Color: Gray

Moon Sign: Taurus
Incense: Sage

16 Wednesday
Fumi-e (Japanese)
Waxing Moon
Moon Phase: Second Quarter
Color: White

Moon Sign: Taurus
Moon enters Gemini 12:18 am
Incense: Coriander

17 Thursday
Quirinalia (Roman)
Waxing Moon
Moon Phase: Second Quarter
Color: Turquoise

Moon Sign: Gemini
Incense: Musk

18 Friday
Saint Bernadette's Second Vision
Waxing Moon
Moon Phase: Second Quarter
Color: Coral

Moon Sign: Gemini
Moon enters Cancer 12:13 pm
Sun enters Pisces 8:32 am
Incense: Ylang ylang

19 Saturday
Pero Palo's Trial (Spanish)
Waxing Moon
Moon Phase: Second Quarter
Color: Blue

Moon Sign: Cancer
Incense: Pine

20 Sunday
Installation of the New Lama (Tibetan)
Waxing Moon
Moon Phase: Second Quarter
Color: Yellow

Moon Sign: Cancer
Incense: Carnation

21 Monday
Presidents' Day (observed)
Waxing Moon
Moon Phase: Second Quarter
Color: Ivory

Moon Sign: Cancer
Moon enters Leo 12:54 am
Incense: Frankincense

Pisces

♓

22 Tuesday
Caristia (Roman)
Waxing Moon
Moon Phase: Second Quarter
Color: Scarlet

Moon Sign: Leo
Incense: Musk

Wednesday
Terminalia (Roman)
Waxing Moon
Moon Phase: Full Moon 11:54 pm
Color: Topaz

Moon Sign: Leo
Moon enters Virgo 12:44 pm
Incense: Cedar

24 Thursday
Regifugium (Roman)
Waning Moon
Moon Phase: Third Quarter
Color: Purple

Moon Sign: Virgo
Incense: Jasmine

25 Friday
Saint Walburga's Day (German)
Waning Moon
Moon Phase: Third Quarter
Color: White

Moon Sign: Virgo
Moon enters Libra 10:59 pm
Incense: Nutmeg

26 Saturday
Zamboanga Festival (Filipino)
Waning Moon
Moon Phase: Third Quarter
Color: Black

Moon Sign: Libra
Incense: Lavender

27 Sunday
Threepenny Day
Waning Moon
Moon Phase: Third Quarter
Color: Amber

Moon Sign: Libra
Incense: Basil

28 Monday
Kalevala Day (Finnish)
Waning Moon
Moon Phase: Third Quarter
Color: Gray

Moon Sign: Libra
Moon enters Scorpio 7:21 am
Incense: Peony

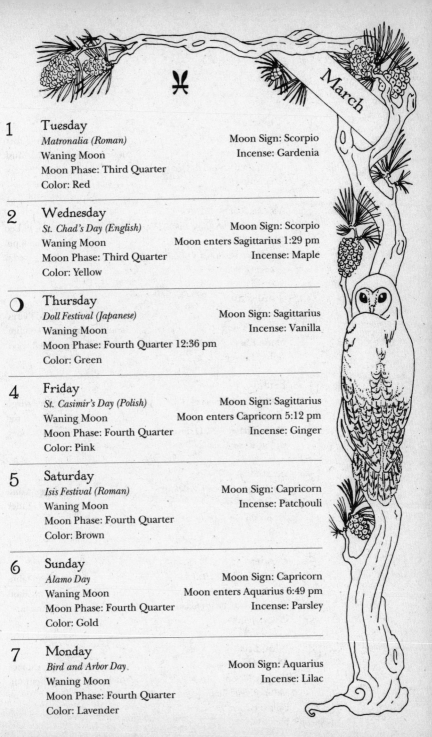

♓

1 Tuesday
Matronalia (Roman)
Waning Moon
Moon Phase: Third Quarter
Color: Red
Moon Sign: Scorpio
Incense: Gardenia

2 Wednesday
St. Chad's Day (English)
Waning Moon
Moon Phase: Third Quarter
Color: Yellow
Moon Sign: Scorpio
Moon enters Sagittarius 1:29 pm
Incense: Maple

3 Thursday
Doll Festival (Japanese)
Waning Moon
Moon Phase: Fourth Quarter 12:36 pm
Color: Green
Moon Sign: Sagittarius
Incense: Vanilla

4 Friday
St. Casimir's Day (Polish)
Waning Moon
Moon Phase: Fourth Quarter
Color: Pink
Moon Sign: Sagittarius
Moon enters Capricorn 5:12 pm
Incense: Ginger

5 Saturday
Isis Festival (Roman)
Waning Moon
Moon Phase: Fourth Quarter
Color: Brown
Moon Sign: Capricorn
Incense: Patchouli

6 Sunday
Alamo Day
Waning Moon
Moon Phase: Fourth Quarter
Color: Gold
Moon Sign: Capricorn
Moon enters Aquarius 6:49 pm
Incense: Parsley

7 Monday
Bird and Arbor Day
Waning Moon
Moon Phase: Fourth Quarter
Color: Lavender
Moon Sign: Aquarius
Incense: Lilac

Pisces ♓

8 Tuesday
International Women's Day
Waning Moon
Moon Phase: Fourth Quarter
Color: Black

Moon Sign: Aquarius
Moon enters Pisces 7:32 pm
Incense: Poplar

9 Wednesday
Forty Saints' Day (Romanian)
Waning Moon
Moon Phase: Fourth Quarter
Color: Brown

Moon Sign: Pisces
Incense: Pine

☽ Thursday
Tibet Day
Waning Moon
Moon Phase: New Moon 4:10 am
Color: Purple

Moon Sign: Pisces
Moon enters Aries 9:03 pm
Incense: Sandalwood

11 Friday
Feast of Gauri (Hindu)
Waxing Moon
Moon Phase: First Quarter
Color: Rose

Moon Sign: Aries
Incense: Rose

12 Saturday
Receiving the Water (Buddhist)
Waxing Moon
Moon Phase: First Quarter
Color: Gray

Moon Sign: Aries
Incense: Lilac

13 Sunday
Purification Feast (Balinese)
Waxing Moon
Moon Phase: First Quarter
Color: Yellow

Moon Sign: Aries
Moon enters Taurus 1:05 am
Incense: Cinnamon

14 Monday
Mamuralia (Roman)
Waxing Moon
Moon Phase: First Quarter
Color: Gray

Moon Sign: Taurus
Incense: Chrysanthemum

15 **Tuesday**
Phallus Festival (Japanese)
Waxing Moon
Moon Phase: First Quarter
Color: Maroon

Moon Sign: Taurus
Moon enters Gemini 8:44 am
Incense: Juniper

16 **Wednesday**
St. Urho's Day (Finnish)
Waxing Moon
Moon Phase: First Quarter
Color: White

Moon Sign: Gemini
Incense: Neroli

Thursday
St. Patrick's Day
Waxing Moon
Moon Phase: Second Quarter 2:19 pm
Color: Turquoise

Moon Sign: Gemini
Moon enters Cancer 7:44 pm
Incense: Carnation

18 **Friday**
Sheelah's Day (Irish)
Waxing Moon
Moon Phase: Second Quarter
Color: Coral

Moon Sign: Cancer
Incense: Dill

19 **Saturday**
St. Joseph's Day (Sicilian)
Waxing Moon
Moon Phase: Second Quarter
Color: Blue

Moon Sign: Cancer
Incense: Pine

20 **Sunday**
Ostara • Spring Equinox • Palm Sunday
Waxing Moon
Moon Phase: Second Quarter
Color: Amber

Moon Sign: Cancer
Moon enters Leo 8:17 am
Sun enters Aries 7:33 am
Incense: Sage

21 **Monday**
Juarez Day (Mexican)
Waxing Moon
Moon Phase: Second Quarter
Color: Silver

Moon Sign: Leo
Incense: Myrrh

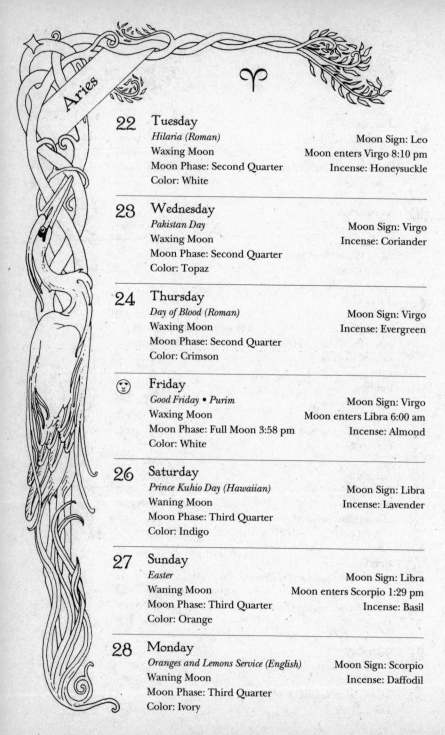

Aries ♈

22 Tuesday
Hilaria (Roman)
Waxing Moon
Moon Phase: Second Quarter
Color: White

Moon Sign: Leo
Moon enters Virgo 8:10 pm
Incense: Honeysuckle

23 Wednesday
Pakistan Day
Waxing Moon
Moon Phase: Second Quarter
Color: Topaz

Moon Sign: Virgo
Incense: Coriander

24 Thursday
Day of Blood (Roman)
Waxing Moon
Moon Phase: Second Quarter
Color: Crimson

Moon Sign: Virgo
Incense: Evergreen

☺ **Friday**
Good Friday • Purim
Waxing Moon
Moon Phase: Full Moon 3:58 pm
Color: White

Moon Sign: Virgo
Moon enters Libra 6:00 am
Incense: Almond

26 Saturday
Prince Kuhio Day (Hawaiian)
Waning Moon
Moon Phase: Third Quarter
Color: Indigo

Moon Sign: Libra
Incense: Lavender

27 Sunday
Easter
Waning Moon
Moon Phase: Third Quarter
Color: Orange

Moon Sign: Libra
Moon enters Scorpio 1:29 pm
Incense: Basil

28 Monday
Oranges and Lemons Service (English)
Waning Moon
Moon Phase: Third Quarter
Color: Ivory

Moon Sign: Scorpio
Incense: Daffodil

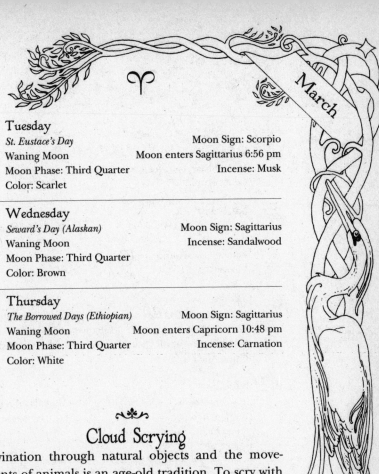

29 Tuesday
St. Eustace's Day   Moon Sign: Scorpio
Waning Moon   Moon enters Sagittarius 6:56 pm
Moon Phase: Third Quarter   Incense: Musk
Color: Scarlet

---

30 Wednesday
Seward's Day (Alaskan)   Moon Sign: Sagittarius
Waning Moon   Incense: Sandalwood
Moon Phase: Third Quarter
Color: Brown

---

31 Thursday
The Borrowed Days (Ethiopian)   Moon Sign: Sagittarius
Waning Moon   Moon enters Capricorn 10:48 pm
Moon Phase: Third Quarter   Incense: Carnation
Color: White

Cloud Scrying

Divination through natural objects and the movements of animals is an age-old tradition. To scry with clouds, scan the sky for a cloud or two that attracts your attention in some way. Close your eyes and bring your question to mind. Evoke all the feelings you hold for this situation, and send this question into the sky on your breath. Pick out three to five images in the clouds, and write or draw each image. Free-associate to explore the energies you associate with these images, and put all that you've written together in a story that answers your question.

—Kristin Madden

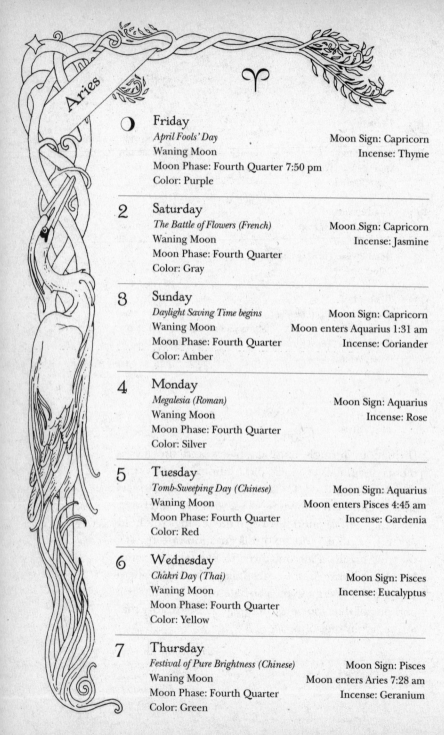

♈

1 Friday ☽
April Fools' Day
Waning Moon
Moon Phase: Fourth Quarter 7:50 pm
Color: Purple

Moon Sign: Capricorn
Incense: Thyme

2 Saturday
The Battle of Flowers (French)
Waning Moon
Moon Phase: Fourth Quarter
Color: Gray

Moon Sign: Capricorn
Incense: Jasmine

3 Sunday
Daylight Saving Time begins
Waning Moon
Moon Phase: Fourth Quarter
Color: Amber

Moon Sign: Capricorn
Moon enters Aquarius 1:31 am
Incense: Coriander

4 Monday
Megalesia (Roman)
Waning Moon
Moon Phase: Fourth Quarter
Color: Silver

Moon Sign: Aquarius
Incense: Rose

5 Tuesday
Tomb-Sweeping Day (Chinese)
Waning Moon
Moon Phase: Fourth Quarter
Color: Red

Moon Sign: Aquarius
Moon enters Pisces 4:45 am
Incense: Gardenia

6 Wednesday
Chakri Day (Thai)
Waning Moon
Moon Phase: Fourth Quarter
Color: Yellow

Moon Sign: Pisces
Incense: Eucalyptus

7 Thursday
Festival of Pure Brightness (Chinese)
Waning Moon
Moon Phase: Fourth Quarter
Color: Green

Moon Sign: Pisces
Moon enters Aries 7:28 am
Incense: Geranium

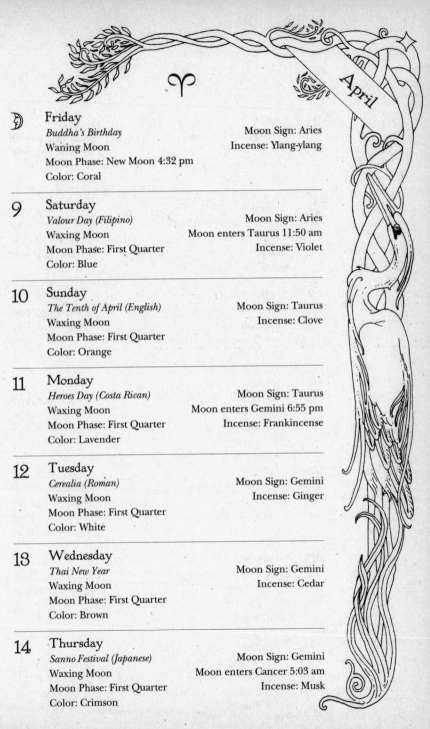

Friday
Buddha's Birthday
Waning Moon
Moon Phase: New Moon 4:32 pm
Color: Coral

Moon Sign: Aries
Incense: Ylang-ylang

9 Saturday
Valour Day (Filipino)
Waxing Moon
Moon Phase: First Quarter
Color: Blue

Moon Sign: Aries
Moon enters Taurus 11:50 am
Incense: Violet

10 Sunday
The Tenth of April (English)
Waxing Moon
Moon Phase: First Quarter
Color: Orange

Moon Sign: Taurus
Incense: Clove

11 Monday
Heroes Day (Costa Rican)
Waxing Moon
Moon Phase: First Quarter
Color: Lavender

Moon Sign: Taurus
Moon enters Gemini 6:55 pm
Incense: Frankincense

12 Tuesday
Cerealia (Roman)
Waxing Moon
Moon Phase: First Quarter
Color: White

Moon Sign: Gemini
Incense: Ginger

13 Wednesday
Thai New Year
Waxing Moon
Moon Phase: First Quarter
Color: Brown

Moon Sign: Gemini
Incense: Cedar

14 Thursday
Sanno Festival (Japanese)
Waxing Moon
Moon Phase: First Quarter
Color: Crimson

Moon Sign: Gemini
Moon enters Cancer 5:03 am
Incense: Musk

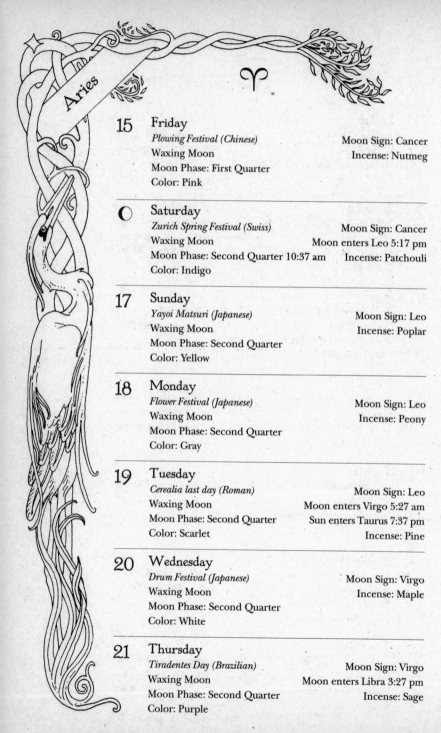

Aries

♈

15 Friday
Plowing Festival (Chinese)
Waxing Moon
Moon Phase: First Quarter
Color: Pink

Moon Sign: Cancer
Incense: Nutmeg

☾ **Saturday**
Zurich Spring Festival (Swiss)
Waxing Moon
Moon Phase: Second Quarter 10:37 am
Color: Indigo

Moon Sign: Cancer
Moon enters Leo 5:17 pm
Incense: Patchouli

17 Sunday
Yayoi Matsuri (Japanese)
Waxing Moon
Moon Phase: Second Quarter
Color: Yellow

Moon Sign: Leo
Incense: Poplar

18 Monday
Flower Festival (Japanese)
Waxing Moon
Moon Phase: Second Quarter
Color: Gray

Moon Sign: Leo
Incense: Peony

19 Tuesday
Cerealia last day (Roman)
Waxing Moon
Moon Phase: Second Quarter
Color: Scarlet

Moon Sign: Leo
Moon enters Virgo 5:27 am
Sun enters Taurus 7:37 pm
Incense: Pine

20 Wednesday
Drum Festival (Japanese)
Waxing Moon
Moon Phase: Second Quarter
Color: White

Moon Sign: Virgo
Incense: Maple

21 Thursday
Tiradentes Day (Brazilian)
Waxing Moon
Moon Phase: Second Quarter
Color: Purple

Moon Sign: Virgo
Moon enters Libra 3:27 pm
Incense: Sage

22 Friday
Earth Day
Waxing Moon
Moon Phase: Second Quarter
Color: Rose

Moon Sign: Libra
Incense: Ginger

23 Saturday
St. George's Day (English)
Waxing Moon
Moon Phase: Second Quarter
Color: Brown

Moon Sign: Gemini
Moon enters Scorpio 10:25 pm
Incense: Lilac

Sunday
Passover begins
Waxing Moon
Moon Phase: Full Moon 6:06 am
Color: Gold

Moon Sign: Scorpio
Incense: Cinnamon

25 Monday
Robigalia (Roman)
Waning Moon
Moon Phase: Third Quarter
Color: Ivory

Moon Sign: Scorpio
Incense: Lavender

26 Tuesday
Arbor Day
Waning Moon
Moon Phase: Third Quarter
Color: Black

Moon Sign: Scorpio
Moon enters Sagittarius 2:46 am
Incense: Juniper

27 Wednesday
Humabon's Conversion (Filipino)
Waning Moon
Moon Phase: Third Quarter
Color: Topaz

Moon Sign: Sagittarius
Incense: Pine

28 Thursday
Floralia (Roman)
Waning Moon
Moon Phase: Third Quarter
Color: Turquoise

Moon Sign: Sagittarius
Moon enters Capricorn 5:33 am
Incense: Jasmine

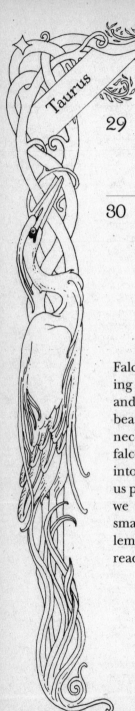

29 Friday
Green Day (Japanese)
Waning Moon
Moon Phase: Third Quarter
Color: White

Moon Sign: Capricorn
Incense: Rose

30 Saturday
Walpurgis Night • May Eve
Waning Moon
Moon Phase: Third Quarter
Color: Blue

Moon Sign: Capricorn
Moon enters Aquarius 7:54 am
Incense: Juniper

Falcon Lore

Falcons are built for speed and agility. As a journeying or meditation guide, falcon brings a swiftness and alertness. Shape-shifting happens in a heartbeat. Goals are reached with blinding speed, and necessary change comes rapidly. The sharp eyes of falcon see deep into the depths. They don't see into the darkness as owl does, but instead they allow us perceive the shadows from a distance. In this way we are alerted before something unexpected smacks us in the face. We are able to avoid problems and speed with agility toward the issues we are ready to handle.

—Kristin Madden

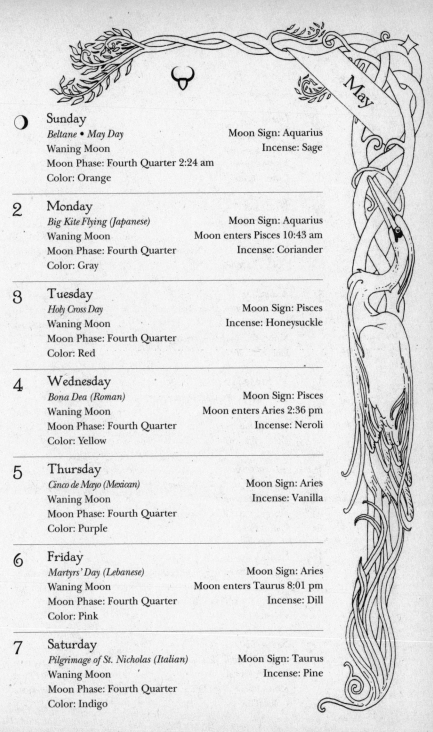

1 Sunday
Beltane • May Day
Waning Moon
Moon Phase: Fourth Quarter 2:24 am
Color: Orange

Moon Sign: Aquarius
Incense: Sage

---

2 Monday
Big Kite Flying (Japanese)
Waning Moon
Moon Phase: Fourth Quarter
Color: Gray

Moon Sign: Aquarius
Moon enters Pisces 10:43 am
Incense: Coriander

---

3 Tuesday
Holy Cross Day
Waning Moon
Moon Phase: Fourth Quarter
Color: Red

Moon Sign: Pisces
Incense: Honeysuckle

---

4 Wednesday
Bona Dea (Roman)
Waning Moon
Moon Phase: Fourth Quarter
Color: Yellow

Moon Sign: Pisces
Moon enters Aries 2:36 pm
Incense: Neroli

---

5 Thursday
Cinco de Mayo (Mexican)
Waning Moon
Moon Phase: Fourth Quarter
Color: Purple

Moon Sign: Aries
Incense: Vanilla

---

6 Friday
Martyrs' Day (Lebanese)
Waning Moon
Moon Phase: Fourth Quarter
Color: Pink

Moon Sign: Aries
Moon enters Taurus 8:01 pm
Incense: Dill

---

7 Saturday
Pilgrimage of St. Nicholas (Italian)
Waning Moon
Moon Phase: Fourth Quarter
Color: Indigo

Moon Sign: Taurus
Incense: Pine

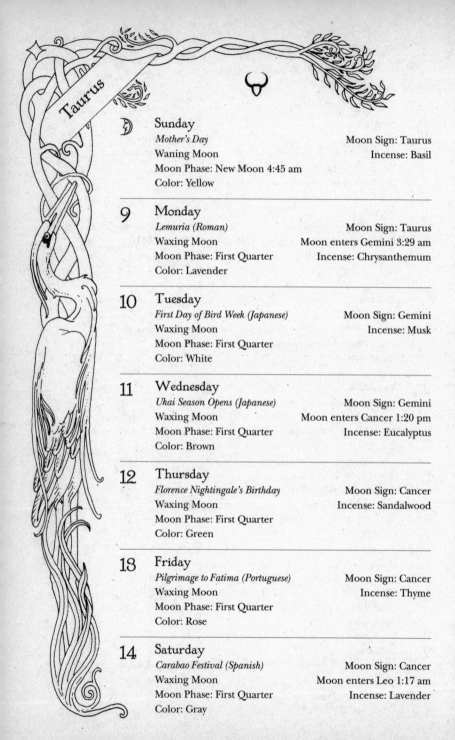

☽ Sunday
Mother's Day   Moon Sign: Taurus
Waning Moon   Incense: Basil
Moon Phase: New Moon 4:45 am
Color: Yellow

9 Monday
Lemuria (Roman)   Moon Sign: Taurus
Waxing Moon   Moon enters Gemini 3:29 am
Moon Phase: First Quarter   Incense: Chrysanthemum
Color: Lavender

10 Tuesday
First Day of Bird Week (Japanese)   Moon Sign: Gemini
Waxing Moon   Incense: Musk
Moon Phase: First Quarter
Color: White

11 Wednesday
Ukai Season Opens (Japanese)   Moon Sign: Gemini
Waxing Moon   Moon enters Cancer 1:20 pm
Moon Phase: First Quarter   Incense: Eucalyptus
Color: Brown

12 Thursday
Florence Nightingale's Birthday   Moon Sign: Cancer
Waxing Moon   Incense: Sandalwood
Moon Phase: First Quarter
Color: Green

13 Friday
Pilgrimage to Fatima (Portuguese)   Moon Sign: Cancer
Waxing Moon   Incense: Thyme
Moon Phase: First Quarter
Color: Rose

14 Saturday
Carabao Festival (Spanish)   Moon Sign: Cancer
Waxing Moon   Moon enters Leo 1:17 am
Moon Phase: First Quarter   Incense: Lavender
Color: Gray

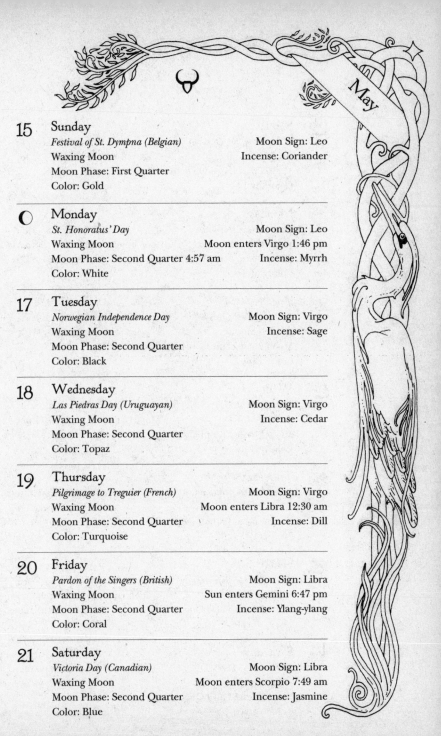

15 Sunday
Festival of St. Dympna (Belgian)
Waxing Moon
Moon Phase: First Quarter
Color: Gold

Moon Sign: Leo
Incense: Coriander

● Monday
St. Honoratus' Day
Waxing Moon
Moon Phase: Second Quarter 4:57 am
Color: White

Moon Sign: Leo
Moon enters Virgo 1:46 pm
Incense: Myrrh

17 Tuesday
Norwegian Independence Day
Waxing Moon
Moon Phase: Second Quarter
Color: Black

Moon Sign: Virgo
Incense: Sage

18 Wednesday
Las Piedras Day (Uruguayan)
Waxing Moon
Moon Phase: Second Quarter
Color: Topaz

Moon Sign: Virgo
Incense: Cedar

19 Thursday
Pilgrimage to Treguier (French)
Waxing Moon
Moon Phase: Second Quarter
Color: Turquoise

Moon Sign: Virgo
Moon enters Libra 12:30 am
Incense: Dill

20 Friday
Pardon of the Singers (British)
Waxing Moon
Moon Phase: Second Quarter
Color: Coral

Moon Sign: Libra
Sun enters Gemini 6:47 pm
Incense: Ylang-ylang

21 Saturday
Victoria Day (Canadian)
Waxing Moon
Moon Phase: Second Quarter
Color: Blue

Moon Sign: Libra
Moon enters Scorpio 7:49 am
Incense: Jasmine

22 Sunday
Heroes' Day (Sri Lankan) — Moon Sign: Scorpio
Waxing Moon — Incense: Parsley
Moon Phase: Second Quarter
Color: Amber

☺ **Monday**
Tubilustrium (Roman) — Moon Sign: Scorpio
Waxing Moon — Moon enters Sagittarius 11:38 am
Moon Phase: Full Moon 4:18 pm — Incense: Daffodil
Color: Silver

---

24 Tuesday
Culture Day (Bulgarian) — Moon Sign: Sagittarius
Waning Moon — Incense: Musk
Moon Phase: Third Quarter
Color: Gray

---

25 Wednesday
Lady Godiva's Day — Moon Sign: Sagittarius
Waning Moon — Moon enters Capricorn 1:11 pm
Moon Phase: Third Quarter — Incense: Maple
Color: White

---

26 Thursday
Pepys' Commemoration (English) — Moon Sign: Capricorn
Waning Moon — Incense: Carnation
Moon Phase: Third Quarter
Color: Crimson

---

27 Friday
St. Augustine of Canterbury's Day — Moon Sign: Capricorn
Waning Moon — Moon enters Aquarius 2:10 pm
Moon Phase: Third Quarter — Incense: Almond
Color: Purple

---

28 Saturday
St. Germain's Day — Moon Sign: Aquarius
Waning Moon — Incense: Violet
Moon Phase: Third Quarter
Color: Brown

29 Sunday
Royal Oak Day (English)
Waning Moon
Moon Phase: Third Quarter
Color: Orange

Moon Sign: Aquarius
Moon enters Pisces 4:09 pm
Incense: Clove

☽ Monday
Memorial Day (observed)
Waning Moon
Moon Phase: Fourth Quarter 7:47 am
Color: Ivory

Moon Sign: Pisces
Incense: Rose

31 Tuesday
Flowers of May
Waning Moon
Moon Phase: Fourth Quarter
Color: Maroon

Moon Sign: Pisces
Moon enters Aries 8:07 pm
Incense: Gardenia

⤚✺⤙

Burdock Healing Lore

Burdock *(Arctium minus/Arctium lappa)* is one of the most powerful blood purifiers available. It has been used for many centuries as a diuretic and to treat skin and scalp problems. Burdock contains vitamins A, B complex, and E along with many trace minerals. It cleanses the liver and lungs and is excellent for digestive and respiratory difficulties. The Chinese use it to treat colds, flu, throat infections, and pneumonia. It has great potential as an alternative cancer treatment and has been successful in preventing kidney and gall stones. Burdock is not recommended for use by pregnant women.

—Kristin Madden

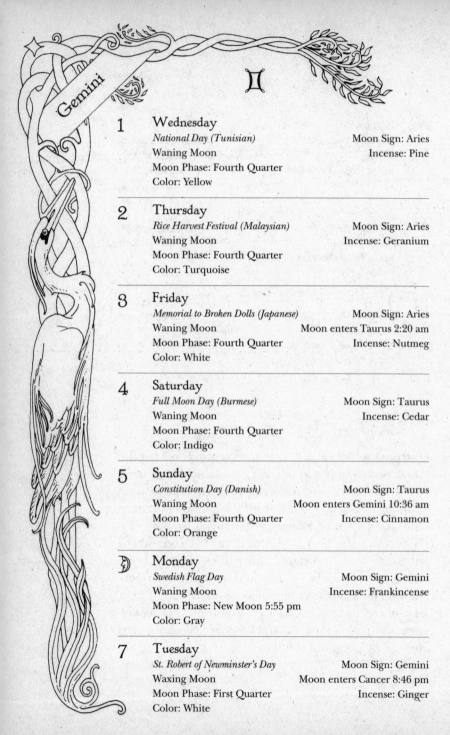

Gemini

♊

1 Wednesday
National Day (Tunisian)
Waning Moon
Moon Phase: Fourth Quarter
Color: Yellow
Moon Sign: Aries
Incense: Pine

2 Thursday
Rice Harvest Festival (Malaysian)
Waning Moon
Moon Phase: Fourth Quarter
Color: Turquoise
Moon Sign: Aries
Incense: Geranium

3 Friday
Memorial to Broken Dolls (Japanese)
Waning Moon
Moon Phase: Fourth Quarter
Color: White
Moon Sign: Aries
Moon enters Taurus 2:20 am
Incense: Nutmeg

4 Saturday
Full Moon Day (Burmese)
Waning Moon
Moon Phase: Fourth Quarter
Color: Indigo
Moon Sign: Taurus
Incense: Cedar

5 Sunday
Constitution Day (Danish)
Waning Moon
Moon Phase: Fourth Quarter
Color: Orange
Moon Sign: Taurus
Moon enters Gemini 10:36 am
Incense: Cinnamon

☽ Monday
Swedish Flag Day
Waning Moon
Moon Phase: New Moon 5:55 pm
Color: Gray
Moon Sign: Gemini
Incense: Frankincense

7 Tuesday
St. Robert of Newminster's Day
Waxing Moon
Moon Phase: First Quarter
Color: White
Moon Sign: Gemini
Moon enters Cancer 8:46 pm
Incense: Ginger

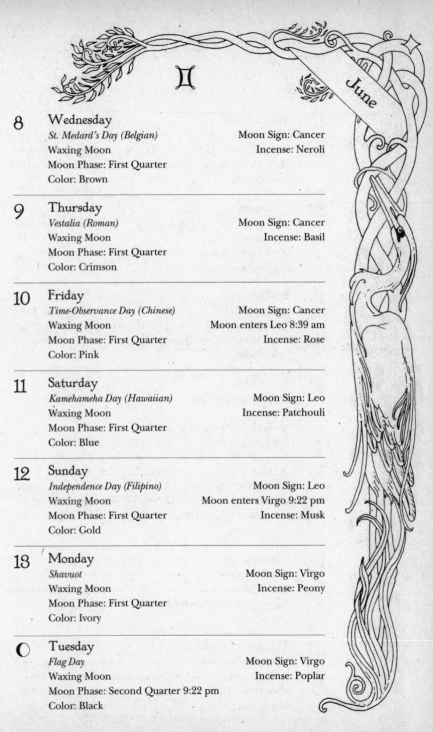

8 Wednesday
St. Medard's Day (Belgian)
Waxing Moon
Moon Phase: First Quarter
Color: Brown

Moon Sign: Cancer
Incense: Neroli

9 Thursday
Vestalia (Roman)
Waxing Moon
Moon Phase: First Quarter
Color: Crimson

Moon Sign: Cancer
Incense: Basil

10 Friday
Time-Observance Day (Chinese)
Waxing Moon
Moon Phase: First Quarter
Color: Pink

Moon Sign: Cancer
Moon enters Leo 8:39 am
Incense: Rose

11 Saturday
Kamehameha Day (Hawaiian)
Waxing Moon
Moon Phase: First Quarter
Color: Blue

Moon Sign: Leo
Incense: Patchouli

12 Sunday
Independence Day (Filipino)
Waxing Moon
Moon Phase: First Quarter
Color: Gold

Moon Sign: Leo
Moon enters Virgo 9:22 pm
Incense: Musk

13 Monday
Shavuot
Waxing Moon
Moon Phase: First Quarter
Color: Ivory

Moon Sign: Virgo
Incense: Peony

☾ Tuesday
Flag Day
Waxing Moon
Moon Phase: Second Quarter 9:22 pm
Color: Black

Moon Sign: Virgo
Incense: Poplar

♊

15 Wednesday
St. Vitus's Day Fires
Waxing Moon
Moon Phase: Second Quarter
Color: White

Moon Sign: Virgo
Moon enters Libra 8:59 am
Incense: Coriander

16 Thursday
Bloomsday (Irish)
Waxing Moon
Moon Phase: Second Quarter
Color: Green

Moon Sign: Libra
Incense: Sage

17 Friday
Bunker Hill Day
Waxing Moon
Moon Phase: Second Quarter
Color: Rose

Moon Sign: Libra
Moon enters Scorpio 5:23 pm
Incense: Dill

18 Saturday
Independence Day (Egyptian)
Waxing Moon
Moon Phase: Second Quarter
Color: Gray

Moon Sign: Scorpio
Incense: Maple

19 Sunday
Juneteenth • Father's Day • Pentecost
Waxing Moon
Moon Phase: Second Quarter
Color: Amber

Moon Sign: Scorpio
Moon enters Sagittarius 9:45 pm
Incense: Parsley

20 Monday
Flag Day (Argentinian)
Waxing Moon
Moon Phase: Second Quarter
Color: Silver

Moon Sign: Sagittarius
Incense: Lavender

21 Tuesday
Litha • Summer Solstice
Waxing Moon
Moon Phase: Second Quarter
Color: Gray

Moon Sign: Sagittarius
Moon enters Capricorn 10:52 pm
Sun enters Cancer 2:46 am
Incense: Juniper

♋

☻ **Wednesday**
Rose Festival (English)
Waxing Moon
Moon Phase: Full Moon 12:14 am
Color: Topaz

Moon Sign: Capricorn
Incense: Sandalwood

---

23 **Thursday**
St. John's Eve
Waning Moon
Moon Phase: Third Quarter
Color: Crimson

Moon Sign: Capricorn
Moon enters Aquarius 10:36 pm
Incense: Carnation

---

24 **Friday**
St. John's Day
Waning Moon
Moon Phase: Third Quarter
Color: Purple

Moon Sign: Aquarius
Incense: Thyme

---

25 **Saturday**
Fiesta of Santa Orosia (Spanish)
Waning Moon
Moon Phase: Third Quarter
Color: Brown

Moon Sign: Aquarius
Moon enters Pisces 11:03 pm
Incense: Lilac

---

26 **Sunday**
Pied Piper Day (German)
Waning Moon
Moon Phase: Third Quarter
Color: Yellow

Moon Sign: Pisces
Incense: Cinnamon

---

27 **Monday**
Day of the Seven Sleepers (Islamic)
Waning Moon
Moon Phase: Third Quarter
Color: Lavender

Moon Sign: Pisces
Incense: Chrysanthemum

☽ **Tuesday**
Paul Bunyan Day
Waning Moon
Moon Phase: Fourth Quarter 2:23 pm
Color: Scarlet

Moon Sign: Pisces
Moon enters Aries 1:51 am
Incense: Honeysuckle

29 **Wednesday**
Saint Peter and Paul's Day   Moon Sign: Aries
Waning Moon   Incense: Eucalyptus
Moon Phase: Fourth Quarter
Color: Brown

---

30 **Thursday**
The Burning of the Three Firs (French)   Moon Sign: Aries
Waning Moon   Moon enters Taurus 7:45 am
Moon Phase: Fourth Quarter   Incense: Geranium
Color: Purple

Pomegranate Chicken Recipe

4 boneless chicken breasts
2 pomegranates, juiced
4 Tbl. flour
½ tsp. salt
¼ tsp. pepper
1 chopped onion
   Olive oil or butter
2 cups chicken broth

Soak the chicken in pomegranate juice for forty-five minutes. Remove chicken and wipe off excess juice. Combine the flour, salt, and pepper, and coat the chicken with this mixture. Keep the juice ready on the side. Saute the chopped onion in olive oil or butter, then add the chicken until browned. Add the juice and broth. Simmer for twenty-five minutes. Add pomegranate seeds just before serving.

—Kristin Madden

1 Friday
Climbing Mount Fuji (Japanese)
Waning Moon
Moon Phase: Fourth Quarter
Color: Coral

Moon Sign: Taurus
Incense: Sandalwood

2 Saturday
Heroes' Day (Zambian)
Waning Moon
Moon Phase: Fourth Quarter
Color: Gray

Moon Sign: Taurus
Moon enters Gemini 4:26 pm
Incense: Juniper

3 Sunday
Indian Sun Dance (Native American)
Waning Moon
Moon Phase: Fourth Quarter
Color: Orange

Moon Sign: Gemini
Incense: Sage

4 Monday
Independence Day
Waning Moon
Moon Phase: Fourth Quarter
Color: White

Moon Sign: Gemini
Incense: Myrrh

5 Tuesday
Tynwald (Nordic)
Waning Moon
Moon Phase: Fourth Quarter
Color: Maroon

Moon Sign: Gemini
Moon enters Cancer 3:07 am
Incense: Evergreen

☽ Wednesday
Khao Phansa Day (Thai)
Waning Moon
Moon Phase: New Moon 8:02 am
Color: Yellow

Moon Sign: Cancer
Incense: Cedar

7 Thursday
Weaver's Festival (Japanese)
Waxing Moon
Moon Phase: First Quarter
Color: Green

Moon Sign: Cancer
Moon enters Leo 3:11 pm
Incense: Musk

8 **Friday**
St. Elizabeth's Day (Portuguese)
Waxing Moon
Moon Phase: First Quarter
Color: White

Moon Sign: Leo
Incense: Ylang-ylang

9 **Saturday**
Battle of Sempach Day (Swiss)
Waxing Moon
Moon Phase: First Quarter
Color: Indigo

Moon Sign: Leo
Incense: Pine

10 **Sunday**
Lady Godiva Day (English)
Waxing Moon
Moon Phase: First Quarter
Color: Amber

Moon Sign: Leo
Moon enters Virgo 3:57 am
Incense: Clove

11 **Monday**
Revolution Day (Mongolian)
Waxing Moon
Moon Phase: First Quarter
Color: Gray

Moon Sign: Virgo
Incense: Rose

12 **Tuesday**
Lobster Carnival (Nova Scotian)
Waxing Moon
Moon Phase: First Quarter
Color: Red

Moon Sign: Virgo
Moon enters Libra 4:09 pm
Incense: Sage

13 **Wednesday**
Festival of the Three Cows (Spanish)
Waxing Moon
Moon Phase: First Quarter
Color: Brown

Moon Sign: Libra
Incense: Maple

☽ **Thursday**
Bastille Day (French)
Waxing Moon
Moon Phase: Second Quarter 11:20 am
Color: Turquoise

Moon Sign: Libra
Incense: Jasmine

15 Friday

St. Swithin's Day   Moon Sign: Libra
Waxing Moon   Moon enters Scorpio 1:51 am
Moon Phase: Second Quarter   Incense: Nutmeg
Color: Pink

16 Saturday

Our Lady of Carmel   Moon Sign: Scorpio
Waxing Moon   Incense: Lavender
Moon Phase: Second Quarter
Color: Blue

17 Sunday

Rivera Day (Puerto Rican)   Moon Sign: Scorpio
Waxing Moon   Moon enters Sagittarius 7:35 am
Moon Phase: Second Quarter   Incense: Basil
Color: Yellow

18 Monday

Gion Matsuri Festival (Japanese)   Moon Sign: Sagittarius
Waxing Moon   Incense: Daffodil
Moon Phase: Second Quarter
Color: Silver

19 Tuesday

Flitch Day (English)   Moon Sign: Sagittarius
Waxing Moon   Moon enters Capricorn 9:26 am
Moon Phase: Second Quarter   Incense: Musk
Color: Black

20 Wednesday

Binding of Wreaths (Lithuanian)   Moon Sign: Capricorn
Waxing Moon   Incense: Pine
Moon Phase: Second Quarter
Color: White

☻ Thursday

National Day (Belgian)   Moon Sign: Capricorn
Waxing Moon   Moon enters Aquarius 8:55 am
Moon Phase: Full Moon 7:00 am   Incense: Chrysanthemum
Color: Purple

22 Friday
St. Mary Magdalene's Day
Waning Moon
Moon Phase: Third Quarter
Color: Rose

Moon Sign: Aquarius
Sun enters Leo 1:41 pm
Incense: Ginger

23 Saturday
Mysteries of Santa Cristina (Italian)
Waning Moon
Moon Phase: Third Quarter
Color: Brown

Moon Sign: Aquarius
Moon enters Pisces 8:12 am
Incense: Violet

24 Sunday
Pioneer Day (Mormon)
Waning Moon
Moon Phase: Third Quarter
Color: Gold

Moon Sign: Pisces
Incense: Coriander

25 Monday
St. James' Day
Waning Moon
Moon Phase: Third Quarter
Color: Ivory

Moon Sign: Pisces
Moon enters Aries 9:23 am
Incense: Peony

26 Tuesday
St. Anne's Day
Waning Moon
Moon Phase: Third Quarter
Color: White

Moon Sign: Aries
Incense: Gardenia

○ Wednesday
Sleepyhead Day (Finnish)
Waning Moon
Moon Phase: Fourth Quarter 11:19 pm
Color: Topaz

Moon Sign: Aries
Moon enters Taurus 1:54 pm
Incense: Neroli

28 Thursday
Independence Day (Peruvian)
Waning Moon
Moon Phase: Fourth Quarter
Color: Crimson

Moon Sign: Taurus
Incense: Evergreen

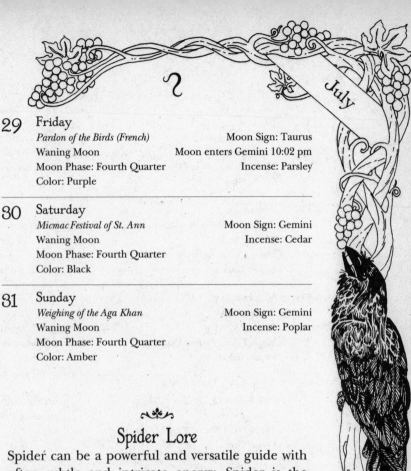

29 Friday
Pardon of the Birds (French)
Waning Moon
Moon Phase: Fourth Quarter
Color: Purple

Moon Sign: Taurus
Moon enters Gemini 10:02 pm
Incense: Parsley

30 Saturday
Micmac Festival of St. Ann
Waning Moon
Moon Phase: Fourth Quarter
Color: Black

Moon Sign: Gemini
Incense: Cedar

31 Sunday
Weighing of the Aga Khan
Waning Moon
Moon Phase: Fourth Quarter
Color: Amber

Moon Sign: Gemini
Incense: Poplar

Spider Lore

Spider can be a powerful and versatile guide with often subtle and intricate energy. Spider is the weaver, the link to past and future, and the keeper of language and creativity. However, spider can also be an indication that you need to pay more attention to the web you are weaving, and you should be aware of the types of energy flowing through it. Spider also reminds us that we can be powerful if we need to, but also that power is not to be used lightly or casually.

—Kristin Madden

Leo ♌

1 Monday
Lammas
Waning Moon
Moon Phase: Fourth Quarter
Color: Gray

Moon Sign: Gemini
Moon enters Cancer 8:52 am
Incense: Lavender

2 Tuesday
Porcingula (Native American)
Waning Moon
Moon Phase: Fourth Quarter
Color: Black

Moon Sign: Cancer
Incense: Ginger

3 Wednesday
Drimes (Greek)
Waning Moon
Moon Phase: Fourth Quarter
Color: Yellow

Moon Sign: Cancer
Moon enters Leo 9:10 pm
Incense: Coriander

☽ Thursday
Cook Islands Constitution Celebration
Waning Moon
Moon Phase: New Moon 11:05 pm
Color: Green

Moon Sign: Leo
Incense: Dill

5 Friday
Benediction of the Sea (French)
Waxing Moon
Moon Phase: First Quarter
Color: White

Moon Sign: Leo
Incense: Rose

6 Saturday
Hiroshima Peace Ceremony
Waxing Moon
Moon Phase: First Quarter
Color: Indigo

Moon Sign: Leo
Moon enters Virgo 9:54 am
Incense: Patchouli

7 Sunday
Republic Day (Ivory Coast)
Waxing Moon
Moon Phase: First Quarter
Color: Orange

Moon Sign: Virgo
Incense: Cinnamon

8 Monday
Dog Days (Japanese)
Waxing Moon
Moon Phase: First Quarter
Color: Lavender

Moon Sign: Virgo
Moon enters Libra 10:08 pm
Incense: Maple

---

9 Tuesday
Nagasaki Peace Ceremony
Waxing Moon
Moon Phase: First Quarter
Color: Gray

Moon Sign: Libra
Incense: Juniper

---

10 Wednesday
St. Lawrence's Day
Waxing Moon
Moon Phase: First Quarter
Color: Brown

Moon Sign: Libra
Incense: Sandalwood

---

11 Thursday
Puck Fair (Irish)
Waxing Moon
Moon Phase: First Quarter
Color: Purple

Moon Sign: Libra
Moon enters Scorpio 8:25 am
Incense: Carnation

☽ Friday
Fiesta of Santa Clara
Waxing Moon
Moon Phase: Second Quarter 10:38 pm
Color: Pink

Moon Sign: Scorpio
Incense: Thyme

---

13 Saturday
Women's Day (Tunisian)
Waxing Moon
Moon Phase: Second Quarter
Color: Black

Moon Sign: Scorpio
Moon enters Sagittarius 3:47 pm
Incense: Lilac

---

14 Sunday
Festival at Sassari
Waxing Moon
Moon Phase: Second Quarter
Color: Amber

Moon Sign: Sagittarius
Incense: Sage

Leo ♌

15 Monday
Assumption Day
Waxing Moon
Moon Phase: Second Quarter
Color: Silver

Moon Sign: Sagittarius
Moon enters Capricorn 7:13 pm
Incense: Chrysanthemum

16 Tuesday
Festival of Minstrels (European)
Waxing Moon
Moon Phase: Second Quarter
Color: Red

Moon Sign: Capricorn
Incense: Honeysuckle

17 Wednesday
Feast of the Hungry Ghosts (Chinese)
Waxing Moon
Moon Phase: Second Quarter
Color: Topaz

Moon Sign: Capricorn
Moon enters Aquarius 7:39 pm
Incense: Eucalyptus

18 Thursday
St. Helen's Day
Waxing Moon
Moon Phase: Second Quarter
Color: Turquoise

Moon Sign: Aquarius
Incense: Geranium

☺ Friday
Rustic Vinalia (Roman)
Waxing Moon
Moon Phase: Full Moon 1:53 pm
Color: Coral

Moon Sign: Aquarius
Moon enters Pisces 6:52 pm
Incense: Sandalwood

20 Saturday
Constitution Day (Hungarian)
Waning Moon
Moon Phase: Third Quarter
Color: Blue

Moon Sign: Pisces
Incense: Juniper

21 Sunday
Consualia (Roman)
Waning Moon
Moon Phase: Third Quarter
Color: Yellow

Moon Sign: Pisces
Moon enters Aries 7:01 pm
Incense: Clove

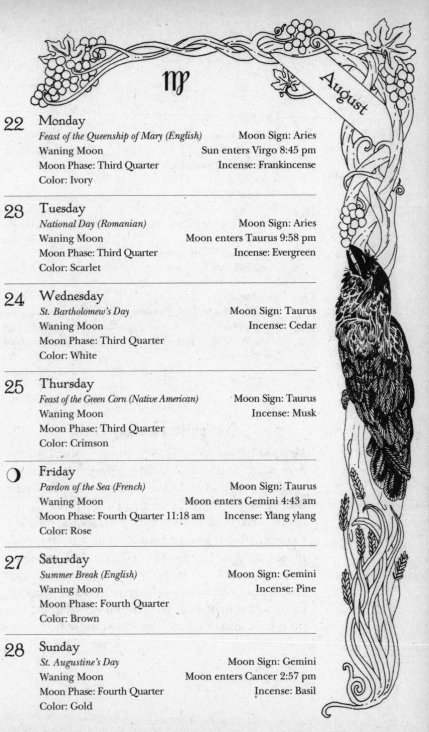

22 Monday
Feast of the Queenship of Mary (English)
Waning Moon
Moon Phase: Third Quarter
Color: Ivory

Moon Sign: Aries
Sun enters Virgo 8:45 pm
Incense: Frankincense

23 Tuesday
National Day (Romanian)
Waning Moon
Moon Phase: Third Quarter
Color: Scarlet

Moon Sign: Aries
Moon enters Taurus 9:58 pm
Incense: Evergreen

24 Wednesday
St. Bartholomew's Day
Waning Moon
Moon Phase: Third Quarter
Color: White

Moon Sign: Taurus
Incense: Cedar

25 Thursday
Feast of the Green Corn (Native American)
Waning Moon
Moon Phase: Third Quarter
Color: Crimson

Moon Sign: Taurus
Incense: Musk

☽ Friday
Pardon of the Sea (French)
Waning Moon
Moon Phase: Fourth Quarter 11:18 am
Color: Rose

Moon Sign: Taurus
Moon enters Gemini 4:43 am
Incense: Ylang ylang

27 Saturday
Summer Break (English)
Waning Moon
Moon Phase: Fourth Quarter
Color: Brown

Moon Sign: Gemini
Incense: Pine

28 Sunday
St. Augustine's Day
Waning Moon
Moon Phase: Fourth Quarter
Color: Gold

Moon Sign: Gemini
Moon enters Cancer 2:57 pm
Incense: Basil

29 Monday
St. John's Beheading
Waning Moon
Moon Phase: Fourth Quarter
Color: Gray

Moon Sign: Cancer
Incense: Myrrh

30 Tuesday
St. Rose of Lima Day (Peruvian)
Waning Moon
Moon Phase: Fourth Quarter
Color: Maroon

Moon Sign: Cancer
Incense: Sage

31 Wednesday
Unto These Hills Pageant (Cherokee)
Waning Moon
Moon Phase: Fourth Quarter
Color: Brown

Moon Sign: Cancer
Moon enters Leo 3:14 am
Incense: Maple

Mesquite Healing Lore

Mesquite *(Prosopis* spp.) is a common shrub of the American Southwest. While commonly used to smoke meats and add flavor to barbecues, mesquite is also widely used for medicinal purposes. It has been used to disinfect cuts and soothe bruises. Excellent for digestive problems and bacterial illnesses, mesquite is also favored as a soothing emollient for ulcers, colitis, and conjunctivitis. Mesquite eases upper respiratory inflammations and supports the development of a healthy immune system. The pods have also been used as a food source.

—Kristin Madden

1 Thursday
Greek New Year
Waning Moon
Moon Phase: Fourth Quarter
Color: White

Moon Sign: Leo
Incense: Jasmine

---

2 Friday
St. Mamas's Day
Waning Moon
Moon Phase: Fourth Quarter
Color: Pink

Moon Sign: Leo
Moon enters Virgo 3:56 pm
Incense: Almond

☽ Saturday
Founder's Day (San Marino)
Waning Moon
Moon Phase: New Moon 2:45 pm
Color: Black

Moon Sign: Virgo
Incense: Lavender

---

4 Sunday
Los Angeles' Birthday
Waxing Moon
Moon Phase: First Quarter
Color: Orange

Moon Sign: Virgo
Incense: Coriander

---

5 Monday
Labor Day (observed)
Waxing Moon
Moon Phase: First Quarter
Color: Lavender

Moon Sign: Virgo
Moon enters Libra 3:52 am
Incense: Rose

---

6 Tuesday
The Virgin of Remedies (Spanish)
Waxing Moon
Moon Phase: First Quarter
Color: Red

Moon Sign: Libra
Incense: Musk

---

7 Wednesday
Festival of the Durga (Hindu)
Waxing Moon
Moon Phase: First Quarter
Color: Yellow

Moon Sign: Libra
Moon enters Scorpio 2:10 pm
Incense: Pine

Virgo ♍

8 Thursday
Birthday of the Virgin Mary
Waxing Moon
Moon Phase: First Quarter
Color: Purple

Moon Sign: Scorpio
Incense: Chrysanthemum

9 Friday
Chrysanthemum Festival (Japanese)
Waxing Moon
Moon Phase: First Quarter
Color: Coral

Moon Sign: Scorpio
Moon enters Sagittarius 10:03 pm
Incense: Nutmeg

10 Saturday
Festival of the Poets (Japanese)
Waxing Moon
Moon Phase: First Quarter
Color: Brown

Moon Sign: Sagittarius
Incense: Jasmine

☽ Sunday
Coptic New Year
Waxing Moon
Moon Phase: Second Quarter 7:37 am
Color: Yellow

Moon Sign: Sagittarius
Incense: Parsley

12 Monday
National Day (Ethiopian)
Waxing Moon
Moon Phase: Second Quarter
Color: Gray

Moon Sign: Sagittarius
Moon enters Capricorn 2:56 am
Incense: Daffodil

13 Tuesday
The Gods' Banquet (Roman)
Waxing Moon
Moon Phase: Second Quarter
Color: Black

Moon Sign: Capricorn
Incense: Gardenia

14 Wednesday
Holy Cross Day
Waxing Moon
Moon Phase: Second Quarter
Color: White

Moon Sign: Capricorn
Moon enters Aquarius 5:02 am
Incense: Neroli

15 Thursday
Birthday of the Moon (Chinese)
Waxing Moon
Moon Phase: Second Quarter
Color: Turquoise

Moon Sign: Aquarius
Incense: Evergreen

16 Friday
Mexican Independence Day
Waxing Moon
Moon Phase: Second Quarter
Color: Rose

Moon Sign: Aquarius
Moon enters Pisces 5:24 am
Incense: Ginger

☺ Saturday
Von Steuben's Day
Waxing Moon
Moon Phase: Full Moon 10:01 pm
Color: Blue

Moon Sign: Pisces
Incense: Violet

18 Sunday
Dr. Johnson's Birthday
Waning Moon
Moon Phase: Third Quarter
Color: Gold

Moon Sign: Pisces
Moon enters Aries 5:43 am
Incense: Poplar

19 Monday
St. Januarius' Day (Italian)
Waning Moon
Moon Phase: Third Quarter
Color: White

Moon Sign: Aries
Incense: Peony

20 Tuesday
St. Eustace's Day
Waning Moon
Moon Phase: Third Quarter
Color: Maroon

Moon Sign: Aries
Moon enters Taurus 7:47 am
Incense: Pine

21 Wednesday
Christ's Hospital Founder's Day (British)
Waning Moon
Moon Phase: Third Quarter
Color: Topaz

Moon Sign: Taurus
Incense: Coriander

Libra ≏

22 Thursday
Mabon • Fall Equinox
Waning Moon
Moon Phase: Third Quarter
Color: Green

Moon Sign: Taurus
Moon enters Gemini 1:07 pm
Sun enters Libra 6:23 pm
Incense: Dill

23 Friday
Shubun no Hi (Chinese)
Waning Moon
Moon Phase: Third Quarter
Color: Purple

Moon Sign: Gemini
Incense: Thyme

24 Saturday
Schwenkenfelder Thanksgiving (Germ.-Amer.)
Waning Moon
Moon Phase: Third Quarter
Color: Indigo

Moon Sign: Gemini
Moon enters Cancer 10:10 pm
Incense: Cedar

◖ Sunday
Doll's Memorial Service (Japanese)
Waning Moon
Moon Phase: Fourth Quarter 2:41 am
Color: Amber

Moon Sign: Cancer
Incense: Cinnamon

26 Monday
Feast of Santa Justina (Mexican)
Waning Moon
Moon Phase: Fourth Quarter
Color: Ivory

Moon Sign: Cancer
Incense: Lavender

27 Tuesday
Saints Cosmas and Damian's Day
Waning Moon
Moon Phase: Fourth Quarter
Color: White

Moon Sign: Cancer
Moon enters Leo 10:03 am
Incense: Juniper

28 Wednesday
Confucius' Birthday
Waning Moon
Moon Phase: Fourth Quarter
Color: Brown

Moon Sign: Leo
Incense: Sandalwood

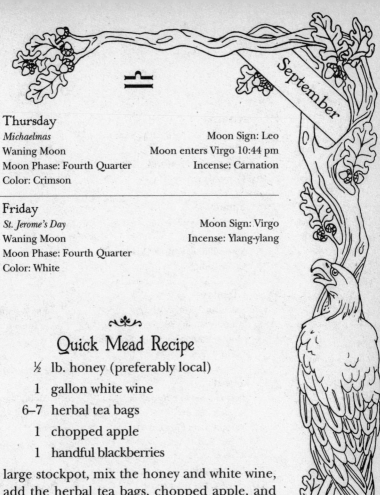

September

29 Thursday
Michaelmas
Waning Moon
Moon Phase: Fourth Quarter
Color: Crimson

Moon Sign: Leo
Moon enters Virgo 10:44 pm
Incense: Carnation

30 Friday
St. Jerome's Day
Waning Moon
Moon Phase: Fourth Quarter
Color: White

Moon Sign: Virgo
Incense: Ylang-ylang

Quick Mead Recipe

½ lb. honey (preferably local)
1 gallon white wine
6–7 herbal tea bags
1 chopped apple
1 handful blackberries

In a large stockpot, mix the honey and white wine, and add the herbal tea bags, chopped apple, and blackberries. Bring the mixture to a boil for one minute, then simmer for 2–3 minutes. Let it cool, then transfer to glass bottles or jars and refrigerate for three days. To make a non-alcoholic meade, boil everything except the wine. When ready to refrigerate, add ginger ale in place of the white wine.

—Kristin Madden

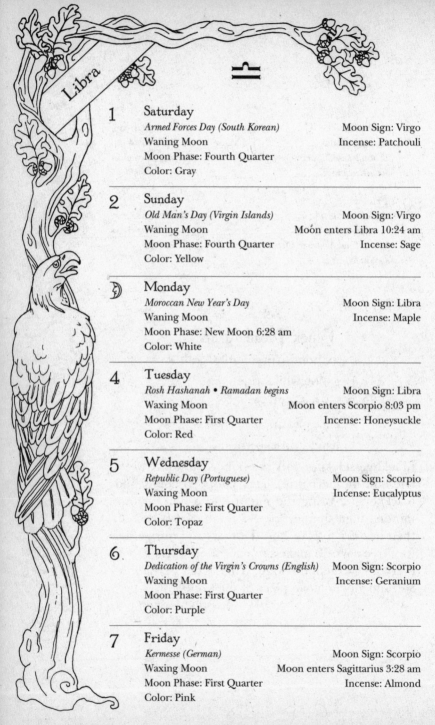

Libra

♎

1 Saturday
Armed Forces Day (South Korean)
Waning Moon
Moon Phase: Fourth Quarter
Color: Gray

Moon Sign: Virgo
Incense: Patchouli

2 Sunday
Old Man's Day (Virgin Islands)
Waning Moon
Moon Phase: Fourth Quarter
Color: Yellow

Moon Sign: Virgo
Moon enters Libra 10:24 am
Incense: Sage

3 Monday
Moroccan New Year's Day
Waning Moon
Moon Phase: New Moon 6:28 am
Color: White

Moon Sign: Libra
Incense: Maple

4 Tuesday
Rosh Hashanah • Ramadan begins
Waxing Moon
Moon Phase: First Quarter
Color: Red

Moon Sign: Libra
Moon enters Scorpio 8:03 pm
Incense: Honeysuckle

5 Wednesday
Republic Day (Portuguese)
Waxing Moon
Moon Phase: First Quarter
Color: Topaz

Moon Sign: Scorpio
Incense: Eucalyptus

6 Thursday
Dedication of the Virgin's Crowns (English)
Waxing Moon
Moon Phase: First Quarter
Color: Purple

Moon Sign: Scorpio
Incense: Geranium

7 Friday
Kermesse (German)
Waxing Moon
Moon Phase: First Quarter
Color: Pink

Moon Sign: Scorpio
Moon enters Sagittarius 3:28 am
Incense: Almond

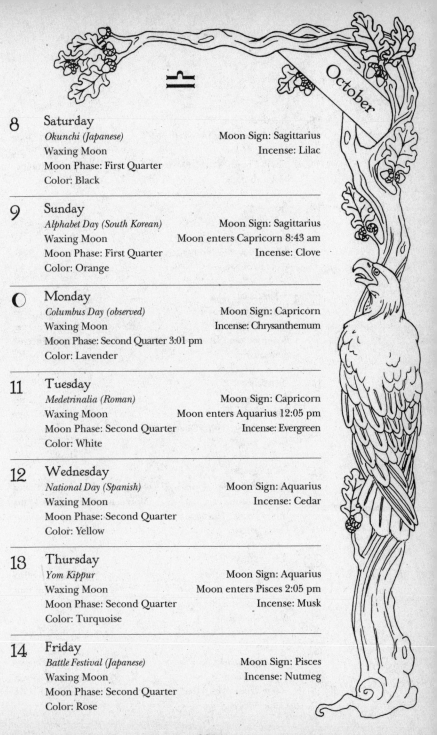

8 Saturday

Okunchi (Japanese)
Waxing Moon
Moon Phase: First Quarter
Color: Black

Moon Sign: Sagittarius
Incense: Lilac

9 Sunday

Alphabet Day (South Korean)
Waxing Moon
Moon Phase: First Quarter
Color: Orange

Moon Sign: Sagittarius
Moon enters Capricorn 8:43 am
Incense: Clove

Monday

Columbus Day (observed)
Waxing Moon
Moon Phase: Second Quarter 3:01 pm
Color: Lavender

Moon Sign: Capricorn
Incense: Chrysanthemum

11 Tuesday

Medetrinalia (Roman)
Waxing Moon
Moon Phase: Second Quarter
Color: White

Moon Sign: Capricorn
Moon enters Aquarius 12:05 pm
Incense: Evergreen

12 Wednesday

National Day (Spanish)
Waxing Moon
Moon Phase: Second Quarter
Color: Yellow

Moon Sign: Aquarius
Incense: Cedar

13 Thursday

Yom Kippur
Waxing Moon
Moon Phase: Second Quarter
Color: Turquoise

Moon Sign: Aquarius
Moon enters Pisces 2:05 pm
Incense: Musk

14 Friday

Battle Festival (Japanese)
Waxing Moon
Moon Phase: Second Quarter
Color: Rose

Moon Sign: Pisces
Incense: Nutmeg

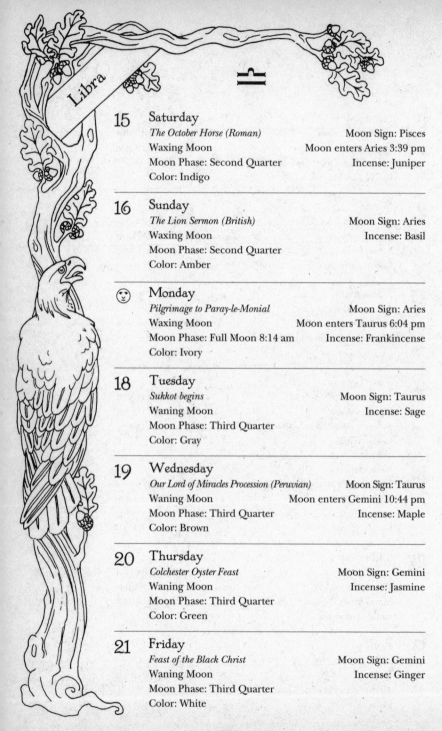

Libra ♎

15 Saturday
The October Horse (Roman)
Waxing Moon
Moon Phase: Second Quarter
Color: Indigo

Moon Sign: Pisces
Moon enters Aries 3:39 pm
Incense: Juniper

16 Sunday
The Lion Sermon (British)
Waxing Moon
Moon Phase: Second Quarter
Color: Amber

Moon Sign: Aries
Incense: Basil

Monday
Pilgrimage to Paray-le-Monial
Waxing Moon
Moon Phase: Full Moon 8:14 am
Color: Ivory

Moon Sign: Aries
Moon enters Taurus 6:04 pm
Incense: Frankincense

18 Tuesday
Sukkot begins
Waning Moon
Moon Phase: Third Quarter
Color: Gray

Moon Sign: Taurus
Incense: Sage

19 Wednesday
Our Lord of Miracles Procession (Peruvian)
Waning Moon
Moon Phase: Third Quarter
Color: Brown

Moon Sign: Taurus
Moon enters Gemini 10:44 pm
Incense: Maple

20 Thursday
Colchester Oyster Feast
Waning Moon
Moon Phase: Third Quarter
Color: Green

Moon Sign: Gemini
Incense: Jasmine

21 Friday
Feast of the Black Christ
Waning Moon
Moon Phase: Third Quarter
Color: White

Moon Sign: Gemini
Incense: Ginger

22 Saturday
Goddess of Mercy Day (Chinese)
Waning Moon
Moon Phase: Third Quarter
Color: Blue

Moon Sign: Gemini
Moon enters Cancer 6:41 am
Incense: Pine

---

23 Sunday
Revolution Day (Hungarian)
Waning Moon
Moon Phase: Third Quarter
Color: Gold

Moon Sign: Cancer
Sun enters Scorpio 3:42 am
Incense: Coriander

Monday
United Nations Day • Sukkot ends
Waning Moon
Moon Phase: Fourth Quarter 9:17 pm
Color: Silver

Moon Sign: Cancer
Moon enters Leo 5:48 pm
Incense: Myrrh

---

25 Tuesday
St. Crispin's Day
Waning Moon
Moon Phase: Fourth Quarter
Color: Scarlet

Moon Sign: Leo
Incense: Musk

---

26 Wednesday
Quit Rent Ceremony (England)
Waning Moon
Moon Phase: Fourth Quarter
Color: White

Moon Sign: Leo
Incense: Neroli

---

27 Thursday
Feast of the Holy Souls
Waning Moon
Moon Phase: Fourth Quarter
Color: Purple

Moon Sign: Leo
Moon enters Virgo 6:28 am
Incense: Vanilla

---

28 Friday
Ochi Day (Greek)
Waning Moon
Moon Phase: Fourth Quarter
Color: Coral

Moon Sign: Virgo
Incense: Parsley

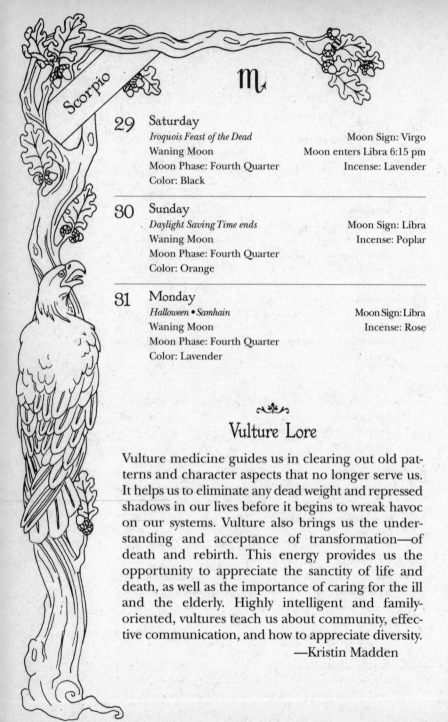

29 Saturday
Iroquois Feast of the Dead   Moon Sign: Virgo
Waning Moon   Moon enters Libra 6:15 pm
Moon Phase: Fourth Quarter   Incense: Lavender
Color: Black

30 Sunday
Daylight Saving Time ends   Moon Sign: Libra
Waning Moon   Incense: Poplar
Moon Phase: Fourth Quarter
Color: Orange

31 Monday
Halloween • Samhain   Moon Sign: Libra
Waning Moon   Incense: Rose
Moon Phase: Fourth Quarter
Color: Lavender

Vulture Lore

Vulture medicine guides us in clearing out old patterns and character aspects that no longer serve us. It helps us to eliminate any dead weight and repressed shadows in our lives before it begins to wreak havoc on our systems. Vulture also brings us the understanding and acceptance of transformation—of death and rebirth. This energy provides us the opportunity to appreciate the sanctity of life and death, as well as the importance of caring for the ill and the elderly. Highly intelligent and family-oriented, vultures teach us about community, effective communication, and how to appreciate diversity.

—Kristin Madden

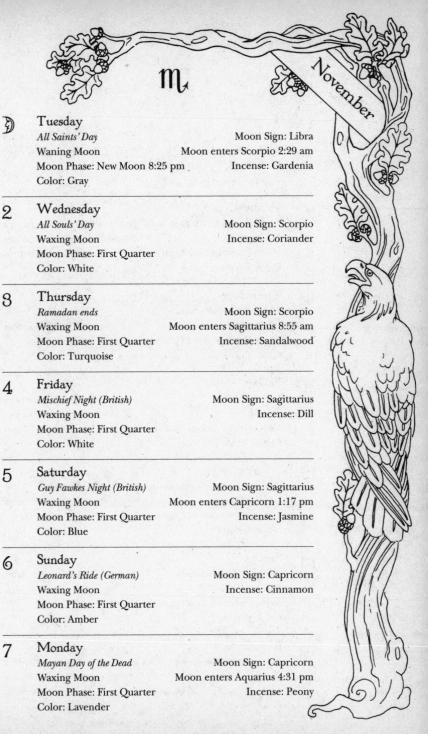

♏

Tuesday
All Saints' Day
Waning Moon
Moon Phase: New Moon 8:25 pm
Color: Gray

Moon Sign: Libra
Moon enters Scorpio 2:29 am
Incense: Gardenia

---

2 Wednesday
All Souls' Day
Waxing Moon
Moon Phase: First Quarter
Color: White

Moon Sign: Scorpio
Incense: Coriander

---

3 Thursday
Ramadan ends
Waxing Moon
Moon Phase: First Quarter
Color: Turquoise

Moon Sign: Scorpio
Moon enters Sagittarius 8:55 am
Incense: Sandalwood

---

4 Friday
Mischief Night (British)
Waxing Moon
Moon Phase: First Quarter
Color: White

Moon Sign: Sagittarius
Incense: Dill

---

5 Saturday
Guy Fawkes Night (British)
Waxing Moon
Moon Phase: First Quarter
Color: Blue

Moon Sign: Sagittarius
Moon enters Capricorn 1:17 pm
Incense: Jasmine

---

6 Sunday
Leonard's Ride (German)
Waxing Moon
Moon Phase: First Quarter
Color: Amber

Moon Sign: Capricorn
Incense: Cinnamon

---

7 Monday
Mayan Day of the Dead
Waxing Moon
Moon Phase: First Quarter
Color: Lavender

Moon Sign: Capricorn
Moon enters Aquarius 4:31 pm
Incense: Peony

Scorpio ♏

Tuesday
Election Day
Waxing Moon
Moon Phase: Second Quarter 8:57 pm
Color: White

Moon Sign: Aquarius
Incense: Ginger

---

9 Wednesday
Lord Mayor's Day (British)
Waxing Moon
Moon Phase: Second Quarter
Color: Brown

Moon Sign: Aquarius
Moon enters Pisces 7:22 pm
Incense: Eucalyptus

---

10 Thursday
Martin Luther's Birthday
Waxing Moon
Moon Phase: Second Quarter
Color: Purple

Moon Sign: Pisces
Incense: Chrysanthemum

---

11 Friday
Veterans Day
Waxing Moon
Moon Phase: Second Quarter
Color: Coral

Moon Sign: Pisces
Moon enters Aries 10:22 pm
Incense: Thyme

---

12 Saturday
Tesuque Feast Day (Native American)
Waxing Moon
Moon Phase: Second Quarter
Color: Indigo

Moon Sign: Aries
Incense: Violet

---

13 Sunday
Festival of Jupiter (Roman)
Waxing Moon
Moon Phase: Second Quarter
Color: Orange

Moon Sign: Aries
Incense: Sage

---

14 Monday
The Little Carnival (Greek)
Waxing Moon
Moon Phase: Second Quarter
Color: Silver

Moon Sign: Aries
Moon enters Taurus 2:02 am
Incense: Lavender

Tuesday
St. Leopold's Day
Waxing Moon
Moon Phase: Full Moon 7:58 pm
Color: Black

Moon Sign: Taurus
Incense: Poplar

---

16 Wednesday
St. Margaret of Scotland's Day
Waning Moon
Moon Phase: Third Quarter
Color: White

Moon Sign: Taurus
Moon enters Gemini 7:10 am
Incense: Cedar

---

17 Thursday
Queen Elizabeth's Day
Waning Moon
Moon Phase: Third Quarter
Color: Crimson

Moon Sign: Gemini
Incense: Evergreen

---

18 Friday
St. Plato's Day
Waning Moon
Moon Phase: Third Quarter
Color: Pink

Moon Sign: Gemini
Moon enters Cancer 2:42 pm
Incense: Sandalwood

---

19 Saturday
Garifuna Day (Belizian)
Waning Moon
Moon Phase: Third Quarter
Color: Gray

Moon Sign: Cancer
Incense: Patchouli

---

20 Sunday
Commerce God Ceremony (Japanese)
Waning Moon
Moon Phase: Third Quarter
Color: Yellow

Moon Sign: Cancer
Incense: Parsley

---

21 Monday
Repentance Day (German)
Waning Moon
Moon Phase: Third Quarter
Color: Ivory

Moon Sign: Cancer
Moon enters Leo 1:10 am
Incense: Maple

Sagittarius

22 Tuesday
St. Cecilia's Day
Waning Moon
Moon Phase: Third Quarter
Color: Maroon

Moon Sign: Leo
Sun enters Sagittarius 12:15 am
Incense: Pine

◑ Wednesday
St. Clement's Day
Waning Moon
Moon Phase: Fourth Quarter 5:11 pm
Color: Topaz

Moon Sign: Leo
Moon enters Virgo 1:41 pm
Incense: Neroli

24 Thursday
Thanksgiving Day
Waning Moon
Moon Phase: Fourth Quarter
Color: Green

Moon Sign: Virgo
Incense: Dill

25 Friday
Saint Catherine of Alexandria's Day
Waning Moon
Moon Phase: Fourth Quarter
Color: Rose

Moon Sign: Virgo
Incense: Ylang-ylang

26 Saturday
Festival of Lights (Tibetan)
Waning Moon
Moon Phase: Fourth Quarter
Color: Black

Moon Sign: Virgo
Moon enters Libra 1:58 am
Incense: Lilac

27 Sunday
Saint Maximus' Day
Waning Moon
Moon Phase: Fourth Quarter
Color: Gold

Moon Sign: Libra
Incense: Basil

28 Monday
Day of the New Dance (Tibetan)
Waning Moon
Moon Phase: Fourth Quarter
Color: Gray

Moon Sign: Libra
Moon enters Scorpio 11:33 am
Incense: Frankincense

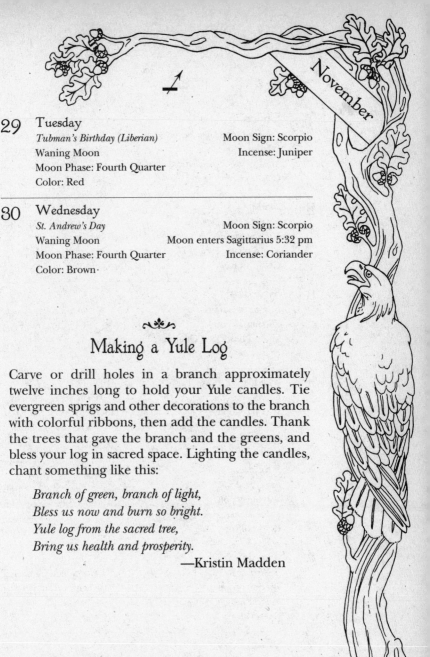

29 Tuesday
Tubman's Birthday (Liberian)   Moon Sign: Scorpio
Waning Moon   Incense: Juniper
Moon Phase: Fourth Quarter
Color: Red

30 Wednesday
St. Andrew's Day   Moon Sign: Scorpio
Waning Moon   Moon enters Sagittarius 5:32 pm
Moon Phase: Fourth Quarter   Incense: Coriander
Color: Brown·

Making a Yule Log

Carve or drill holes in a branch approximately twelve inches long to hold your Yule candles. Tie evergreen sprigs and other decorations to the branch with colorful ribbons, then add the candles. Thank the trees that gave the branch and the greens, and bless your log in sacred space. Lighting the candles, chant something like this:

> *Branch of green, branch of light,*
> *Bless us now and burn so bright.*
> *Yule log from the sacred tree,*
> *Bring us health and prosperity.*

—Kristin Madden

Sagittarius

Thursday
Big Tea Party (Japanese)
Waning Moon
Moon Phase: New Moon 10:01 am
Color: Purple

Moon Sign: Sagittarius
Incense: Carnation

2 Friday
Republic Day (Laotian)
Waxing Moon
Moon Phase: First Quarter
Color: Coral

Moon Sign: Sagittarius
Moon enters Capricorn 8:42 pm
Incense: Nutmeg

3 Saturday
St. Francis Xavier's Day
Waxing Moon
Moon Phase: First Quarter
Color: Brown

Moon Sign: Capricorn
Incense: Pine

4 Sunday
St. Barbara's Day
Waxing Moon
Moon Phase: First Quarter
Color: Yellow

Moon Sign: Capricorn
Moon enters Aquarius 10:36 pm
Incense: Parsley

5 Monday
Eve of St. Nicholas' Day
Waxing Moon
Moon Phase: First Quarter
Color: Silver

Moon Sign: Aquarius
Incense: Myrrh

6 Tuesday
St. Nicholas' Day
Waxing Moon
Moon Phase: First Quarter
Color: Black

Moon Sign: Aquarius
Incense: Honeysuckle

7 Wednesday
Burning the Devil (Guatemalan)
Waxing Moon
Moon Phase: First Quarter
Color: White

Moon Sign: Aquarius
Moon enters Pisces 12:44 am
Incense: Sandalwood

December

◐ **Thursday**
Feast of the Immaculate Conception
Waxing Moon
Moon Phase: Second Quarter 4:36 am
Color: Turquoise

Moon Sign: Pisces
Incense: Geranium

9 **Friday**
St. Leocadia's Day
Waxing Moon
Moon Phase: Second Quarter
Color: White

Moon Sign: Pisces
Moon enters Aries 4:02 am
Incense: Ginger

10 **Saturday**
Nobel Day
Waxing Moon
Moon Phase: Second Quarter
Color: Gray

Moon Sign: Aries
Incense: Lavender

11 **Sunday**
Pilgrimage at Tortugas
Waxing Moon
Moon Phase: Second Quarter
Color: Orange

Moon Sign: Aries
Moon enters Taurus 8:46 am
Incense: Poplar

12 **Monday**
Fiesta of Our Lady of Guadalupe
Waxing Moon
Moon Phase: Second Quarter
Color: Lavender

Moon Sign: Taurus
Incense: Rose

13 **Tuesday**
St. Lucy's Day (Swedish)
Waxing Moon
Moon Phase: Second Quarter
Color: Maroon

Moon Sign: Taurus
Moon enters Gemini 2:59 pm
Incense: Evergreen

14 **Wednesday**
Warriors' Memorial (Japanese)
Waxing Moon
Moon Phase: Second Quarter
Color: Brown

Moon Sign: Gemini
Incense: Eucalyptus

Sagittarius

Thursday
Consualia (Roman)
Waxing Moon
Moon Phase: Full Moon 11:16 am
Color: Green

Moon Sign: Gemini
Moon enters Cancer 11:01 pm
Incense: Musk

16 Friday
Posadas (Mexican)
Waning Moon
Moon Phase: Third Quarter
Color: Pink

Moon Sign: Cancer
Incense: Almond

17 Saturday
Saturnalia (Roman)
Waning Moon
Moon Phase: Third Quarter
Color: Blue

Moon Sign: Cancer
Incense: Pine

18 Sunday
Feast of the Virgin of Solitude
Waning Moon
Moon Phase: Third Quarter
Color: Amber

Moon Sign: Cancer
Moon enters Leo 9:18 am
Incense: Cinnamon

19 Monday
Opalia (Roman)
Waning Moon
Moon Phase: Third Quarter
Color: Gray

Moon Sign: Leo
Incense: Peony

20 Tuesday
Commerce God Festival (Japanese)
Waning Moon
Moon Phase: Third Quarter
Color: Red

Moon Sign: Leo
Moon enters Virgo 9:39 pm
Incense: Sage

21 Wednesday
Yule • Winter Solstice
Waning Moon
Moon Phase: Third Quarter
Color: Yellow

Moon Sign: Virgo
Sun enters Capricorn 1:35 pm
Incense: Cedar

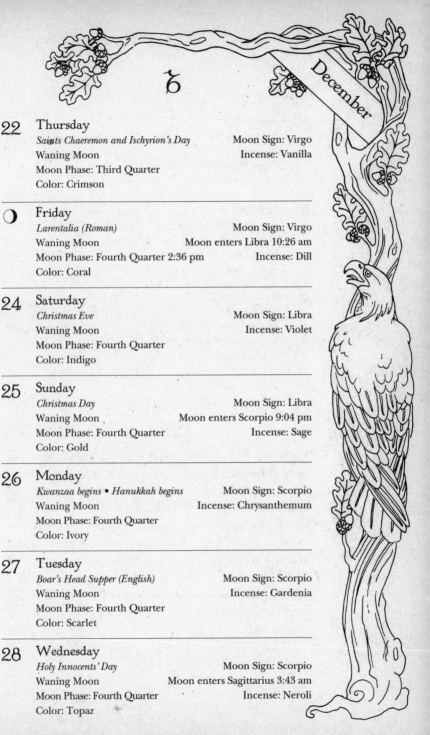

♑ December

22 **Thursday**
Saints Chaeremon and Ischyrion's Day Moon Sign: Virgo
Waning Moon Incense: Vanilla
Moon Phase: Third Quarter
Color: Crimson

☽ Friday
Larentalia (Roman) Moon Sign: Virgo
Waning Moon Moon enters Libra 10:26 am
Moon Phase: Fourth Quarter 2:36 pm Incense: Dill
Color: Coral

24 **Saturday**
Christmas Eve Moon Sign: Libra
Waning Moon Incense: Violet
Moon Phase: Fourth Quarter
Color: Indigo

25 **Sunday**
Christmas Day Moon Sign: Libra
Waning Moon Moon enters Scorpio 9:04 pm
Moon Phase: Fourth Quarter Incense: Sage
Color: Gold

26 **Monday**
Kwanzaa begins • Hanukkah begins Moon Sign: Scorpio
Waning Moon Incense: Chrysanthemum
Moon Phase: Fourth Quarter
Color: Ivory

27 **Tuesday**
Boar's Head Supper (English) Moon Sign: Scorpio
Waning Moon Incense: Gardenia
Moon Phase: Fourth Quarter
Color: Scarlet

28 **Wednesday**
Holy Innocents' Day Moon Sign: Scorpio
Waning Moon Moon enters Sagittarius 3:43 am
Moon Phase: Fourth Quarter Incense: Neroli
Color: Topaz

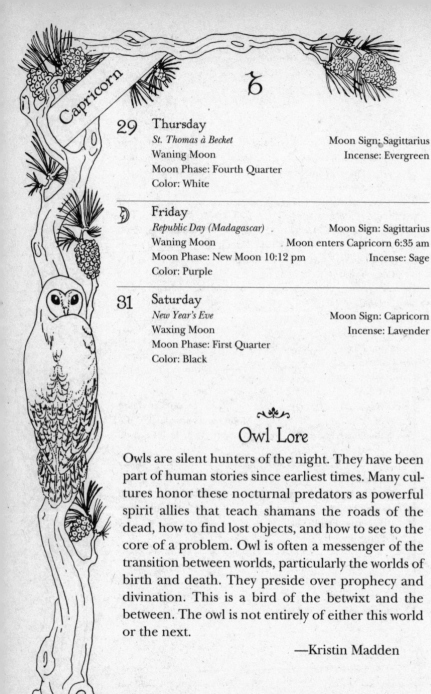

29 Thursday
St. Thomas à Becket   Moon Sign: Sagittarius
Waning Moon   Incense: Evergreen
Moon Phase: Fourth Quarter
Color: White

☽ Friday
Republic Day (Madagascar)   Moon Sign: Sagittarius
Waning Moon   Moon enters Capricorn 6:35 am
Moon Phase: New Moon 10:12 pm   Incense: Sage
Color: Purple

31 Saturday
New Year's Eve   Moon Sign: Capricorn
Waxing Moon   Incense: Lavender
Moon Phase: First Quarter
Color: Black

Owl Lore

Owls are silent hunters of the night. They have been part of human stories since earliest times. Many cultures honor these nocturnal predators as powerful spirit allies that teach shamans the roads of the dead, how to find lost objects, and how to see to the core of a problem. Owl is often a messenger of the transition between worlds, particularly the worlds of birth and death. They preside over prophecy and divination. This is a bird of the betwixt and the between. The owl is not entirely of either this world or the next.

—Kristin Madden

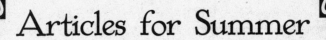

Articles for Summer

Iaká, the Women, and the Crocodile

by Mavesper Cy Ceridwen
(translated from Portuguese by Ana Maria Bahiana)

The Carajá Indians tell the story of a village where the men brought home very little game and then kept most of it for themselves. The women were starving, so they decided to leave early in the morning and go fishing. On the riverbank there was a talking crocodile who fell in love with them.

The crocodile brought the women a great quantity of fish, and the women had plenty to eat. They were so happy that they made love to the crocodile, and when the men came back, the women didn't want to eat or make love to them. This situation lasted for a while, and the men became increasingly suspicious, sending a boy to spy on the women. He saw everything and told the men, who, the very next morning, followed the women to the riverbank, hiding in the reeds.

When the women left, the men captured and killed the talking crocodile. The next day, the women arrived and began calling for the crocodile, but he was nowhere to be found. The women went looking for him and found him where the men had left him, dead. In anger, they swore to avenge this creature who was good to them, and they went into the forest to make spears, bows, and arrows. The men laughed and mocked the women, believing they were incapable of fighting. They even belittled the women by turning their arrowheads backward— so as not to kill the women, only hurt them.

In one version of the myth, all the women are killed. In another version, the women kill all the men, except for two or three who survive and flee. The women, their wrath avenged, cut off one breast in mourning for the murdered crocodile. When they throw their cut breasts in the river, the breasts turn into the pink dolphins *(botos)* common in the rivers of the Amazon basin.

A Comment on This Myth

The Carajá myth about Iaká, the talking crocodile, is one of women rebelling against male oppression. The crocodile is symbol of the power of the womb, similar to the dragon or the serpent in similar myths. That is, we find women overcoming male oppression in the stories of Tiamat in Babylon, Ua-zit in Egypt, the Serpent Goddess of Crete, and the Serpent Woman of the Native Americans.

In all of these stories, as with the Icamiabás (the Amazonas warrior goddesses of the Iaká myth), their anger over the murder of the crocodile lead them to revenge. The Iaká myth can encourage us to bring forth our capabilities and overcome a lack of self-esteem and confidence. In the version of the myth where their cut flesh is transformed into river dolphins, we see the theme of anger and hate turning into creative power.

Other Goddesses who create from anger, like the Iaká women, are the Hawaiian Pele, the Mexican Cipactli, and Olosa, the crocodile goddess of Haiti. The Iaká women can also be invoked in matters of injustice, retribution, and compensation.

Iaká Women Ritual

On your altar, spread a green altar cloth, a crocodile statue, green candles, one green quartz, some rosemary incense and rue leaves, and one thin, flexible branch approximately three feet in length. Also have ready a blend of mineral oil and guarana powder.

Draw the circle and invoke the Iaká women:

On this night, O Iaká women,
I call on you to heal.
Make injustices and insecurities
Fall like dust under your heels.
On this beautiful starry night,
Teach us courage and bring us your might.
Welcome!

Use the rue leaves to cleanse negative energies from yourself and the space around you. Lie on your stomach on the floor, with your legs together and arms at your sides. Relax and slowly lift your torso with your arms bent at the elbows, assuming a crocodile posture. Feel connected to the earth and to water, and breathe—bringing the energy completely to your center.

If you are a woman, relive the story of the crocodile women as if you were one of them. Concentrate on connecting with the crocodile, who stands for the magical power of the womb and the earth. Feel the power of triumph and righteous victory. Bear an Iaká women spear.

If you are a man, first relive the story of the crocodile women as if you were one of the tribesmen, and then as the crocodile. As one of the Carajá men, note your attitudes toward the powers and capabilities of women, and check how many times you engage in biased points of view, belittling women's abilities, As the crocodile, who personifies your connection with Mother Earth, notice if you are removed from your source of real power by your machismo and preconceived notions. Connect with this new power, and see how it can change your life.

Spells

Power Lance Spell

Make a spear with the twig and the crystal. Decorate it with crocodile pictures and symbols. Make anointing oil by adding ground nettle or fog tree leaves to the mineral oil and guarana. Anoint your lance and the crocodile statue with this mixture, charging them to bring you strength, determination, and courage.

Iaká War Water

Add one green crystal, thirteen iron nails, and one small crocodile icon—a small statue or a toy—to some source water. Use this war water to drive away enemies and protect yourself from threats of any kind.

Iaká Women's Bread

Add ground cashew nuts to any bread recipe. Mold it into the shape of a crocodile. Bless it and eat it ritually, visualizing personal power, self-confidence, and determination coming into you.

Iaká Women's Protective Charm

During a Iaká women ritual described above, charge one skeleton quartz or crocodile quartz (also known as celestial quartz). Leave it wherever you feel protection is needed. Thank the Iaká women by throwing flowers in a lake or into any running water. Raise a power cone, and feast on pineapple and papaya.

Bring the ritual to a close by opening the circle.

A Calendula Skin Balm

by Laurel Reufner

Its beautiful golden-orange flowers turned toward the warming Sun, *Calendula officinalis* opens her gorgeous petals to greet the day. By midday they are starting to close up, cheerfully waiting the next dawn.

Bright and happy wherever they happen to be growing, calendula also has culinary and medicinal uses that make it a valuable addition to your garden. In the *Countrie Farme,* a book written in 1699, calendula is prescribed for headache, jaundice, red eyes, toothache, ague, and weakness of heart. The flowers were dried and added to all manner of soups, pottages, and broths. They were also used as a dye to make yellow cheeses.

Perhaps some of the best uses of calendula are in preparations for the skin. Juice from the leaves is excellent used on bee stings, bruises, and assorted bug bites. An oil decoction makes a wonderful balm for dry skin and some rashes, including diaper rash. What follows is my recipe for a calendula balm, known to friends as "Tilly's Butt Balm." It's been field-tested on both of my daughters, who still request it when their little bottoms are sore. If you don't want to make the balm, simply keep some calendula oil on hand in your fridge and pour it on the affected area whenever it flares up.

Calendula Balm

   2 oz. cocoa butter

   1 tsp. beeswax

   5 oz. calendula oil (see below)

500 I.U. vitamin E oil

   2 oz. rose water

In a double boiler melt the cocoa butter, beeswax, and calendula oil over low heat until they are well blended. If you don't have a double boiler, take a small heat-resistant glass bowl, and place it in a small pan with about an inch of water in the pan. Remove from heat and stir in the vitamin E oil.

Pour the rose water into a small bowl, and then slowly add the cocoa butter mixture. Begin stirring the mixture, preferably clockwise in order to infuse it with healing energies. I like to use a whisk, but a spoon will do as well. The change in composition that occurs is subtle, but noticeable. The cream will appear a little thicker. The separation of oil and water will have pretty much disappeared. A little of the balm on the end of your finger will feel more creamy than oily when you rub it into your skin.

While the cream is still warm, pour it into clean containers. Allow the cream to cool completely before you close up the containers—this helps keep excess moisture from being trapped with the cream. I like to store mine in the refrigerator, but any cool and dark place will do.

Label and date the bottles. With proper storage and a little luck, your containers of cream should stay fresh for at least a year. If they start to smell bad or you notice mold, get rid of them, and if the oil and water start to separate, just stir everything back together again and you're good to go.

The Thunder God

by Kristin Madden

Hail Thor,
Hallower and guardian,
Son of the Earth Mother and the All-Father,
Strong and noble wielder of thunder and lightning,
Red-bearded friend to us all.
Guide us through the seasons and the cycles of life.
Bring the gift of fertility to the land,
As we love and honor you.
Let us find strength and wisdom within us,
Hail Thor!

Thor is best known as the Norse thunder god whose magical hammer create lightning. He is often seen as a huge, rather dull-witted, and extremely short-tempered man with red hair. The truth about Thor goes well beyond that common perception.

The Many Names of Thor

Possibly the most widely worshiped god among the ancient Norse people, Thor was known by many names. To the Norse, he was Thor. To the Germanic tribes, he was called Donner and Donar. The Anglo-Saxons paid him homage as Thunor. Many people even believe that the Sami Horagalles is a version of Thor.

His worship extended from Scandinavia and northern Europe down into Iceland. His greatest temple was constructed at Uppsala in Sweden, and place names throughout these areas bear his name. Even our modern Thursday is named after the thunder god ("Thor's day").

Thor was so popular that hammer-shaped amulets were still worn during the early years of the Christianization of Scandinavia. Several sources state that molds from that time have been found containing both the hammer and cross shapes, to be cast into the same piece of jewelry. The hammer is his symbol and his worshippers continue to wear Thor's hammer on chains around their necks.

A member of the Aesir, Thor is the defender of Asgard. This was where the Aesir gods had their mansions. Asgard lay at the top of Bifrost, the Rainbow Bridge that connected Midgard (our world) with the abode of the Aesir. Asgard is said to be resplendent with silver and gold. From his tower in Asgard, Thor's father and leader of the Aesir, Odin could see into all the nine worlds of the Norse cosmology.

Thor's hall in Asgard is said to be enormous. He holds great feasts in his luxurious five hundred and forty rooms and eats very well along with his guests. At home, Thor is known as a generous and loving family man. His wife is Sif of the Golden Hair. Thor is the stepfather of Sif's son Ull, the god of skiers, snowshoes, and hunting. Thrud, sometimes named among the Valkyrie, is a daughter of Thor. Thor also had two sons, Modi and Magni, with the giantess Jarnsaxa.

Stories of Thor

Thor travels about in a chariot drawn by two magical goats. Sparks fly from the hooves of Tanngniost (Toothgnasher) and Tanngrisnir (Toothgrinder), and the chariot's wheels create thunder as it passes through the heavens. These two fierce goats provide an endless supply of food that Thor has been known to offer to humans in need. His only requirement is that the bones be kept intact and together. After the meal, Thor raises Mjollnir, his hammer, over the bones and the goats are magically brought back to life.

The main enemies of Asgard are found among the Jotnar, or the giants. In battling his enemies, Thor wields Mjollnir. It was crafted by dwarves and symbolizes both Thor's immense strength and the thunderbolt. It is considered to be one of the Aesir's most valuable treasures. Its great power allows Thor to defend Asgard on his own without the assistance of any other Aesir.

The red-hot Mjollnir always strikes its target with a clap of thunder and returns to Thor's hand for another throw. Although he is the strongest Aesir next to Odin, the All-Father, Thor requires a special belt and iron gloves to wield such a weapon as Mjollnir. With his belt or girdle, Megingardir, Thor's incredible strength is doubled.

As defender of Asgard, Thor is a protective warrior, and he defends humans from the often frightening forces of the world. His worshippers have included farmers, artisans, and common folk. His strength supports peaceful communities and hard-working people that hold fast to their promises. He is known as a god of justice and law due to his strenuous disapproval of oath breaking.

Thor is the son of Jord, the Earth Mother, and his might includes some of her magical lineage. He is commonly known to control the weather, bringing both storms and fair weather. He is a fertility god and his wife, Sif, is the goddess of the harvest and of fertility.

His associations with fertility extend both to the crops of the land and to humans. Mjollnir is believed to be a symbol of fertility and renewal. During traditional Norse wedding ceremonies, the bride holds the hammer in her lap to ensure a fertile partnership. She is also frequently given a hammer necklace for protection.

This fertility association is based on the relationship between the weather and the health of the crops. An old superstition that summer lightning contributes to the ripening of crops has found modern evidence to support it. Studies suggest that lightning does play a role in the fertilization of the land. Fire, often sparked by lightning, is necessary for certain types of trees to reproduce.

As the son of the Earth Mother, it is no surprise that Thor is associated with certain trees and animals. Oak trees are sacred to many thunder gods, including Thor. St. Boniface, an Englishman that was consecrated as a German bishop, cut down a sacred oak where Thor was honored in a place called Geismar to put an end to the heathen religion. As was the norm during the Christian conversions, the foundation for a new church was laid in its place. There is also some evidence to suggest an affiliation with rowan trees, sometimes referred to as "Thor's salvation."

The Images on the Hammer

Eagle images often appear on Thor's hammer, perhaps due to their nearly universal connections with lightning and fire. In "The Lay of Hymir," Thor caught Jormungandr, the world serpent, on a fishing trip. According to Snorri Sturluson's version of this story, Thor's failure to kill the serpent paved the way for the end of the world. Other scholars have differing views on this, though the point remains that because of this story Thor is forever associated with serpents and dragons. These symbols often appear on Thor's hammer today.

Thor is the hallower and the giver of blessings. He was the god invoked to hallow the runes inscribed on burial stones. When gentle Balder, beloved of the Aesir, was killed, Thor hallowed the funeral pyre with Mjollnir. This hallowing sanctifies the object or place. Many modern Norse practitioners will open their rites with a hammer hallowing.

It has been suggested that Thor may have shamanic associations. Certain lines in old stories and poems may indicate his participation in the seidh of the ancient Norse. Whether this is true or not, Thor was invoked for protection by travelers, particularly before a sea journey. Thor himself made great journeys throughout the worlds. His strength and compassion for humans makes him an ideal guide and guardian, whether you are taking a physical journey or embarking on a shamanic one.

By now, it should be obvious that the thunder god is a multifaceted and complex being deserving of a more understanding. He is not a simple-minded, hot-tempered madman as he is too often depicted. Thor can be gentle and clever, cunning and creative. He is the people's god and, as such, his worship continues to thrive among a wide variety of heathens and Pagans today.

Through the Looking Glass: An Exploration of Mirrors

by Elizabeth Barrette

Since the invention of mirrors, this tool has ranked high as an object of magical and spiritual power. After all, mirrors allow us do something that no human being can do without assistance—see our own faces.

From the familiar silvered glass to the mystery of tinted decoratives and the subtle murk of polished obsidian, mirrors capture our interest just as they were once believed to capture souls. In addition to their rich history, they remain a popular altar tool today.

The Background of the Mirror

Our ancestors had to content themselves with imperfect reflectors. Clear mirrors were not portable, and the portable ones were not clear. People could see themselves in still, dark water or in ice. Sometimes a piece of dark stone or wood could be rubbed smooth to produce a vague picture. And that was it, for millennia.

Because people considered the reflection to represent their soul or other self, they believed that any injury to it could impact them—hence the dire predictions of bad luck upon the dropping or breaking of a mirror.

Later, smiths hammered metal into flat sheets. There were more effective as mirrors, but the readily available metal sheets—in brass and copper—gave a noticeable tint to the image. Silver gave the truest reflection, but few could afford that metal. The Bible cites mirrors made from brass, and papyrus records mention silver ones in Egypt. In the late Middle Ages came a new style of mirror based on tin, and dressed with silver nitrate and mercury, which improved image quality a great deal.

The modern mirror, made from clear glass with a very thin silvery backing, was invented in Vienna during the late seventeenth century. It quickly spread throughout Europe despite its expense. Small mirrors soon became favored trade items in far-off lands.

Mirrors and Divinity

Cultures around the world consider the mirror a symbol of feminine power, especially divine power. Many goddesses appear with a mirror as part of their regalia, and mirrors are popular artifacts for temples, shrines, and altars. The round, shimmery surface of a mirror suggests its connection to the Moon and to the element of water.

For example, the Tibetans represent their goddess Lasya with a mirror. Lasya oversees matters of beauty and the Moon. In central Asia, the Moon is the mirror that reflects everything in the world. Indian mythology refers to the great goddess as the "Mirror of the Abyss," who holds the reflection of Shiva. In the Egyptian language, the word for "mirror" and "life" is one and the same. Also the ankh is sometimes seen as representing a mirror. The "Mirror of Hathor" appears in temple paintings and statuary as an emblem of that goddess.

In Greece, the goddess Venus rules the vagaries of love and beauty. Her special metal is copper, and copper mirrors adorned her shrines. In fact, the familiar circle-and-cross emblem of Venus and femininity is also the alchemical symbol for copper. People still use copper mirrors as the preferred type for love magic, or for divination on Friday, the day ruled by Venus.

The Afro-Caribbean goddess Yemaya is traditionally depicted holding a mirror as she rides the ocean waves on her twin fish-tails. Many mermaid legends involve a mirror. Sometimes this merely represents the creature's vanity, but more often it embodies her magical power. If a man steals a mermaid's mirror, he can force her to stay with him as his wife—at least until she finds her missing artifact and returns to the sea.

Mirror Scrying

The most popular use of a magic mirror is for scrying. Scholars refer to this as crystallomancy or catoptromancy, and Romans called skilled readers *specularii*. Techniques include viewing distant scenes in the present, gazing into the past or the future, and summoning symbolic visions. Many occult shops sell mirrors for this purpose—often expensive ones made from black glass, obsidian, or onyx—but you can also make your own. Different types suit different objectives. For instance, use a mirror framed on only three sides to see over long distances.

Whether made for the purpose or appropriated from a cosmetic counter, a mirror should be prepared before magical use. These processes varies from simple to complex, depending on the source you consult. Most include several common elements: washing the mirror in water, exposing it to moonlight, and storing it in a bag to protect it. Many Pagans believe that you should never allow sunlight to fall on your magic mirror, especially if you use it for scrying. Instead, scry at night, or in a darkened room lit by candles.

A scrying mirror may reveal such things as a lover's illicit affair, good or bad news from afar, preventable or inevitable misfortune to come, the history of events or objects, messages from spirits or patron deities, the face of a future spouse, whether a sick person will live or die, the veracity of statements made before it, and so forth. The morality or immorality of the power largely depends on the user's actions.

Other Magical and Spiritual Uses

The mirror is generally regarded as a window or door to other realms. Most mirrors are flat, but some are concave (good for catching things) or convex (good for repelling things). Mirror applications include astral projection, conjuring spirits, viewing past lives, capturing souls, and speaking with distant persons. Indeed, the realm of the dead is sometimes known as "the Hall of Mirrors."

Some of these uses suggest the reason behind the custom of covering any mirrors in a room where someone is ill or has died. That is, this practice prevents the mirror from trapping the person's soul, or providing a conduit for other spirits to enter the room. Celtic women were buried with their personal mirrors, as they believed these objects carried their souls.

Because of their constant association with personal appearance, mirrors play a role in some love spells. They can enhance beauty and psychic abilities, but they can also encourage vanity. If you have the strength of will to face your flaws honestly, however, the mirror can be a powerful tool for self-improvement.

Another aspect of mirrors is their ability to reflect and turn things back the way they came—hence their use as protective talismans. One popular binding involves fastening the photograph of a harasser between two mirrors placed face-to-face. Another is to put an object symbolic of the problem into a "mirror box," which is exactly what it sounds like: a box lined entirely with mirrors. All harm thus reflects back on itself.

The oriental art of feng shui takes these principles to a sophisticated level, using many types of mirrors and other reflective objects. These mirror can attract positive energy, repel or redirect negative energy, duplicate prosperity, and compensate for inauspicious features in a room or building. The eight-sided bagua mirror brings harmony, abundance, and protection. Its sides embody attributes of marriage, fame, wealth, family, career, new knowledge, and children.

Conclusions

The magic mirror still holds a place of honor among contemporary practitioners, and is well worth acquiring. However, mirrors can prove tricky to handle, so they may be best reserved for intermediate to advanced practitioners. Novices might find themselves facing more than they know how to deal with.

The most important warning, of course, is the one that applies to all types of divination: Don't ask questions you don't want to know the answers to.

An Anniversary Ritual

by Twilight Bard

Anniversaries are a very special occasion for couples. Whether they exchanged vows at a civil ceremony, before their high priest or priestess in a circle of friends, or alone together under the light of the Moon, anniversaries mark a full turn of a wheel that was set in motion by their commitment to a life together.

A Beginning and an Ending

The word "anniversary" comes from the Latin *annus* ("year") and *versus* ("to turn"). Like New Year's Day, an

anniversary is an ending and a beginning entwined. One way to make an anniversary celebration special is to mark it with a ritual invoking Janus, the Roman god of gates and doorways. He was called on to celebrate beginnings, with the understanding that one cycle must end for another to begin. The first month of the new year, January, was derived from his name. He is depicted with two faces: one that looks back on things past, and the other that looks ahead toward what is to come.

Planning and Performing an Anniversary Ritual

When planning the ritual, prepare a white pillar candle with carvings or painted designs that are meaningful to both participants. This could be runes or symbols (hearts, flowers, and so on) that you feel represent your relationship. Also gather two taper candles (each lover choosing a color they feel appropriate), a cup filled with wine or some rich nectar (perhaps a cup from your wedding or some other special occasion), and an athame (a ritual knife). If you do not have an athame, a kitchen knife, wand, or similar instrument will do.

Find a peaceful setting that will be conducive to loving energies—be it outdoors in a sacred woodland clearing, or in your bedroom surrounded by romantic candle light. Be sure you have enough privacy so that you both can focus on the ritual (and each other) without disturbance, and be as intimate as you like without concern of prying eyes. The transitional hours of dusk or dawn on the day of the occasion are particularly potent and beautiful. If you really want to go all out, dress up in romantic garb, ritual robes, or, if the location allows for the privacy, be skyclad.

Sit or kneel facing one another, the unlit candles, filled cup, and athame (or your chosen instrument) between you. Calm and center yourselves completely, taking several deep breaths if necessary.

When ready, each person grasps in his or her left hand the right hand of the other—so that you are forming a small circle. Both of you will visualize the love you have welling up in your heart, and you will send the feeling across your chest, down your right arm and into your partner's left hand, toward your beloved's heart. Be open to your mate's energy seeping into your right hand and making its way up to your heart.

Let the energy flow in a circle through you both, mingling together as it runs up one arm, through the heart, and down the other arm. Envision this energy as stream of light, either colored green (the color associated with the heart chakra) or pink (the color associated with love). Let it encircle you both, connecting you until you can't tell where one person's energy stops and the other's energy begins.

An Invocation to Janus

When ready, raise your hands together toward the heavens, invoking the god Janus with words like these:

We stand together, hand in hand,
On the threshold of a new year.
We look to the past,
Remembering the love we have shared
And learning from the mistakes we have made.
We look to the future,
Anticipating joys and sorrows
That we will face together.
We call you, great Janus,
Keeper of the gate,
Who oversees transitions,

Looking backward and forward simultaneously;
Be with us and bless our rite
As another year comes full circle
And we set the wheel in motion again!

Each of you should then take up your colored taper. Speaking one at a time, renew your vows for another year, either by repeating the same promises you made on the day you first solidified your commitment, or with new words appropriate to circumstances and changing needs. As each person finishes speaking, light the taper and say:

By this flame,
Like the passion that burns within me,
I freely dedicate myself to you.

When your vows are spoken, together use the tapers to light the pillar candle, saying:

As these flames join to become one,
We set the wheel of our years in motion again.

Blow out the tapers. Gaze at the candle together, or close your eyes, and meditate on the coming year, which will be filled with unity, harmony, and passion.

When you're both ready, take up the cup between you, each holding it with your left hand. Above it and pointing downward toward the cup, hold the athame (or instrument you have chosen) together with your right hands. Say in unison:

The lover comes willingly,
The beloved accepts openly,
And together they are as one!

Then plunge the blade into the liquid. This act stands in for the Great Rite (sex), and so is a powerful blessing on the union of opposites. Remove the blade. Each takes a sip from the cup, leaving the rest as an offering to Janus, thanking the god for his presence.

Spend some time being tender with each other. Talk intimately, kiss and stroke each other lovingly, or, if your privacy is secure, make love and so consummate your renewed vows. Celebrating each anniversary with a ritual such as this continuously reaffirms your commitment to walking down life's path together.

Creating a Fetch

by Karen Follett

In the mid 1960s, a toy manufacturer introduced a line of tiny dolls that fit into jewelry lockets. This jewelry represented the ultimate "height of fashion" to every trend-conscious six-year-old of that era. These little locket dolls represented much more to those of us who tended to view objects a bit differently.

By day, these lockets transformed us "atypicals" into bejeweled queens of fashion. By night, the dolls emerged from their lockets and were sent on quests for information. These dolls-turned-messengers were charged with bringing back information about test questions, the whereabouts of lost objects, and other knowledge of concern to children of our age. While I think that it would be a fair statement to say that many of us lacked the vocabulary to label what we were doing, we were, in fact, creating "fetches" of these dolls.

What Is a Fetch?

A fetch is a nonphysical entity that is created for the purpose of gathering the information that lies beyond our physical boundaries. As the creator of the fetch, you decide the form, task, and life span of this energy. In addition to the power that you assert in the creation of the fetch, you also have the ultimate responsibility and accountability for the ethical use of the fetch.

The word "poppet" is used to label many types of dolls. For our purposes, a poppet is a tangible vessel that houses the fetch. The poppet can be as simplistic as a piece of jewelry or as elaborate as a doll that has been hand crafted, embedded with herbs and gemstones, initiated, and completed in conjunction with astrological influences.

While the following instructions are geared for the creation of a fetch and poppet from the "ground floor" and up, I believe that there are many ways to achieve a goal. So, unless you are learning a specific technique as ascribed by a specific tradition, let your intuition be your guide in this creation. After all, it has been nearly forty years since I sent my doll-turned-messenger on her first mission, and to this day, she still houses my fetch.

The energy manifestation of the fetch and the physical manifestation poppet is interdependent, and created in tandem. In addition to housing the fetch, the poppet acts to nourish, ground, and protect the fetch's energy and attributes.

Before you begin constructing your poppet, focus on the reasons why you are creating your fetch. This focus will aid in your deciding which attributes to infuse into the poppet. (Write these attributes on paper, as they will be used in the consecration of the fetch.) For the gathering of information, you may want attributes such as clear sight and the ability to receive and impart communication clearly. You may even gather herbs, stones, and metals possessing the qualities that you want to infuse into your fetch.

Next, you will assign to your fetch the visualized form that you want this energy to take. This can be a ball of energy or a totem animal or any visualization of form that bridges the gap from concept to manifested reality.

The physical construction of the poppet can be as simplistic or as elaborate as you choose. You can sew, knit, crochet, or even draw a doll-like "vessel" from any material. The choice of material should take the fetch's attributes in consideration. (There is much speculation that natural materials tend to hold energy more efficiently than synthetic materials.) You can add facial and anatomical features, even an "umbilical cord" to represent the connection between you and your fetch.

Every step that you take in the creation of your poppet is a step that has the potential of charging the energy of your fetch. You can focus form and intent with each seam you sew or each swipe of the pen. You can infuse clear sight while you create the eyes, clear hearing while you attach the ears, and clear communication while you fashion a mouth. Artistic ability is not the essential element in the creation of the poppet. As with any magical working, your focused intent is the only "essential" ingredient for success.

If you are creating a fabric or a stitched poppet, leave a small portion of the poppet open for stuffing. Gather the herbs, stones, metals, and oils that you want to use to further enhance the fetch. Cotton balls make an excellent and economical stuffing for the poppet. If you are drawing your poppet, anoint the finished work with oil or smudge with herbs. Again, focused intent is more important than technique as you complete the poppet.

The consecration of the fetch and poppet is very similar to the consecration of any other working tool of the craft. Cast your circle, call the quarters, and petition your deity of choice. Present your poppet to each element and to the deity, asking that the desired characteristics be imparted to your fetch.

State to the fetch that it will be protected and sealed into this poppet until it is released by you, and only you. State to the fetch that it will always return to the poppet upon completion of each and every task. Instruct that, upon its return to the poppet, it will lie dormant until you command otherwise. Thank the elements and deity and release the circle.

Your fetch is now ready for its first mission. Instructed the fetch as you would instruct a small child—with clear, concise, and specific instructions. You will also want to state the terms of communication with your fetch. Instruct your fetch that it will only obey your voice and intent. Your fetch can impart its information in visual, auditory, and sensory forms. Information can be relinquished during your waking hours and while asleep.

As with any new skill, there is a period of a "learning curve" where you may need to learn a new symbolic language, or you may need to adjust your communication techniques with your fetch. Your fetch and poppet are valuable tools and should be treated as such. Use the knowledge wisely.

Dandelion Spell for Beating Bad Habits

by Janina Renée

If you are at home during the day, and if you have some sort of repetitive bad habit—such as biting your nails, picking your nose, chewing on pencils, etc.—you can decrease the incidence of this kind of behavior. Simply do this: Whenever you catch yourself in the act, immediately go out in your yard, pluck a small leaf off of a dandelion, and eat it on the spot while saying:

Dandelion, tooth of the lion, as you build my strength and cleanse my blood, so help me to build my will and rid myself of bad impulses.

Performing this spell is not as uncomfortable as it may seem. Dandelion leaves don't taste all that bad, and they're less bitter in early spring and late fall.

It is the action of interrupting whatever you are doing, going out of doors, and going through the other motions that serves as a spell by making an impression on your unconscious. And whether it works for you or not, you'll get a little something out of it because dandelions supply many nutrients, such as vitamin A and potassium, while also acting as a detoxifier.

By the way, this is also something you can do if you are trying to break small children of bad habits. If you gently walk them through this rite, it will do them no harm.

The Enlightened Salad

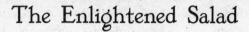

by Shira Bee

During the heyday of drive-in movie theaters and roller derbies, salads consisted of iceberg lettuce coated in globs of opaque, fat-laden dressing. Salads were relegated to appetizer status, side dishes quickly consumed before a greasy main course.

The cultural revolution of the 1960s included the emergence of earth-revering religions and holistic movements, as well as widespread health consciousness. TV dinners and the five food groups were no longer considered the end-all, be-all of nutrition. A greener, more holistic culinary aesthetic emerged.

Nowadays, an attractive, well-balanced salad is accepted as a entrée in its own right. (Meat and potatoes need not follow!) Enlightened salads—those harmoniously balanced in terms of taste, presentation, and nutritional content—have long been an integral component of European and Mediterranean diets. Enlightened salads incorporate fresh, mix-and-match greens, and an interplay of colors, flavors, and textures.

Magical rituals and practices—be it a tarot reading for a client or friend, an invocation, consecration, spell, chant, or participation in a seasonal festival— can be physically and emotionally draining, as these activities draw from our core psychic energies. Therefore, it is important to maintain healthful eating habits that provide us with the energy to both enact our magic and replenish us in the aftermath. A wholesome diet has always played a key role in the path to enlightenment.

The more nourished our bodies, the clearer our minds, and the more heightened our magical powers and perceptions.

"I focus on what combinations I can assemble to make interesting, delicious salads," says Annie Somerville, executive chef of Greens, a nationally renowned San Francisco–based vegetarian restaurant and author of *Fields of Greens: New Vegetarian Recipes from the Celebrated Greens Restaurant.* Greens' seemingly endless variety of salad entrees are crafted from fresh, locally grown, organic ingredients. Their typical garden salad contains crispy romaine lettuce, red mustard, arugula, sweet cherry tomatoes, cucumbers, radishes, pine nuts, and a drizzle of champagne mustard vinaigrette topped with rich gorgonzola cheese.

Enlightened salads range from the simplistic (i.e., a handful of elements such as butter lettuce, cherry tomatoes, and grated carrot topped with fresh lemon juice and ground pepper) to the whimsical and complex (baby spinach leaves, tufts of spring green kale, dark-colored radicchio, heirloom tomatoes, sliced raw apples and walnut bits all topped with champagne vinaigrette and crumbled blue cheese).

Equal importance is placed on all components, from the dominant green leaf to the smidgen of garnish. Disparate flavors and textures—from bitter greens to sweet veggies to tangy dressings—balance each other out in delightful equilibrium. Enlightened salads also welcome diversity, happily incorporating both Eastern and Western sensibilities. The inclusion of Asian shiitake mushrooms and sesame or ginger-based dressing, for example, adds Eastern flair to an otherwise rural garden mix. It is well-known that salads are a staple in Greece, southern Europe, and the Middle East. Annie credits Mediterranean cuisine as her primary salad influence, but also acknowledges the flavors of Mexico and Asian countries.

Enlightened salads also pack nutritional punch. Greens are an excellent source of antioxidant vitamins A and C (rule of thumb is the darker the leaf, the more vitamin rich its content), iron, and folic acid. Toss sunflowers and cherry tomatoes into the mix for added source of phytochemicals and vitamin E. For added protein, include grilled chicken, tuna, tofu, or a cooked egg. Extra virgin olive oil and avocados supply an excellent source of heart-healthy monounsaturated fat. Enlightened salads, with their seemingly endless combination of ingredients, are the saving grace of both omnivorous and vegetarian Pagans alike!

Creating an enlightened salad can be just as rewarding as eating one, as there are no set rules and an impressive array of potential ingredients, including: greens (baby spinach leaves, romaine hearts, arugula, endive, radicchio, watercress, dandelion greens, frisee, and escarole); vegetables (cherry and heirloom tomatoes, carrots, cucumber, zucchini, and apple slices, avocado, mushrooms); herbs (cilantro, dill, parsley); and garnishes (walnuts, thinly sliced almonds, pumpkin seeds, croutons, grated blue cheese, goat cheese, olives).

Delicious greens also need to be dressed in something flavorful and bright. The sky's the limit when it comes to selecting an olive oil or vinegar based dressing. Choose from an array of vinaigrettes made from balsamic lemon, red-wine, champagne mustard, sherry, or pear vinegars. Blended olive oils, those infused with shallots, garlic, citrus juices, chili peppers, and so on, also make for a delectable coating. Greens employs a constantly evolving array of homemade olive oil and vinegar-based dressings for their health-conscious clientele. The key to dressing an enlightened salad is to add just enough to infuse flavor throughout the salad, while not drowning the mix or weighting the greens.

Whipping up an enlightened salad is an art form, but if you're pressed for time, simply utilize one dominant green, toss in some cherry tomatoes, drizzle with olive oil, squeeze in a dash of lemon, and sprinkle liberally with sunflower seeds. For an even simpler variation, skip the oil altogether and opt for a balsamic vinaigrette dressing. A few quality ingredients go a long way and inventiveness is key.

Enlightened salads stand on their own as a culinary phenomenon. They make for healthful eating any time of the day. They are an ideal pre- or post-ritual meal, and perfect for solo practitioners and groups alike. So do your taste buds and your body a favor by making the transition from dull to daring greens! It's a change that will leave your body and soul feeling enlightened.

The Enlightened Salad Healthiness List

For greens, use these varieties: red leaf, green leaf, romaine, butter-head lettuce, spinach, escarole, collards, radicchio, mache, arugula, watercress, dandelion, kale.

And avoid these greens: iceberg lettuce (miniscule nutritional value).

For garnishes and dressings, use: goat cheese, feta cheese, veggies, avocado (use sparingly), diced apple, orange slices, basil leaves, dill, fennel, chives, cilantro, mint, sunflower seeds, pine nuts, walnuts, olives, capers, nasturtium leaves, edible chrysanthemums, pansies, balsamic vinaigrette, citrus- or wine-based vinaigrettes, olive oil, lemon and lime juice, pepper.

Avoid these garnishes and dressings: cubed cheddar cheese, ham (both are high in saturated fat and cholesterol), croutons, bacon-bits, ranch, bleu cheese, thousand island, caesar salad dressings.

Sports Goddesses

by Cerridwen Iris Shea

As we become more aware of the necessity for exercise in promoting good health, it seems only appropriate to turn to sports goddesses to oversee our forays into fitness. But what are our choices?

Nike is the goddess most commonly referred to regarding sports in this day and age. Nike is a Greek goddess of victory. She didn't just keep her eye on the athletic field, she was busy on the battlefield as well.

Her Roman counterpart is Victoria. This goddess also had wings and carried trophies she'd acquired in the defeat of her enemies. Her likeness appeared on Roman coins until the third century AD.

Cybele, also part of the Roman pantheon, had the Megalesian games held in her honor every April. This festival consisted of six days of feasting and competition. Theatre was an important part of the festival.

If you consider hunting a sport rather than a way to put a meal on the table, you could turn to Diana, goddess of the hunt, or to Atalanta, a free-spirited and independent goddess who covers hunt, travel, and adventure.

Epona looks after horses and horse breeding. Macha beat horses in a race while pregnant, and then she cursed nine generations of the men of Ulster when she gave birth to twins at the finish line and died. Much of the Morrigan's ferocity is physical. Warrior goddesses have to be vigorous, or they couldn't accomplish all those feats on the battlefield.

Come to think of it, goddesses seem pretty darned healthy. They come in all shapes and sizes, but they're physically and mentally fit. Goddessing is not a vocation for the faint of heart—both in terms of body energy and the spirit. They have to be ready for anything—wars, games, love, shape-changing. There's never a dull moment, after all. All the time spent loving and feuding keeps them robust.

So to whom do you turn for inspiration when you're ready to make the commitment to your own health and fitness? That's the beauty of it—you have many options.

If you prefer, you can give the goddess of ten thousand names still another name. Abflexia will help you through your crunches. Fleeta will keep those feet moving as you run. Cycla can give you that extra oomph on the stationary bike. If you come up with a goddess for ice hockey, send her my way, please.

Alternatively, you can step out of goddess energy to call on the male entities of Hermes/Mercury, or of Lugh. Lugh was famous for mastering anything to which he set his mind to, and that's pretty strong magic to tap into when exercising.

If you're more comfortable with a traditional deity, you can work with one of the goddesses previously mentioned. You could call on Hygeia, who is in charge of overall health and hygiene. Or you can sit down and have a chat with your patron goddess. Even if she's not known for games held in her honor or archery or battle, she's able-bodied enough to add strength and resolve to your commitment to your own well-being.

When embarking on a new fitness regime, you're often encouraged to partner up with someone who strives for similar goals. Who would make a better than your patron goddess?

Often you connect to your deities through stillness. You meditate, you write in your journal, and you listen. Listening is still important when finding your sports goddess, but in this case, you're more likely to find her while you're doing.

Next time you exercise, try to do so mindfully. Turn the way you prepare for your exercise session—the changing of clothes, setting up or traveling to space, warming up—as a mini-ritual. As you concentrate on your workout, be aware of the sights, sounds, scents, and voices around you. In your mind's eye, does a particular vision appear? In your eyes, does something or someone inspire you? Do you hear a particular goddess calling you?

Use your cool-down, shower, and other post-exercise time as a mini-ritual to return you to the mundane world. Turn your exercise time into sacred time and sacred space. Even a noisy, smelly gym can be sacred when approached with mindfulness and playfulness. It may be work, but it also has to be fun, or you won't stick with it.

There's an exciting wealth of energy to tap into. The most important thing when working with a sports goddess is to make the commitment to a healthier lifestyle to yourself and your goddess. Then she can help you see it through. By living the most positive lifestyle we can, we are celebrating her in all her forms.

Summer's Bounty

by Laurel Reufner

Make this summer zucchini bread in disposable aluminum loaf pans for easy freezing. Then you can easily enjoy a taste of summer in the middle of winter.

- 1½ cups flour
- 1 tsp. ground cinnamon
- ½ tsp. baking soda
- ½ tsp. salt
- ½ tsp. baking powder
- ½ tsp. ground nutmeg
- 1 cup brown sugar
- 1 cup zucchini or yellow squash, unpeeled and finely shredded
- ½ cup olive oil
- 1 egg
- ½ cup raisins or chocolate chips (optional)

In a large bowl combine the flour, cinnamon, baking soda, salt, baking powder, and nutmeg. If you are using chocolate chips, you may add them now or at the end. In another bowl mix together the sugar, zucchini, oil, egg, and raisins or chocolate chips (if using). Stir well to combine, and then add to the flour mixture. Stir until everything is mixed and all ingredients are moist. Pour your batter into a greased and floured loaf pan, and bake in a 350°F oven for fifty-five to sixty minutes or until a toothpick poked in the center comes out batter clean. Cool for about ten minutes before removing the loaf from the pan. Let it finish cooling on a wire rack.

Sarakka

by Kristin Madden

Sarakka is an important goddess to the Sami people. Commonly known by the derogatory terms "Lapps" or "Laplanders", the Sami are indigenous to northern Scandinavia and the Russian Kola Peninsula. They are probably best known as largely nomadic reindeer herders.

The Sami have been recognized for their magical and shamanic culture for thousands of years. Known throughout the Western world, Sami sorcerers or shamans were reputed to be able to stop ships under full sail, keeping foreigners from their shores. Sami diviners were able to foretell events, know what was occurring at great distances, and even bring back tangible evidence of their journeys out of body. Sami wind wizards were both feared and sought for the magical ropes that held three winds of increasing strength.

From this culture emerges a goddess that is important to both men and women, as well as to the animals the culture relied upon. Because the Sami people are not a homogenous culture, there are several Sami languages, some of which are mutually unintelligible. In spite of this, Sarakka is still Sarakka to most Sami—though the literature may spell her name as Saracha or Saraahka.

Sarakka is the daughter of Madderakka. Madderakka is the Sami earth mother. She is a creator goddess, sharing responsibility for the original creation of humans with Beive, the Sun goddess. Sarakka has two sisters, also daughters of Madderakka. Juksakka is the bow woman who determines the sex of the child by turning female fetuses to males in the mother's womb. She watches over children from birth through early childhood. She is a special protector of young boys, and she teaches the hunting arts, particularly archery. Uksakka is the door woman. She resides under the door of the home and protects the newborn.

Known as the shaper, Sarakka is sometimes believed to create the body around the soul. In other stories, it is Madderakka that receives energy from the great spirit and creates the body of the fetus in her womb. She then passes it on to Sarakka, who places the body in the mother's womb and watches over it until birth.

Sarakka is first and foremost a birthing goddess. As dividing-woman and separation-mother, she rules the separation of the baby's body from the mother's at birth. She is depicted on the Sami shamanic drum along with Madderakka, holding a forked stick. Some say this stick is a symbol of the separation of mother and child.

It is said that Sarakka feels the pain of the mother in labor. It is customary to make an offering of brandy to her once labor begins. In some areas, wood was chopped outside the birthing tent to help her open the way for the baby to be born.

Once the baby is born, Sarakka's porridge, often made with breast milk, is eaten to honor the great midwife. In some areas, this porridge is eaten as a divinatory food. Three sticks are hidden in the porridge. A white stick indicates good luck. A black stick means death, and a forked stick signifies success.

Sarakka is worshiped by both men and women. In some areas, she is believed to be the most important of the gods. She is still popular among the Sami today. She is the protector of the family and home. As a fertility goddess, she is known as the fertility caretaker for men and women. She not only protects animals, particularly reindeer calves, but she also ensures the fertility of these creatures.

Taking up residence under the hearth, Sarakka occupies a place of particular importance and is honored as a fire goddess. In traditional Sami homes, the fireplace is in the center. Traditional Sami homes are circular, resembling the Native American tepee, or eight-sided, like the Navajo hogan. The internal spaces of the home each have a specific significance. The fireplace is known as the *arran*. Areas behind the arran, opposite the entrance, are sacred.

During pregnancy, Sami mothers pray to Sarakka in the hope of discovering the child's name. The name often comes to the mother during dreaming. In other cases, the mother consults the *noaidi*, or Sami shaman, to ensure that the child receives its true name.

According to Hâkan Rydving in *The End of Drum Time*, Sami naming rituals are found throughout the Sami tribes. Among the south Sami, this ceremony was documented in the 1720s as *Sarakka-sjadset*, meaning "Sarakka water." Because the Sami at the time were required to participate in Christian rites, Sami children were baptized with a Christian name.

In some areas, the Christian name was believed to cause illness in children—so it was important that it be washed off. In many areas, the Christian name was offensive and was only used when interacting with Scandinavians. Therefore, the Sarakka-sjadset frequently followed the Christian baptism.

The Sami naming was also a water-pouring ritual most often performed by a woman or girl. The necessary ritual sacrifices were the responsibility of the child's father. The child received a brass or silver amulet that served as proof that the Christian name had been cleared.

During this time, the Sami were also required to attend Christian communion ceremonies. The conflict this created for many Sami has been well documented. Some Sami would ask permission of the shaman's drum before going to communion, not that they had much choice in the matter. Even if the drum gave permission, many Sami still knelt at the church steps to ask forgiveness from Sarakka for their participation in the Christian rite. A south Sami ritual specific to this experience was associated predominantly with Sarakka.

Before and sometimes the day after attending compulsory communion, south Sami people performed a "communion" of bread, meat, cheese and water, liquor, or beer. As they ate, they prayed over Sarakka's blood (the beverages) and Sarakka's flesh (the food). Some sources say that this took place at the first water, presumably a river or lake, on the way to the church. Other sources indicate that this ritual was held at home.

Sarakka is a complex and powerful goddess of the Sami. Like the Celtic Brighid, she is a healer and fire goddess that survived the Christianization and ethnic "cleansing" of her people.

To this day, Sarakka is a widely honored and respected goddess that is helping many people reconnect with a spirituality that could never be fully eradicated.

A Divine Marriage

by Elizabeth Barrette

The Greeks gave us the term *hieros gamos,* which means "divine marriage" or "sacred union." A more modern contraction, hierogamy, means the same thing. It covers a range of activities: the marriage of deities, the marriage of humans, intermarriage between the two, and even human performances based on wedding myths.

Some form of this appears in most religions around the world. In various guises, it plays a major role in contemporary Paganism as well.

Marriage Between Gods and Goddesses

The first version of divine marriage is literally a match made in heaven, and many of these are creation stories. They may tell how a union of god and goddess made the Earth or populated the pantheon with their children. Others relate examples of divine magic.

One of the most famous Greek myths is that of Rhea and Chronos. Chronos had the obnoxious habit of swallowing his children as infants. Rhea managed to hide Zeus, who later caused Chronos to vomit up the other deities. Look at the realms ruled by the various gods and goddesses, and you see how these two create between them all that is . . . though not always peacefully.

Enough of Sumerian liturgy survived to give us a pretty clear picture of Inanna and Dumuzi. Read the lyrically explicit poetry about their love and lovemaking to get a sense of how historical cultures viewed marriage. Inanna and Dumuzi adorn themselves for each other's pleasure, speak enthusiastically about their own and each other's bodies, and have a wonderful time. Other myths in their cycle follow the seasons of Sumerian agriculture as Dumuzi becomes a "dying and rising" god.

In Egypt, the marriage of Isis and Osiris ran into trouble due to his jealous brother Set, who cut Osiris into pieces. Isis managed to find all the pieces except for the phallus. She fashioned a substitute, resurrected her husband, and with him conceived their son Horus. The seasonal rites of Egyptian architecture regularly incorporate this myth.

India is especially rich in images of holy union. Pairs include Vishnu and Lakshmi, Krishna and Rada, Rama and Sita, and Shiva with either Shakti or Kali. In fact, the Shiva/Shakti pairing has its own name: *yabyum*. Most often, the couple appears face-to-face, with the goddess sitting in the god's lap and the two making love.

Marriage Between Deities and Humans

Another version of divine marriage occurs when a god or goddess falls in love (or lust) with a beautiful maid or a handsome man. Many traditions, for example, particularly posit a union between the sacred king and the goddess of the land.

The Greek god Zeus is famous for his serial adultery, and his wife Hera is famous for her jealous temper. Zeus dallies with one attractive mortal after another, and Hera attempts vengeance on husband and lover alike throughout much of the mythology. He often leaves the women pregnant with half-mortal, half-divine heroes—such as is the case with Hercules. Still, somehow the marriage of Zeus and Hera endures.

The Cherokee tell a story about a sky maiden or star maiden, who came down to Earth to play. When their ball rolled away, a human man picked it up, and the sky maiden who chased it got left behind when her other divine friends fled. She marries the man and they have two children, but in time she grows homesick—so she returns to the sky. The husband attempts to get the sky maiden to return, but in the process he gets himself killed. She and her children stay in their village on Earth ever afterward. Many tribes have similar stories of humans marrying sky people, animal spirits, and other divine entities.

In Ireland, the legend of Niall relates how a group of brothers, tired and thirsty after a long hunt, wished to drink from a stream. The guardian of the stream demanded a kiss in payment for the water. Niall's brothers all refused, but Niall consented—whereupon the guardian transformed into a beautiful maiden, the embodiment of Ireland herself. Niall thus became high king, winning her love as well as a drink. The sacred king needs wisdom and compassion in order to have a strong connection to the land and its power; he must see beyond the surface.

Marriage Among Humans

A third version involves humans enacting their own wedding as a holy bond, or reenacting the kind of divine marriage that involves one or more deities. This is especially popular in seasonal festivals with a priest and priestess represents the God and Goddess.

Handfasting is an ancient custom of betrothal or wedding, highly popular in the contemporary Paganism.

Couples often view this as echoing the divine marriage between the God and Goddess. They may take on roles, dress in ethnic garments, and draw liturgy from myths about the divine marriage—Boann and Dagda, Ishtar and Tammuz, Psyche and Cupid, all are good choices. This rich imagery imparts prosperity and happiness to the newlyweds, and fertility to the land. Greek weddings traditionally included two parts: the *engue* (legal vows) and the *ekdosis* (bride moving into groom's house).

Couples liked to hold the ekdosis during the month of Gamelion (December–January), near the festival of Gamelia, which celebrated the divine marriage of Hera and Zeus.

People also stage holiday rituals based on the divine marriage. The dates vary by culture, but the rituals usually happen in spring—the season of renewed life. In Sumeria, the divine marriage of Inanna and Dumuzi was performed in the spring. Saxon tradition centers on the lunar goddess Eostre and her union with the Sun god, from whose name we derive our holiday Ostara (the Spring Equinox). A more generally Celtic and European date for the marriage of God and Goddess is Beltane (May 1).

Historic and contemporary Pagans have also used marriage and lovemaking for worship, raising magical power, or spiritual growth. In India, tantra encourages practitioners to develop self-control and enjoy sustained pleasure not necessarily ending in orgasm (it sometimes lasts for hours). Wiccans observe the great rite, an act of symbolic or literal sex, in ritual. Furthermore, the charge of the goddess states in part: ". . . all acts of love and pleasure are my rituals."

Conclusions

Hierogamy embodies one of the many ways we seek to identify with the divine. Sometimes we do it by telling stories of sacred unions within a pantheon, other times by pairing deities with humans or staging the myths ourselves. All of these bring us closer to the God and Goddess.

The divine marriage truly demonstrates the adage "As above, so below."

Magic in the Gloaming

by Nuala Drago

From sunset to nightfall and from daybreak until dawn, the rhythm of the earth diminishes, yielding to the primordial cycles of darkness and light. This is the gloaming, when twilight hovers between the boundaries of day and night. It is an eerie, shadowy time of transformation and release. It is a quiet time to commune with natural forces in an atmosphere of mystery and enchantment. Some call it witchlight, because there is magic in the gloaming and otherworldly creatures are adrift.

The ancient Celts, like most early cultures, possessed a deep reverence for nature. They viewed the natural world as being alive with gods and goddesses, conscious spirits, ancestral ghosts, familiars, phantoms, fairies, and demons that haunted the twilight. They believed that the gloaming was a sacred time when the meeting of opposites (day and night) temporarily suspended the laws of nature, allowing the veil between the human world and the supernatural realms to dissolve into the mist, briefly mingling the boundaries of time and space for both humans and elementals.

In the half-light of the gloaming, supernatural beings had the ability to shape-shift and pass from their own consciousness and reality into that of the human realm. Often, they would appear as crepuscular creatures, who are active only at dusk and dawn— meaning bats, cats, owls, badgers, skunks, and coyotes to name but a few. In their animal forms, these spirits sometimes became familiars and guides for those who sought them out and knew how to open themselves to such encounters.

The Druids dedicated much of their training to this art. Those who were adept at uniting their spirits with the forces of nature and communing with the ghosts of their ancestors were said to have the ability to permeate any of the elemental realms (in the esoteric sense) to make allies of the spirits and deities who dwelt there. In so doing, they were able to learn secrets—such as the best time to plant crops, when to hunt, when to make war, how to make medicines, and how to heal. This type of magic was as important in the daily lives of their people as it was during times of festivals and celebrations, not merely for their spiritual well-being, but because their very existence depended upon it.

Perhaps no less vital was the fact that, for our ancestors, the atmosphere of gloaming fired the imagination. Traditionally, it became a time of storytelling and passing on the legends of gods and goddesses, great heroes, cultural history, and tall tales. Even yarns of swords and sorcerers, highwaymen, smugglers, poachers, pirates, ill-fated lovers, great warriors, and restless ghosts enriched daily life, helped folks to cope with societal constraints, and gave the ordinary individual something to aspire to.

As twilight fell, the workday was done and clans gathered around the hearth or campfire. The stories they shared transported them outside the limits of their own fears and troubles to a higher plane—one wherein creative visualization, spiritual growth, and enlightenment were among the possibilities.

Fortunately, for most of us in the modern world, our physical survival is not so difficult. We still have problems to overcome and stresses to cope with, however, and, because of our everyday work lives, our spiritual needs are often overlooked. We feel there just isn't enough time anymore. There is magic in the gloaming and we don't even have to make a great effort to experience it.

Even the colors of twilight can influence mood—deep indigo, gold, purple, violet, gray, silver, and black all vibrate with energy and symbolism as the first and brightest stars appear in the darkening sky. The cycle of death and rebirth is played out daily as the energy of the Sun is relinquished to the serenity of the Moon in the in-between time of shadows.

In the gloaming, we fall under the spell of Mercury and Venus shining brilliantly above the horizon. Mercury is akin to quicksilver, magic, and illusion, while Venus, known both as the morning star and the evening star, is associated with love and feminine mystery. To add to the enchantment, the air is rich with the sweet fragrance of noctiflora—moonflower, four o'clocks, jessamine, and certain water lilies. Fireflies glimmer and night birds glide silently between the imposing silhouettes of trees. Gentle breezes caress the face, and cricket chirp.

Twice each day, the gloaming gifts us with a time of almost limitless possibility if only we have the will to open our hearts to them. It is a perfect time for lover's trysts, storytelling, and other voyages of the imagination. It is a time for fairies and familiars, prayer, mediation, self-discovery, centering oneself, or adding greater spiritual meaning to one's life through bonding with nature. It is a time when even pausing briefly to gaze out a window can allow the magic to be felt.

Of course the best place to experience the magic of the gloaming is out of doors in a natural setting. Probably the most propitious locations for twilight magic are those that are places where opposites meet—such as a sandy beach, the mouth of a cave, the edge of a cliff, a clearing in a grove, and so on. The Druids believed that the best place to commune with one's ancestors in the twilight was a cairn or other burial place, but you needn't go to such places in the physical sense. Visualization is often enough.

If you aren't one to venture into the greater outdoors, perhaps you have space to create a small twilight garden in your yard, on a rooftop, or on a porch or patio. There are many plants that bloom at dusk, such as flowering tobacco, sweet rocket, evening primrose, dames violet, and scented geraniums. There are so many plants to choose from for your twilight garden that you can vary them by color, size, scent, their symbolic meanings, or whatever other trait you desire.

All these plants attract the creatures that dwell in the twilight as well. You may want to keep a notebook on the animals, insects, and birds that visit your garden in the gloaming. Try to find out their symbolic meanings as well, and see if their presence was a harbinger for something that has happened in your life. Make note of how the visitors change with the seasons. Try to perceive them as our ancestors did.

Perhaps you don't have the space for a garden or, for some reason, you can't be outdoors safely or don't wish to be outdoors at all. In that case, moonflowers can be grown in a container and placed next to a window and even allowed to twine around the casement. Each captivating, silvery blossom that opens at dusk can grow up to eight inches in width and will perfume the air. From your window, you can still record all that you see and experience in the gloaming.

Remember that the gloaming can be a gateway to other realms. Since all magic depends on the spirits and deities of nature that dwell within those realms, it is wise to stay on friendly terms with them.

When you think you have been treading on supernatural turf, it is a good idea to leave an offering behind—a bit of bread or milk will do. When you are outdoors in the twilight hours, try to disturb as little as possible. Speak softly in the gloaming. Watch and listen. Slow down. Be still. Close your eyes and breathe.

There, now, was that an owl hooting a message from the otherworld?

A Handfasting Ceremony

by Nina Lee Braden

This ceremony was written for a handfasting using two officials, a high priest, and a high priestess. However, it can also be performed by one official. It can be used for a legal religious wedding, a nonlegal religious handfasting, or for a commitment ceremony for same-sex couples. In this ceremony, I will refer to the couple as Moonpiper and Windsong since those names are non-gender specific. It can also be adapted to reflect a more specialized spiritual path.

Casting of the Circle

(Both officials stand at the altar.) **High priestess**: Let us recognize the sacredness of this space. All space is sacred, and all times are sacred. Let us consciously acknowledge and recognize the sacredness that exists all around us today, here, now.

High priest (walking to the east): Let us recognize the sacredness of the east and the element of air. The breeze that caresses our cheeks is sacred. The perfume of flowers is sacred. Our very breath is sacred. Breathe and honor the sacredness of air.

(Walking to the south): Let us recognize the sacredness of the south and the element of fire. The flame that lights the candle is sacred. The fire that cooks our food is sacred. The passion in our hearts is sacred. Feel your passions, and honor the sacredness of fire.

High priestess (walking to the west): Let us recognize the sacredness of the west and the element of water. The salt water of the ocean is sacred. The drop of dew on the leaf is sacred. The fluids that flow through our bodies are sacred. Recognize and honor the sacredness of water.

(Walking to the north): Let us recognize the sacredness of the north and the element of earth. The ground that we walk on is sacred. The trees and mountains and sand are sacred. Our bones are sacred. Acknowledge the strength of your bones, and honor the sacredness of earth. (Both officials move to the center or altar.)

High priestess: We ask that the Lord and Lady, the divine masculine and feminine, shine on us today and lend their love.

High priest: All days are sacred, but today is especially so. We come together today to honor the vows of love and commitment of Moonpiper and Windsong. Let us join today with joyous hearts, sending out love to Moonpiper and Windsong and to all who would welcome a gift of joy.

High priestess: Who stands in support of Moonpiper and Windsong? (Here their friends, attendants, witnesses, or family can speak briefly or merely say "We do." You may insert a poem or quotation that is a favorite of the handfast couple or one appropriate to the season or to a specific spiritual tradition.)

High priestess: What are the benefits of being handfasted? Why should two people make a commitment to each other?

High priest: Being handfasted is not easy, even when you are handfasted to a wonderful person. Why become handfasted?

High priestess: Because it is an opportunity for growth. Moonpiper, in committing to Windsong, you commit to studying yourself so that you may be the best person possible. You also commit to studying Windsong in order to help in his/her growth.

Windsong, in committing to Moonpiper, you commit to studying yourself so that you may be the best person possible. You also commit to studying Moonpiper in order to help in his/her growth.

High priest: You grow in self-knowledge, and you grow in knowledge of others. You will learn to see life from others' points of view, and your life will be enriched. Knowledge leads to wisdom and power. Wisdom and power require responsibility. Use your wisdom and power always with love, always with responsibility.

High priestess: Handfasting is also an opportunity for worship. Through the vows you make to each other and the lives that you live together, you show your worship of the lord and lady.

High priest: Handfasting is an opportunity to establish a tradition. Through the home that you make together, you blend your personal paths and traditions into a new tradition. In so doing, you add to the spiritual growth of all.

High priestess: Moonpiper, do you have any words that you want to speak to Windsong at this time? (Here Moonpiper may speak extemporaneously or may read from a prepared speech.)

Windsong, do you have any words that you want to speak to Moonpiper at this time? (Here Windsong may speak extemporaneously or may read from a prepared speech.)

High priestess: Like the gentle breezes of east, caress each other gently.

High priest: Like the fierce winds of the east, proclaim with power your love for one another.

High priestess: Like the warm sunlight of a summer morning, give warmth and encouragement to each other.

High priest: Like the strong Sun of a summer midday, let your love shine undimmed and high overhead.

High priestess: Like the sweet rain that nurtures our souls, may you nurture one another.

High priest: Like the ocean, may your love for each other be powerful and deep, the undercurrent to all else in your lives.

High priestess: Like the fruits and vegetables of the earth, may you feed each other.

High priest: Like the mountains and rocks, may you protect each other.

High priestess: Like the Lady, may you be unending in your love and wisdom.

High priest: Like the Lord, may you be fierce in your love and passion.

High priest: Do you have tokens you wish to exchange at this time as a symbol of your love and commitment to each other? (Couples may exchange rings, amulets, or other sacred objects.)

High priestess: Moonpiper, please repeat after me: "I, Moonpiper, give thee Windsong this token of my love for you. I promise to be sensitive to your needs. I will strive to give you space when you need it. I will strive to give you comfort when you need it. I will strive to give you encouragement when you need it. My love for you is honest. My love for you is passionate. My love for you is human. My love for you is divine. I will be your partner in creating a home and sacred sanctuary for us to share in our worship of the lord and lady. I will strive to give you love always."

High priest: Windsong, please repeat after me: "I, Windsong, give thee Moonpiper this token of my love for you. I promise to be sensitive to your needs. I will strive to give you space when you need it. I will strive to give you comfort when you need it. I will strive to give you encouragement when you need it. My love for you is honest. My love for you is passionate. My love for you is human. My love for you is divine. I will be your partner in creating a home and sacred sanctuary for us to share in our worship of the lord and lady. I will strive to give you love always."

High priestess: Wherever Moonpiper and Windsong go, they go united, and they are united even when they are apart. May they rest always at home, even when physically separated. Let home be a sanctuary and a haven, a place of healing and growth.

High priest: Let home be a place of courage and integrity. Let fears be expressed honestly and promptly. Let anger be expressed healthily and not allowed to poison the relationship. Be strong in your love for yourselves and in your love for each other.

(At this point, if desired, the couple may perform the Great Rite or may jump over a broom. At this point also, a cord may be bound around the wrists of the couple as the officials speak.)

High priestess: Let this cord represent that you are united, two individuals with one common cause, one hope, one dream.

High priest: Let this cord represent that you enter into this partnership willingly, and that this knot is tied in accordance to your wishes.

High priestess: I pronounce you a wedded couple. You may kiss to seal your pledge.

High priest: We thank the elements of air, fire, water, and earth for their attendance this day and ask that the spirits of the elements go forth and herald this union. These two lives are now joined in one unbroken circle. We thank the lord and lady for blessing us with their divine presence.

High priestess: The circle is open but unbroken. Go in peace and love, taking the joy and celebration of this ceremony with you as you leave.

Tarot and the Eleusinian Mysteries

by Anthony Louis

The tarot deck that was conceived by British occultist Arthur Edward Waite (1857–1942) and illustrated by American artist Pamela Colman Smith (1878–1951) has been the most influential of the past century. It made its debut in 1910 through Rider & Company, a London publisher, and has come to be known as the Rider-Waite-Smith Tarot. Many of the images in this deck allude to the mystery teachings of Eleusis, a religious movement that held sway in the ancient Greek and Roman world for over two thousand years and influenced the development of Western occult traditions and modern Christianity.

Arthur Edward Waite was a member of the short-lived but influential Hermetic Order of the Golden Dawn, a secret society dedicated to the study of Western esoteric traditions. Other members included such notables as Irish poet William Butler Yeats and English occultist Aleister Crowley. In developing his tarot deck, Waite placed primary importance on the use of symbols to communicate esoteric principles. For example, the veil on the High Priestess card contains images of pomegranates, a direct reference to Persephone's ties to the underworld. Waite outlines his interpretations of the cards in his text *The Key to the Tarot*, which is sometimes published with pictorial reproductions of the cards under the title *The Pictorial Key to the Tarot*.

Gertrude Moakley, in her introduction to *Waite's Pictorial Key to the Tarot*, states that Waite's tarot "was intended primarily to convey to the Order's members the secret tradition taught by the ancient mysteries." Waite left no esoteric stone unturned. He explored ceremonial magic, alchemy, theosophy, Rosicrucianism, the grail legends, the Qabala, and most importantly freemasonry. The Masonic teachings, which drew directly from the Eleusinian mysteries, strongly colored his view of the new tarot deck he was developing. The freemasons appear to have borrowed their hierarchy of levels of initiation directly from the ancient mystery schools.

The sacred Eleusinian mysteries, conducted annually in honor of Demeter and Persephone, were instituted in the city of Eleusis, about fourteen miles west of Athens. Worshippers came from throughout the ancient Greek world to make the holy pilgrimage between Athens and Eleusis and participate in the secret ceremonies. Little is known for certain about the details of the rites, because initiates were sworn to secrecy about the activities in the temple of Demeter and violation of that oath was a capital offense.

The "Homeric Hymn to Demeter," written in the seventh century AD, chronicles the myth of Demeter and her doings in the city of Eleusis. Demeter, the goddess of grain (called Ceres by the Romans), was grief-stricken when Hades in his chariot abducted her daughter Persephone (Kore, the Maiden) and conducted her to his home in the underworld. Demeter's search for Persephone took her to Eleusis where, disguised in mortal form, she became a nursemaid for the local ruler's son. Demeter began to perform sacred rites of anointing the boy with ambrosia and purifying him in the fire to make him immortal. When the boy's mother discovered her son being held in the flames, she screamed in fright. Demeter, in anger, ceased the sacred rite that would have made the boy immortal. The goddess then demanded that a temple be built in her honor to practice her rituals, which could lead to eventual immortality.

Remaining in Eleusis and grieving for her daughter, Demeter ceased her divine function of making the crops grow. The entire world fell into famine, and humans could no longer make offerings to the gods. Zeus, who had originally approved the abduction of Persephone, sent his messenger Hermes (the magician) to intercede with Hades for her release. According to the Homeric epic, the god Hades agreed to release Persephone but only after he "secretly gave her sweet pomegranate seeds to eat, taking care for himself that she might not remain continually with grave, dark-robed Demeter." Having eaten pomegranate in the underworld, Persephone was bound to spend a third of each year with Hades beneath the earth. Thus the seasons of the year originated.

To participate in the Eleusinian rites, one was required to speak Greek and to never have shed blood (or if one had, one had to be ritually purified). Initiates were assigned a sponsor to guide them into the mysteries of the religion. The initiation process was overseen by the high priest or hierophant (which means "revealer of sacred things"). And only the Hierophant was allowed to enter the inner sanctum of the temple where the sacred objects *(Hiera)* of Demeter were kept.

There were two sets of secret mysteries (or arcana, from the Latin *arcanus* meaning "secret")—the lesser and the greater. The Lesser Mysteries (Minor Arcana) were a preliminary or introductory set of rites performed at Agrae in the springtime. Six months later, in September, the Greater Mysteries (Major Arcana) were celebrated at Eleusis over a period of nine days (or a *novena*) at harvest time.

The allegorical meaning of the mysteries appears to have derived from the cycle of birth, death, and rebirth as evidenced in the growing of crops, their death and harvesting, and their rebirth in the spring. The Eleusinian influence is seen in the Christian New Testament in the statement that unless a grain of wheat falls into the ground and dies, it cannot grow. By analogy, the cult of Demeter viewed the human soul as needing to pass through a series of tests and trials on this earthly plane so that it can proceed to a higher level of existence and ultimately to immortality.

Part of the celebration of the Greater Mysteries was a dramatic reenactment of the story of Demeter and Persephone, in which the maiden dies, descends into the underworld, and is resurrected through the intercession of the father god Zeus. Some form of communion was probably involved as the high priestess, playing the role of the goddess Demeter in the mystery play, drank beer from a cup, symbolizing the fruits of the goddess poured forth for humankind. The initiates promised to dedicate their lives to the goddess and to live up to her high moral code. In exchange the goddess promised life after death. The ceremonies ended when the hierophant gave his final address called the *Logos* (or "the Word").

Although Waite was eclectic in his choice of symbols for his new tarot deck, it is clear that he made extensive use of the Eleusinian mystery religion and Freemasonry in his conception of the cards. Approaching the cards from the perspective of this ancient mystery religion gives us a deeper understanding of Waite's symbolism and a greater appreciation of the mythical underpinnings of his deck.

Angels Are Like Buses: A Quick Field Guide to Invisible Beings

by Raven Kaldera and Tannin Schwartzstein

The astral plane. A barren hill. The back alley behind the Wal-Mart—these are places you might encounter noncorporeal beings. Learning to identify them, their motives, and their relationship to the world of humans has been a subject of speculation for hundreds of years. We can't promise that this little field guide is anything close to exhaustive, but we can certainly give you some tips based on our personal encounters with noncorporeal beings.

For simplicity, we are focusing this article on entities that were never human (i.e. nonghosts) and not divine. This information may mesh well with some existing sources and conflict with others, but such is the nature of human contact with the beings we have chosen to dub "noncorporeals"—every human's psychic sensitivity and method of information processing is as unique as their brain structure. The way we "see" these beings is not necessarily the way that you will perceive them.

What is most important to remember is that these creatures are not human, were never human, and do not react in human ways. Sometimes their responses may seem deceptively close to a human's, but this is a coincidence. Their ideas, values, experiences, and sense of time are entirely different from ours.

For the sake of expedience, we can divide nonhuman noncorporeals into two rough groups: earthly and unearthly. Earthly spirits share our planet with us, and they originated here. Some may be prehuman. Common earthly spirits include elementals, and the earthly spirits that have been referred to as the "little people" or the "little mysteries." Although we may or may not be able to see them, they are always around us.

Unearthly creatures, such as angels, did not originate on this physical plane of existence, though they may travel here for various reasons. To some of them, Midgard is a travel port, a plane whose edges touch a lot of other planes. Others may be in exile, on the run from something, or on personal quests of their own that have nothing to do with us.

The first assumption to eschew is the notion that any entity you encounter has materialized for your benefit or to bring you a message. Most often, this being has little interest in you. Sometimes when we encounter these creatures, it is akin to two airplanes passing each other in close proximity. It is good to be observant about such events, but it's most important that we don't knock into the other spirit and cause an unnecessary accident. This means that when you encounter a noncorporeal, it is generally wise to take care and keep a distance.

Angels

The beings most popularly referred to as angels have been visualized in many forms over the last three thousand years. Some orders of angels were pictured in ancient lore as giant balls of eyes and wings—a far cry from the fat, cheerful babies we often see on greeting cards today. In our experience, angels are more like large unstoppable balls of power—passing by one is like being hit by a bus. They are massive, energetic, and vaguely hollow inside. Also like buses, angels have specific routes and stops, and it is very difficult to sway them from their assigned purpose.

Angels are a classic example of a nonhuman intelligence. Angels are cogs in the giant machine that we call the universe; each one is like a living, troubleshooting computer program for a specific parameter. Some, such as the archangel Michael, are in charge of defense. Some, like the angel Azrael, are in charge of recycling. Like bees, they have a complex hierarchy and chain of command, outside of which they are incapable of functioning. While they have very individualized jobs, they don't have much actual personality. They exude a great amount of energy and can set things right in amazing ways—but only in ways that they are ordered to. Angels do not live within our time scale, though they seem aware that we live and die. Unlike earthly hive creatures, they are very good at interfacing with other creature species—it's part of their job. During such interactions, you may temporarily feel as if you are hooked into a giant weblike network. It's usually a one-way interface devoid of much extraneous information.

As to the idea of "fallen angels," for purposes of this article, we are separating them from the multitude of entities referred to as "demons." Think of fallen angels as pieces of the universal code that have degraded and become error-ridden. They tend to give false information and undo things that shouldn't be undone—not out of malice, but out of malfunction. It's best to leave them alone.

Demons

The term "demon" has been assigned for centuries to any minor creature that humans couldn't immediately identify or place. The word comes from the Greek *daemon,* which simply means "spirit." We are going to limit the word "demon" to one category of astral critter: otherworldly entities that survive in our world by feeding on the life force of humans. Sometimes they are fleeing something in their own worlds an are in exile; occasionally they have been summoned by careless or ignorant humans (these can be quite angry and malicious).

Demons are opportunistic, and will be attracted to sources of free-flowing energy such as chronic fear and anger. We tend to blame them for things going wrong, but more often than not they are attracted to someone who is sick, weak, or already riddled with problems. Their motivation is entirely selfish. If they stir things up in an already mucky situation, it's to get more food, but they are unlikely to be at the root of the actual problem.

Demons can experience our time scale quite variously, depending. Some are smaller than humans and live much shorter lives; others can adapt to our sense of time. Their appearance will vary with what will get an emotional energy rise out of you— whether anger, laughter, horror, and so on. They will promise you all sorts of ridiculous things, most of which they will not be able to deliver, in order to get past your shields. The more intelligent they are, the more effective are their lies. There is no spell in existence that can absolutely guarantee to make them tell the truth, the whole truth, and nothing but the truth. The best way to deal with them is to work a cool, no-nonsense banishing.

Fairies

The fairy worlds lie alongside ours. Fairies are very attractive to humans, partly because they possess powerful glamour magic (the ability to disguise things or people with illusions), and partly because they come across as seeming more human than angels or demons. Fairies are quirky, like humans, but they don't resemble us in more than cursory ways. Fairies are full of paradoxes. They can appear sexy or sexless, powerful or powerless, wise or foolish—sometimes all at the same time.

Because their time sense is linked to that in their worlds, fairies don't understand our time very well. Fairies often have little to no respect for property and living space, so it isn't wise to invite them into your home. Their refusal to adhere to or comprehend human rules and values makes them seem fickle, dishonest, and amoral, by our standards (and they often are). Take any fairy promise with a grain of salt.

On the positive side, fairies can be very wise and give good (if occasionally disjointed) advice. When they are inclined to be straight with you, they can be very insightful. Fairies seem to understand modern technology. They are also creative and imaginative, and are masters of the art of manifestation. They can inspire artists and craftspeople to new heights. Fairies can create entire tiny worlds out of almost nothing; like all fairy paradoxes, this can manifest as a form of self-delusion They have ability to vanish and leave no trace, so ecologically we can learn a lot from them about caring for natural beauty.

Fairies are highly emotional beings, although their emotional responses to things may seem alien to us. If a fairy becomes your friend and ally for more than a superficial period of time, it will be because you have touched them in some emotional way, not because they feel any sense of honor, duty, or obligation to you.

Elementals

Elemental spirits are living, sentient intelligences that inhabit specific types of matter and energy. The most common are those associated with fire, water, air, and earth. Each of these groups have multiple subgroups too numerous to mention or catalogue. Elemental spirits aren't very bright or creative, and they have very short attention spans. They are all knowing in their spheres and completely ignorant of anything outside of them. They live in our time, but at a much faster or slower pace. Fire and air elementals vibrate at a rate that is almost too fast to communicate with us,. Water elementals will vibrate at a fast or slow rate depending on its state. Earth elementals are the slowest of all. Tree elementals are also slow as well.

Elementals can be useful in helping you achieve certain emotional states. Air elementals give excitement and clarity, while fire elementals give energy. Water elementals can give peace and fluidity, and earth elementals are excellent for stabilizing, slowing down, and keeping in touch with what's "real."

The tiny swarms of creatures that we call "little people" or "little mysteries" are a distantly related form of earth elemental. We tend to associate them with fairies, but that's mostly because fairies get on well with them. Unlike fairies, they understand such concepts as duty, honor, death, and commitment. They are very community oriented and work together well in groups. Their magic is oriented toward small details rather than huge miracles.

In Conclusion

As spiritualists, whether we are Witches, magicians, or mediums, we do sometimes have to share our world with other creatures. Overall, it's important to do your homework and your field research before bothering any such invisible being. Noncorporeals, at their best, can help us to see our world and our existence from new perspectives, and we can do the same for them.

While it's fun to have flights of fancy, whether they are movies, TV, or the written word, sometimes those flights of fancy can be like white noise, getting in the way of actually hearing what they have to say. Learn to listen and observe before making assumptions about the most majestic angel and the humblest stone elemental. They are not our pets, and never will be. Respect them if you don't want to end up being their playthings, or their adversaries. We have a lot to learn from them, but only if we are willing to pay attention.

Navratna, Talisman of Nine Precious Gems

by S. Y. Zenith

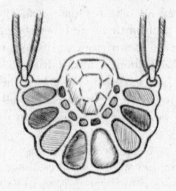

According to Indian gemology, there are eighty-four gem stones. Of these, only nine are considered precious stones by vedic or jyotish astrologers. The nine are ruby, white pearl, red coral, yellow sapphire, emerald, diamond, blue sapphire, cinnamon stone (or hessonite), and cat's-eye.

When these nine gems are mounted in a specific synergistic combination, they are collectively known as the Navratna—a renowned and time-proven talisman for pacifying the nine planets of the jyotish astrology system. The Navratna is commonly set in rings mounted in such a way that each stone touches the skin of the middle finger on the right hand. It is also available as pendants, bracelets, bangles, necklaces, *malas* (rosaries), and pendulums.

Traditionalists believe that all Navratna jewelry is most potent when all nine gems touch the skin. Wealthy individuals of Indian heritage prefer to set the gems in gold. The less affluent may wear the talisman set in silver or five metals. No matter the setting, many attest to the effectiveness of the Navratna in dispelling negative circumstances from their lives. The nine gems filter negative rays from the nine planets, allowing only benefic rays to enter the body. It is also said that this talisman attracts pleasures of money, name, fame, glory, honor, progeny, family, and happiness. It destroys calamities, rids diseases, and increases lifespan.

In my experience wearing a Navratna mala for the past two years, I have found that each time the mala snaps off or breaks, a major malefic influence had been successfully deflected. These malevolent situations usually become known within nine days of the mala snapping. Every such occurrence heralds auspiciousness. I have since repaired the mala several times using strong thread, twenty-pound fishing line, and jeweler's wire.

Planets Represented in the Human Body

Seven planets influence human life and the body continuously. The Sun represents the soul. The Moon represents the mind. Mars represents perseverance. Mercury represents voice. Jupiter represents wisdom (learning). Venus represents love and nurturing. Saturn represents sobriety and thoughtfulness.

In addition to these seven planets, there are two "shadow planets"—known as Rahu and Ketu—that also impact upon human existence. They are not heavenly bodies but calculated points in the planetary orbit, located 180 degrees apart from each other. In astronomy and Western astrology, Rahu is known as "Dragon's Head" or the north node of the Moon. It is the tip where the Moon's orbit crosses the ecliptic. Ketu is the "Dragon's Tail" or the descending south node of the moon. It is said to produce comets and meteors.

A Hindu myth tells of the beginning of creation when the god Lord Vishnu conferred immortality on all planetary beings by feeding them a special potion called *amrita*. A serpent demon entered the room and drank the potion. The Sun and Moon alerted Lord Vishnu who cut the demon in two with his sword. However, the serpent demon had already gained immortality, and thus now was split into two halves. Rahu is the head of the serpent demon and represents insatiable cravings and burning desires for worldly success. Ketu, the body of the demon, represents realms of the spiritual, astral, and otherworldly. Ketu causing disturbances to earthly and practical matters.

Gem Planetary Rulers

The nine gems of the Navratna are governed respectively by the Sun, Moon, Mars, Jupiter, Mercury, Venus, Saturn, Rahu, and Ketu. The Sun's gem is ruby. The Moon's gem is white pearl, and

for fiery Mars it is red coral. Yellow sapphire is Jupiter's stone. Emerald is ruled by Mercury, and diamond by Venus. Blue sapphire is governed by Saturn, and is considered to represent darkness, the enemy of light. Rahu's gem is the cinnamon stone (hessonite). Ketu's gem is cat's-eye from the gem mineral chrysoberyl.

In the *Tantra Sara,* one of the most famous tantric scriptures, the human body is said to be an "island of nine gems" corresponding with nine constituents.

Flesh: Yellow sapphire

Hair: Blue sapphire

Skin: Cat's-eye

Blood: Red coral

Bone: Pearl

Marrow: Emerald

Fat: Cinnamon stone

Semen: Diamond

Vitality: Ruby

When advocating the use of Navratna, many traditional practitioners deem finger joints to be the most sensitive parts where a network of nerve fibers and lymphatic fluid together serve as assimilators of energies emitted by gems. With slight and constant contact with the skin, they draw changes in body chemistry by interaction with the body's energy field that is permeated by a complex electromagnetic field.

Navratna Mystical Powers

Each of the nine gems in the Navratna exhibits specific mystical powers, somewhat based on its planetary influence.

Ruby (Sun): Bestows name, fame, vigor, virtue, warmth, and capacity to command. It has the potential to raise an individual above his/her status. A symbol of love and passion, and beneficial to aspirants for high office. Good for success in all ventures.

Pearl (Moon): Strengthens mental faculties, calms emotions, and increases peace of mind. Ensures harmonious conjugal life and protects from widowhood.

Red Coral (Mars): Promotes courage, fame, career success, and protects from elemental calamities such as floods, fires, and storms. Helps eradicate difficulties.

Emerald (Mercury): Improves memory, communication, intuition, and sharpens the intellect and ability to absorb information. Also bestows sufficient wealth.

Yellow Sapphire (Jupiter): Enhances financial status, bestows adequate wealth, good health, name, honor, and fame.

Diamond (Venus): Confers longevity, advancement in life, intelligence, wealth, luxury, success in undertakings, and good fortune.

Blue Sapphire (Saturn): A note of caution here from the Indian astrological perspective: Although blue sapphires can be beneficial for some individuals, it may not produce positive results for others. A trial of several days will provide indications whether it is appropriate for a person. If suitable for an individual, this gem attracts happiness, prosperity, career achievements, and favors from high officials. It counteracts envy from others and eliminates misfortune. If in doubt, consult a jyotish astrologer or a knowledgeable gemologist.

Cinnamon Stone (Rahu): Draws prosperity, good health, and triumph over adversaries. Bestows intelligence and knowledge. Assists in business development and professional improvement. Banishes evil influences. Protects from sudden misfortunes.

Cat's-Eye (Ketu): Believed to be a quick-action gem for ridding poverty and diseases. Restores lost wealth. Grants philosophical disposition and serenity. Also protects from hidden enemies, dangers, and diseases.

Gems for Success

Each profession is presided over by a planet and its related gem. Wearing a lucky gem specifically connected to an occupational category gives the career a boost, based on the following list.

Ruby: Politicians, civil servants, social service workers, public welfare officers, actors, film producers, and movie directors.

Pearl: For those in metal industries, engineering supplies, computer fields, music, and musical instrument production.

Red Coral: Military personnel, police officers, security service authorities, hotel employees, real-estate professionals, and those engaged in electrical work.

Emerald: Agency staffers, contract workers, cloth or clothing traders, fashion designers, decorators, writers, and business owners of paper product industries.

Yellow Sapphire: Artists, teachers, lecturers, those working in financial establishments, entertainers in performing arts, and religious leaders.

Diamond: Administrative professionals, agriculturists and farmers specializing in poultry, dairy products, fruits, and vegetables.

Blue Sapphire: For those in iron and steel enterprises, real-estate agents, property brokers, construction or building material manufacturers and suppliers.

Cinnamon Stone: Politicians, astrologers, dancers, palmists, and individuals working in metaphysical environments.

Cat's-Eye: Journalists, writers, publishers, lawyers, movie producers and directors, actors, and those in medical professions and printing industries.

Gem Substitutes

As precious gems of high-quality grades are not easily affordable for many of us, substitutes of medium grade or semiprecious gems can be used as follows.

Ruby: Garnet, red tourmaline, red spinel, star ruby

Pearl: Moonstone, clear quartz

Red Coral: Carnelian, red jasper

Emerald: Aquamarine, green agate, jade, peridot, green tourmaline

Yellow Sapphire: Topaz, citrine, yellow tourmaline

Diamond: White sapphire, white zircon

Blue Sapphire: Amethyst, lapis lazuli, blue zircon, blue tourmaline

Cinnamon Stone: Hessonite garnet

Cat's-Eye: Tiger's-eye.

Greek Gods for the Modern Age

by Laura LaVoie

When we were children, most of us were taught the rich history of the Greek and Roman mythologies. As adult Pagans, we are now in the position of connecting with these deities on a personal level, but in an age of computers, fast food, and SUVs, some of us find it difficult to relate to an ancient god of agriculture or a vengeful goddess of specific crimes. Still, as we have evolved past agrarian culture into the current age of overwhelming technology, we can imagine the gods did so as well. Though many of the ancient gods and goddesses were tied to specific functions, with a little creative thinking we can incorporate them into our busy modern lives.

In this article I'll lay the groundwork for exploring the Greek pantheon's place in our hectic lives. This is meant to be a basic primer—the options are truly limitless. Have a look at the following Olympian deities and their possible correlation with twenty-first-century living

The Greek Gods Today

Artemis

This twin goddess is related to the animals, the hunt, and childbirth. An obvious application is for the expectant parents to keep an image of her available to protect the child and ease childbirth. Why not call upon her to help keep our animal companions safe? When I am at work during the day, I know that my cat is protected by the energies of Artemis.

Apollo

The Sun to Artemis' Moon, this twin god is also known for music, prophecy, and healing. A simple application of his energies is to request his help if you're feeling ill. If you find yourself at work with a killer headache, have a short conversation with Apollo and allow him to give you relief.

Aphrodite

Everyone is familiar with the goddess of love, beauty, desire, and sexuality. Today, though, Aphrodite can be seen as a deity of self-love and self-esteem. At our jobs and at home we often have moments of feeling inadequate. A short conversation with Aphrodite is sure to give you that boost of self-confidence to get through the situation.

Ares

Ares is known as the god of war, but more specifically he rules over the frenzy of life. In my life, I realized how useful his energies could be when I was in a disagreement. Certainly we need to rein in our emotions for the purpose of interacting with individuals throughout our day, but we all know that keeping those feelings bottled up isn't healthy. Vent your frustration to Ares and let him help you with your rage.

Athena

Athena has always been pictured as the warrior. Her spheres of influence include wisdom, military victory, and the domestic arts. A little help on the domestic front never hurt anyone, especially today when we have very little time to spend handling our household. Ask for Athena's help when doing anything around the house.

Demeter

Surely the goddess of grain is not as crucial to our twenty-first century sensibility as to folk of yore. Yet in Demeter we can seek ancient wisdom. Although our meals often come from boxes and cartons, somewhere in the chain agricultural roots still exist. A simple prayer before mealtime can ensure that Demeter will be looking after you to keep you fed.

Dionysus

Reminiscent of a fraternity brother, Dionysus is the god of wine and intoxication. When applied with a liberal dose of common sense, he can help us to be responsible drinkers.

Hades

As the ruler of the underworld, Hades passes through our lives in shadows, only to be seen when we are struck with tragedy. We as Pagans know that death is merely a completion of a cycle, but this doesn't dull the pain of loss. Despite Hades' bad reputation, he does occasionally exhibit compassion, and he can be called upon to watch over those who have left us behind.

Hephaestus

Hephaestus is the god of fire and crafts, which roughly translates to blacksmithing. Though one might think that modern Pagans have little use for this art, the element of fire does not need to be taken literally. Today, one might consider assembly line workers to be contemporary blacksmiths. Their work affects our lives as we entrust our safety to the automobiles that we drive. Call on Hephaestus to look over the autoworkers that assembled your car and help them take care in their work. Employ him also to protect your car as you drive it, respecting it for the fire craft that it truly is.

Hera

The wife of Zeus is known as the patron of marriage. In a world where half of all marriages are doomed to fail, we could use some of Hera's influence. Ask her for blessings for your own marriage or the union of friends and family. Having a goddess like this on your side is always a good idea.

Hermes

Hermes is the messenger god of the Olympians. This gives him an important place in modern life. Today, many of us rely on the Internet to communicate. We instant-message our friends and family, and use e-mail to do our jobs. Hermes' "messenger" influence can help speed web-based communication along to its recipient and be sure that all e-mails and messages are communicated gracefully.

Persephone

The daughter of Demeter, Persephone has long been viewed as the representation of the seasonal cycle. The young goddess of spring was born to the agricultural deity. When she disappears into the underworld, the earth feels the consequences and falls into winter. Even today our lives are affected by the seasonal cycle. Weather patterns dictate our weekend plans or affect our moods. Befriending the goddess of spring can help balance these elemental energies.

Poseidon

Integral to the stories of the *Iliad* and *Odyssey*, this angry sea god holds a fascination for people of all cultures. As we have evolved beyond the use of sea navigation for our main source of travel, it seems Poseidon's realm might have been replaced by travel through the air. The sea is part of a delicate balance of the earth's ecosystem, and in many places it is perishing. Employ Poseidon's sea energies to help the earth heal itself from years of human carelessness. Even the pond in your own back yard could use a little energy boost.

Zeus

The Olympians' supreme ruler, Zeus, holds authority over all the realms previously mentioned. Being a great leader and powerful god, he is a natural to call upon when making important decisions regarding politics and career development. Ask for his guidance before an interview to help yourself look and act more confident. With Zeus on your side, who would say no?

Each of these deities has limitless applications for twenty-first-century living. When we apply a little imagination, we can see they influence our world just as they did ancient Greece centuries ago.

Crystal Wire Stars

by Laurel Reufner

Imagine a row of wire stars hanging in a picture window, their crystals sparkling in the sunlight. Or picture dozens of stars dangling from your Yule tree, waiting for you to pass them out to visitors to take home. These little stars are super easy to make. And with a little imagination you can make them stand out from any other holiday craft items.

Materials You Will Need

Wire. Craft wire available at your local craft store will work for these stars, as will prepackaged wire that can be found at most hardware stores. Eighteen to twenty-two gauge wire is the best range for this project. Anything thinner will make the stars too flimsy to hold their shape. A craft store will yield more color choices, but the hardware store is probably cheaper.

Nails. You will need ten nails, plus the hammer to pound them in place. A nail that is relatively thin and one to two inches in length will be fine.

Board. A six-by-six-by-one-half-inch pine board is the perfect size for wrapping your wire. Feel free to use a bigger or smaller piece of wood, but this size really is good for holding.

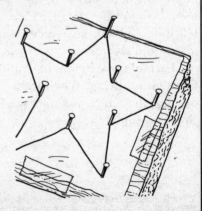

Wire Cutters and Pliers.

Star Pattern. One to two inches across is a good size star for this project. The pattern will be nailed down to a board, so

306

you might want to make a photocopy or a tracing on scrap paper to position your nails.

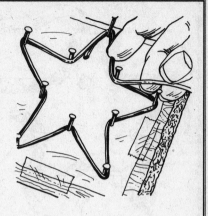

Crystals, Beads, Etc. Use assorted goodies to thread on to or hang from your finished star. These additions are purely optional, so feel free to leave them out if you wish.

Making the Stars

The first step is to transfer the pattern to your board. I use a bit of tape to hold my star pattern in place. Another option, if you are using a soft wood such as pine, is to trace over your pattern with a stylus or pencil until the lines are visible on the wood. Once your pattern is in place, hammer nails at each of the five outer points and the five inner points. This forms the template for wrapping the wire into a star shape.

Start with three to four feet of wire. This may seem like a lot, but it is easier if you do not have to keep stopping to hide the ends of wires. Also, you'll have fewer sharp ends to contend with.

Place one end around an outer point, and begin weaving the wire in and out around the nails. At the outer points, the wire should be on the outside of the nail, and on the inner points it should be on the inside. Keep wrapping until your star is at least six strands thick for a good, solid shape. More than that is also fine, but less wire makes for a flimsy star. Once you have the wire wrapped around your nails to a

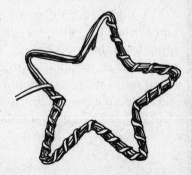

thickness you like, clip the end of the wire with the wire cutters and tuck the end back between the strands. Take the claw end of a hammer and pull out a few nails so it is easier to remove the wire from your pattern. Gently pull the star from around the nails. If needed, you can reshape it once you have the wires off of the board.

Cut about a four- to five-foot length of wire in either the same color as what you used to wrap around the nails or in a contrasting color. Tuck an end down into the wire strands and begin wrapping the new wire around those wires making up your star shape. Feel free to get a little sloppy, letting some kinks and small curls make their way into your ornament—this adds character. Wrap the whole thing at least three times, and more if you feel like it. Trim any excess wire, and you are pretty much finished with the basic ornament. Tie a length of ribbon or fishing line around one of the star's points for hanging.

If you like things basic, leave your star as it is. Personally, I like to add a small quartz crystal to the center. Just thread a piece of monofilament through the wire and then tie it off close to the crystal.

To make an even more elaborate star, simply add more embellishments. More crystals, or other types of stones, can be hung from the star's points. Beads can be strung on the wire while you are wrapping your stars. You could thread some beads on to string or monofilament and hang them from the star, or use the beaded thread to form a more elaborate hanger than plain ribbon or monofilament.

Be creative and have fun.

Articles for Fall

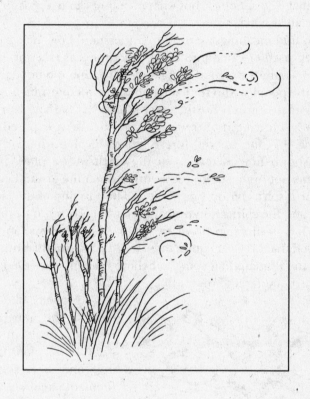

Corn Dollies for City Dwellers

by Lily Gardner

Many of us are hard-pressed to come up with satisfying rituals for Lughnasah. In the height of summer, it is difficult to think of autumn's harvest and decline. The books on sabbats tell us to make corn dollies, but what meaning can that possibly have for us city dwellers?

To find meaning, we need to understand how the corn dolly or corn mother came into being. We moderns take for granted that agriculture is a good thing, but cultivation did not come easily to the peoples who settled north of the Mediterranean. When the Romans moved north to settle the "barbarian" land, they began by clearing it of trees. Stubbled fields lay exposed to the wind where once sacred forests stood. Further, the barbarians were shown how to tear open the earth with a plow. Did the Romans not understand that splitting open the ground enraged the earth spirits beyond reckoning? This farming of the land was theft, and the spirits would steal back what was taken from them.

What it all came down to was the Norse, Slavs, and Celts believed the forces of nature to be more powerful than humanity, while the Romans had come to believe humans were the lords of nature, bending it to their will.

To pacify the earth deities, the northerners needed rituals to soften each act of plowing, sowing, and harvesting. To them, the field was a living being. They laid an egg before the plow on the first day of cultivation. If the egg broke before the plow, the earth was willing to accept being dug up. The spirits of the wind had to be sacrificed to for the sowing to be successful. Strict rules governed traffic through the farmland. Women who had recently given birth and people who were ill were not allowed near a sown field.

But the real fears began in the height of summer when the grain ripened. The spirits of the grain knew that their time was near and so they grew vengeful. The bright Sun of noontime was said to be when the corn mother traveled through her fields of grain. This spirit was malevolent.

On the day of harvest farmer sharpened their sickles and ran out into the fields shouting and doing battle with the spirits of the corn. The stalks of grain fell under the sickle as they hacked their way through the land. More and more of the enemy spirits were cut down until they met with the last sheaf—where the spirits of grain had fled. This last sheaf would become the corn dolly. Depending on the country, the rituals varied.

In some places, the dolly was jeered at and beaten with sticks, and the unlucky person who cut her down was also beaten and called names. In some parts of the country she was brought into the barn or home and was honored there as a good luck talisman. In other lands, the sheaf was dressed in white and appeared in the field at midnight, where she fertilized the grain by passing through it.

As interesting as this history may be, the modern Pagan must ask what relevance the corn dolly has in the age of electricity and supermarkets. Though few of us labor in the fields, most of us work at something that takes up much of our day. Many of us have goals at our jobs that require some favorable outcome. And even with electricity, most of us notice by the first of August the decline of light. Many of us plan for our last summer holiday before school begins again. All life grows, peaks, and declines.

The corn dolly for us symbolizes the peak of summer, and the strength and protection of the summer months. The corn dolly is the distillation of that spirit, and that is her power. As harvest talisman, she wears symbols of the work we perform during the year.

And how does one make a corn dolly when there isn't a field of grain for miles? One way is to buy raffia at the local craft store, and have on hand ribbons, leather cord, and fabric. Gather decorative weeds from your neighborhood for the corn dolly's staff and skirt.

Pull a large handful of raffia from the bag and straighten the strands so that the ends roughly line up. Fold these in half, and cinch the folded strands up toward the fold to form the dolly's head. Tie this form up with either a ribbon or a leather cord. Cinch in further down the fold to form a waist and tie with ribbon. To make the arms, pull a smaller handful of raffia from the bag, fold in half, cut to a proportionate length for arms, and tie at each end to form hands. Slip it between the head and waist of the folded raffia. Decorate your corn dolly with a bit of fabric for clothes, and with feathers, beads, or dried flowers. The more personally meaningful the materials that are used to create the dolly, the more powerful the magic.

My corn dollies always resemble a human form, but many people feel more comfortable making an abstract form—a braid, fan, or sheaf. To bless the corn dolly, wave her sunwise in the smoke of the Lughnasah bonfire, and say:

> *Spirits of the ripening grain, harvest queen!*
> *Bless our labor, bless our home and family,*
> *Keep us safe.*
> *Free us from worry, want, and woe.*
> *From this harvest to the next*
> *Our gratitude and prayers reside in you.*
> *Blessed be!*

Hang the dolly in the kitchen to watch over you through the year. The following Lughnasah, thank the corn dolly for your safety and good fortune, and throw her on the Lughnasah fire.

Creating Magic in the Kitchen

by Tammy Sullivan

When you prepare a meal for yourself or your family, you have the makings of magic. If you feel you need to cast a circle before doing any sort of spell work, feel free to do so. It is best to go with your instinct on this. Each time you cook, you have the four elements at work—fire from the heat of your stove; air from the steam; earth from the seasonings, herbs, vegetable, or grains, and water from the liquid used in preparation.

You may also add the magical correspondences of certain food to your intent. A love spell, for instance, would be an excellent choice when baking brownies: You have cocoa, vanilla, sugar, and eggs in almost any brownie recipe, and all of these ingredients share the correspondence of love. Because of the association of love with apples and cinnamon, apple pie would also be a great example. Food contains emotional and magical triggers and can invoke feelings of love, joy, etc. If someone is upset, you can bet an oven-fresh chocolate chip cookie will have him or her smiling again.

Herbal correspondences are appropriate concerns when planning your menus. Keep your needs in mind. If you are a little lacking in the financial area, you might want to make a dish rich in the spices and herbs that correspond to money. You can plan entire meals or just a main dish to accomplish this.

You may also incorporate stirring patterns based on what you wish to accomplish—that is, stir deosil for drawing and widdershin for repelling. You may also want to bake or place a fetish into the food. Mardi Gras chefs bake a symbolic baby into each "king" cake, and fortune cookies of course have fortunes baked in. Use your creativity. If you don't do a lot of baking, you can put fetishes, when appropriate, to work by dropping them in the stewpot, or placing them beside the stove. If you like, you can write small verses of blessings, roll them up, and bake them into cookies.

In a clear voice while you work, state the purpose of the food. I don't mean telling the food that it will nourish you—that is a given. I mean assigning a magical task to it. If the food is meant to be a healing spell, state it plainly. Chicken soup, for example, is only chicken soup until you tell it to be a healing potion. Also, it is a good idea when simmering or boiling to instruct the food to retain the vitamins your body needs.

You may trace magical symbols into the food. This is easier with baked goods, but the symbol does not have to show in order to work. Decorate your cookies, pastries, pies, and cakes with icing symbols. If making a stew or pasta you can incorporate the symbol into your stirring pattern. Don't discount the shape of your pan—pans come in all shapes and sizes today, and you can use this to suit your purpose. Also, candy decorations for cookies and cakes come in many shapes.

You can use your ritual tools in the preparation of the food, but a knife from the kitchen will work just as well as your athame. I recommend keeping a separate mortar and pestle to be used strictly for cooking. Some herbs used in spell work can be poisonous, and you don't want to risk having traces of them in your kitchen and in your food.

A small altar, placed by your workspace, can be a wonderful addition to your kitchen. You may honor deity by placing a small bit of the food there before serving. Consider placing a permanently lit candle on your kitchen altar. This will watch over your home and bless it. A seven-day novena-type candle, replaced once a week, works well for this.

It is said to be helpful to place clear quartz crystals near the stove—this will make the food taste better. You may choose a selection of stones, according to intent if you like, or keep certain ones around to impart specific energies constantly. I suggest having at least one protective stone.

It is beneficial to meditate on gratitude while you prepare the table. Preparing the table can be a continuation of the spell or not, depending on your choice. You may choose to make use of candles and corresponding colors in your linens. Flowers that serve your magical intent are excellent in a centerpiece for your table. A few last magical dining tips follow.

Always place the salt on the table first, and remove it last.

Pass dishes deosil to continue spreading positive vibrations.

Always leave a sip of wine in your glass for the fairy folk.

Always leave a morsel of food on your plate to ensure you are never without.

Before you dine, it is a good idea to honor deity and bless the meal. A simple verse of thanks will do.

May your home be blessed with many magical meals and a joyful kitchen.

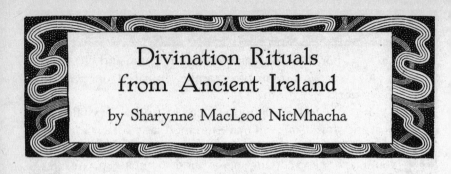

Divination Rituals from Ancient Ireland

by Sharynne MacLeod NicMhacha

In ancient Celtic society there were three classes of sacred or esteemed persons—Druids, seers, and bards. The Druids presided over rituals and judgments, communicated with the gods on behalf of their people, studied natural and moral philosophy, and provided training for druidic students. The seers performed divination and made prophecies, organizing special ceremonies and watching and interpreting the omens of the natural world. The bards composed poetry, much of which was in praise of (or criticized) their kings, heroes, or patrons. They also preserved traditional lore pertaining to the culture, its religion, and to the ancestors.

The power of the poets was very great, and many were said to have the power of prophecy. This connection between poetry and prophecy existed in a number of other ancient cultures as well. In early Ireland, the power of prophecy and divination was attributed to all three groups of sacred people (to varying degrees). Here are three interesting divination rituals from ancient Irish tradition.

Imbas Forosnai: The Illumination of Foresight

Imbas forosnai (pronounced IMM–muss FORE–uss–nah) means literally "great wisdom of illumination." It is also frequently translated as "wisdom or illumination of foresight." In the great Irish epic *Táin Bó Cuailgne* ("The Cattle Raid of Cooley"), the warrior queen Medb consults a female prophetess regarding the outcome of an upcoming battle. The seeress, who is named Fedelm, is described as a beautiful woman wearing a speckled cloak with a gold pin and a red-embroidered hooded tunic. She wore her hair in "three tresses" or braids, two wound upward on her head and the third hanging down her back. She held a gold weaving rod in her hand, illustrating the symbolic connection between spinning and weaving and prophecy, and her eyes had triple irises—perhaps indicating that she could "see" into the three worlds of sky, earth, and the sea/underworld.

Medb asks where she is coming from, and the young woman replies: "From learning verse and vision in Alba (Scotland)." Medb inquires if she has the imbas forosnai, the "light of foresight," and the girl replies that she does. She then asks Fedelm to look into the future and see what will become of her army. Fedelm replies, "I see it crimson, I see it red." Medb does not want to believe this, and questions her three times. Fedelm's answer remains the same. Medb goes to battle in spite of the girl's prophecy and is defeated.

Illuminating inspiration was one of the three things which characterized a fully trained and empowered poet. In the ninth-century text known as *Cormac's Glossary*, imbas forosnai is said to make known to the poet whatever thing he or she wished (and whatever it was expedient to reveal). In this ritual, the poet-seer, or *fili* in Old Irish, chews a piece of raw animal flesh and then places it on a stone behind the door, chanting a spell over it. He offers it to the gods and summons them to him, staying with them until the following day. He then chants over his two palms and again summons the deities. He covers his cheeks with his two palms and enters into a trance. People watch over him during this sacred sleep to make sure that he is not disturbed. When he wakes, whatever he has asked is revealed.

On first glance, this mysterious and somewhat cryptic ritual seems to be an attempt to obtain revelation or wisdom directly from the gods. This may, in fact, be what it entails. However, scholars are at a loss to explain why the poet would chew a piece of "flesh" prior to his mantic sleep and prophetic vision. This chewing of flesh brings to mind the well-known motif of Finn mac Cumall chewing his thumb or putting his thumb under his "tooth of wisdom" to obtain prophetic wisdom. I suspect that these mythological elements may be referring to the chewing and consumption of dried *amanita muscaria* mushrooms prior to the shaman's trance (which often results in divine knowledge or prophetic utterances). The flesh of these mushrooms are red, and in a number of cultures psychotropic plants or entheogens are referred to by secret code names.

The word for Finn's "tooth of wisdom" could also be translated as a "morsel of flesh." In addition, there are several stories in which people attempt to attain otherworld knowledge by seeking or consuming red "bubbles" *(bolg)*, a word that is used to describe some mushrooms in Gaelic languages. The ritual, when viewed in this light, is a direct parallel with shamanic rites known from other cultures.

Teinm Laeda: Revealing the Core of Knowledge

Another method of poetic divination was called *teinm laeda* (TEN–um LIE–thuh). The term literally means the "breaking open" or "pith" or "marrow" of something. One story tells how Finn mac Cumall put his thumb in his mouth and chanted through this method to obtain whatever knowledge he required. He was also sometimes said to chew on his thumb to acquire wisdom. It is possible that this ritual may have also involved the use of shamanic mushrooms. One of the codes or symbols used in Irish myths for the *amanita muscaria* mushroom is the hazelnut. The tree has reddish or purplish leaves and the nuts in some stories are also said to be red. To obtain knowledge, the salmon of wisdom who live at the well of divine knowledge are said to "break open" the hazelnuts that fall from the sacred purple hazel trees. This may be a description of the sacred concepts that lie behind these rituals.

In addition, Finn was said to chew his thumb in the following manner: "From the bone to the marrow, and from the marrow to the innermost core or sap." This seems to allude to the juice or powerful inner essence of the mushrooms themselves. Teinm laeda also involved chanting of some kind (as with the imbas forosnai ritual). However, it may have been a more personal or spontaneous ritual, somewhat different from the formal ritual associated with imbas forosnai. Like imbas forosnai, this method of divination may have involved the invocation of Pagan gods. St. Patrick evidently outlawed both imbas forosnai and teinm laeda because they involved offerings to Pagan spirits or deities.

Díchetal di Chennaib: Spontaneous Incantations and Spells

The name of this third kind of divination (pronounced DEE–ched–ull di CHENN–uv, with the "ch" as in "Bach," not as in "choose") means an inspired and spontaneous ("off the top of one's head") incantation or spell. It is sometimes translated as "spontaneous chanting of foreknowledge." Both the Druids and the poets were said to make use of this method, which was said to be one of the fourteen "streams of knowledge" (rivers and bodies of water were often associated with the pursuit of divine wisdom).

Since this kind of divination happened very spontaneously and was therefore a highly personal experience, we do not have a description of the rituals associated with it. However, sometimes the name of the divinatory method is spelled in a different way *(díchetal do chollaib cenn),* which could be translated as an incantation or spell made by way of "the ends of the hazel tree"—perhaps referring to the hazelnut. In early myths and later folklore, the hazel was associated with divine wisdom. Hazelnuts were used in divination rites at Samhain well into the last century. Once again, amanita mushrooms could be involved here, or perhaps other forms of inspiration, such as meditations on bodies of water, personal ritual at a sacred natural site, the use of hazel wands or hazelnuts, and so on.

The Sacred Sleep of the Gods

The concept of a "sacred sleep," or trance-state during which the seeker communicates with the gods or spirits, is a common religious element worldwide. It occurs in the ancient Irish divination ritual of imbas forosnai and was also found in early Wales. The medieval writer Gerald of Wales describes a group of unique people who existed in Wales called Awenyddion, a word that means "those who have *awen* (poetic inspiration)." These people, who were "led by their innate understanding," were consulted about various matters. They then behaved as if they were taken over by some spirit, and they uttered their prophecies through riddles and cryptic language (a common occurrence with many oracles). After their ecstatic experience, they were roused by others "as if from a deep sleep," much as in the Irish rite.

This concept of mantic sleep associated with illumination or inspiration continued as part of Celtic sacred tradition for many centuries. In the 1600s, poetic candidates in Scotland were placed in a darkened room where they lay down and wrapped their tartan garments around their head to block out the light. (A darkened state is common in shamanic rituals). With a stone on their belly—perhaps to regulate the breath, which would facilitate a trance state)—they remained like this all day. At evening time, the young poets gathered to recite their poetic creations to their teacher.

A similar practice also existed in Ireland during the early 1700s. Interesting folk rituals associated with prophecy and the acquisition of divine knowledge still existed in Scotland into the last century. A person who was specially selected from the community was taken to a secluded place (in some cases near a waterfall), where he or she was left alone to receive wisdom and guidance from the spirits. The roots of these ancient prophetic rituals are with us still, and the guidance of the gods and the spirits may still be sought in lonely, secluded places or during our own rites of divination.

Aboriginal Dreaming

by Emely Flak

For more than forty-thousand years, the Australian Aborigines lived in harmony with the harsh environment of the Great Southern Land. The arrival of white settlers to Australia introduced a conflicting set of environmental values to their peaceful existence. When the Union Jack was raised in Botany Bay just over two hundred years ago, it marked the beginning of a process of dispossession. The displacement caused by the new settlers violated the Aborigines' sacred connection to the land.

The Eurocentric and arrogant mindset of the new arrivals assumed that there was no religion among the aboriginal people. They could not understand that the native culture was one rich in spiritual tradition, nor comprehend that the lifestyles of the indigenous people was one based on a deep respect for the land and on sophisticated preservation of natural resources.

Two prominent features of Aboriginal spirituality are the dreaming and totemism.

The Dreaming

Although there were believed to be around five hundred indigenous tribes in precolonial Australia, the one common theme in their spiritual lives is the dreaming, also sometimes called the dreamtime.

The dreaming is based on the Aboriginal theory of creation. In the time of the dreaming, spirit ancestors roamed the land. In their journey, they created natural features in the landscape in the form of rock, mountains, valleys, and waterways. They laid down the law for social order among all living things. Each clan respected tribal boundaries that defined their sacred sites. Territorial versions of the descriptive and colorful dreaming stories vary in accordance to their landmarks and unique features. To each Aborigine, their tribal land is their "dreaming."

One spirit ancestor from the dreaming that is known across many Aboriginal clans is the rainbow serpent. The rainbow serpent formed waterways such as rivers, creeks, and lakes. Its spirit is honored as a powerful force. In rock art, it is typically depicted as a snake. Representing the dual force of creation and destruction, the spirit essence of water is essential for sustaining life— though at its extreme, in flooding or other climactic disasters, it also threatens life.

The Law

The spirit ancestors handed down the law in the dreaming, as a template for establishing a societal order. The law is a sacred set of tribal laws and social taboos to live by. Through regional interpretations, each clan established its tribal codes and taboos. Some social taboos impose a rule of avoidance in social interaction. For example, one strict rule is that an Aboriginal man and his mother-in-law are not permitted to speak to one another with eye contact. When verbal communication occurs they must lower their eyes and minimize all dialogue or attempt to communicate through a go-between.

Totemism

The Aborigines believe that each man and woman, through the dreaming, carries a spiritual link to his or her totem. The totem is most commonly an animal, though it can also be a plant or object. Each person is assigned a totem, often by the expectant mother, who finds the symbol through a dream or synchronistic event. This equates to a form of divination for the totem selection of the unborn child. The totem is more than a link with the past. It also validates a link with the natural environment and becomes a source of strength and inspiration. When an Aborigine needs retreat or spiritual guidance, he or she will often find a place that represents his or her totem. For instance, if the totem is the kookaburra bird, then the foot of a gum tree where one often finds kookaburras is a place of contemplation.

In ritual, Aborigines emulate the movement, posture, and appearance of their totem. Totemism promotes a sense of identity and connection with others. People who share the same totem are considered to be "brothers" and "sisters." In most tribes, if the totem is an animal, then killing or eating the flesh of that animal is taboo.

Ritual

Aboriginal ritual is as diverse as the regional clans that occupied Australia. Each group recreates their relationship with the dreaming through the oral tradition of dance and song. This art form is designed to affirm the people's sacred connection to the land. By emulating their spirit ancestor's journey, they transform from human to animal to land form. Ceremonies also visually explain tribal law and custom. There are rituals for rites of passage such as birth, puberty, coupling, and death.

In the context of the dreaming, many places and rituals are so sacred that they are protected by secrecy. For this reason, very few, if any, non-Aboriginal people (or *Piranypa*) will witness an authentic dreaming ritual. Instead of donning ritual clothing, the Aborigines decorate their bodies with paint and feathers. It is not unusual to see the use of blood to glue feathers to the skin.

The *corroboree,* often mistaken for a social gathering, is a ceremonial dance depicting a story that is staged along with the hypnotic sound of the wood instrument made from a hollow branch, the didgeridoo. Some corroborees are performed for deep spiritual purposes, and others depict contemporary stories featuring recent themes like aircraft and the invasion of white settlers.

This is a spiritual path with no defined gods, goddesses, or religious leaders. The closest thing to a deity or god is of course the spirit ancestor. Aboriginal spirituality has been described as "nontheist," as it's based on intimate connection with the land rather than an affinity with a deity. Through elaborate ceremonial reenactment of the dreaming, the Aborigines see themselves as embodiments of their spirit ancestors or their totemic identity. This in turn empowers them with spiritual authority. Their ancestor heroes permeate through every living thing and every landscape feature.

Sacred Sites

Of the thousands of sacred sites around the country, one of the most famous internationally is Ayers Rock in central Australia. In 1985, this largest monolith in the world was symbolically "handed over" to its Aboriginal owners, the Anangu, who then reintroduced its Aboriginal name—Uluru. The Anagu believe that the great rock is inhabited by ancestral spirits who have left their mark at numerous places. Their energy force has left an imprint on the landscape. This handing over, however, has not stopped tourists from climbing the rock, as it remains a popular holiday destination.

The Influence of Christianity

In their well-meaning attempts to "civilize" the indigenous Australians, Christian missionaries established the Aboriginal Christian Church. To reconcile the differences between Aboriginal spirituality and Christianity, the church integrates rainbow spirit themes. Aboriginal art decorates places of worship and the Gospel links to the dreaming stories. Rainbow spirit theology assumes that a God, as supreme creator, communed with the Australian Aborigines from the beginning of time. For some Aborigines, particularly in urban areas, this has been an acceptable approach to preserve their spiritual identity. To Christian Aborigines, Christ is Aboriginal.

Only in the last couple of decades has the white Australian taken a genuine interest in the Aboriginal spiritual tradition and its explicit link to the country's landscape. We now look to indigenous wisdom for land management strategies to protect our frail environment. We value their indigenous art and craft that captures the essence of the Australian landscape.

The Aboriginal flag was recognized by the federal government in 1995 and continues to remind us of this deep respect for the environment. In its simplicity, it symbolizes the identity of the Australian Aboriginal people and their relationship to the land. Black represents their race; red the earth; and yellow the Sun.

Despite the fact that the white settlers undermined the native spiritual culture, the resilient dreamtime tradition occupies a place in the hearts and minds of all aboriginal people today. The dreaming, to Australian aboriginals, is both myth and reality. The creative force that commenced in the dreaming continues today as it transgresses the concept of time.

The vast difference between Judeo-Christian spiritual expression and that of the indigenous Australians has been summed up in this poem by Muta, a Murinbata Aborigine:

> *White man got no Dreaming*
> *Him go 'nother way*
> *White man, him go different*
> *Him got road belong himself.*

Energy of Place

by Cerridwen Iris Shea

Have you ever walked into a house or onto a piece of land and felt strong emotions—either a profound connection or a forceful revulsion? Have you ever traveled someplace and felt as though you'd come home—even though you'd never been there before? Welcome to the energy of place.

The energy of place is one reason there are blessing, cleansing, and housecleaning rituals in our craft. Every building you enter, every vehicle you drive, every piece of land on which you step has its own unique energy. Working with these energies helps us walk our path with greater ease.

What makes up the energy? I believe it is a combination of factors. Each area has its own energy, often guarded by a spirit or deva. There's a debate whether the deva creates the energy or vice versa. Everyone who passes through a place leaves some bit of personal, residual energy behind. Sacred sites with lots of traffic feed on the faith of their pilgrims. A site of a massacre feeds on the energy of every visitor's horror. An empty house will have traces of the lives of former inhabitants and visitors mixed in with its own energies.

Sometimes the deva of a place will warn you if something or someone unhealthy is approaching, thus giving you time to get out. A place's energy has as many layers as an onion, which can make working with it both difficult and rewarding. As magical people, we may not be able to transform the energy of a battlefield such as Gettysburg, but we can certainly work with the energies of the spaces we live in, work in, and, to some extent, visit.

Sorting Through Energy Layers

How do you sort through the layers and figure out the essence of a place? Listening with all the senses is a good starting point. For example, imagine you are house hunting. You walk into an older house and fall in love with it. You like the structure and the grounds, and this is where you want to live. Ask the realtor if you can have a few minutes on your own. Walk through the house by yourself in silence. Listen to the creaks and groans. How does the house smell? Are there temperature variations? What feelings do you get as you move from room to room? Don't forget to check closets, chimneys, attics, and the basement. Check out the garage. Check any outbuildings. Walk the perimeter of the property and see what the spirits of the place have to tell you. Tell them you'd like to make this your home. This can all be done silently (in case your realtor doesn't understand this sort of work). See what answer comes back to you.

Moving rituals (as in rituals for a house move, not merely a powerful ritual) are an important part of connecting with the energy of place. It's important to remember not only to do a ritual with the space you move into, but also the space you're moving out of. Your energy melds with the indigenous energy of place. It's up to you to make sure you leave something positive for the next inhabitants. Explain why you're leaving. Thank the space for offering you shelter. Even if the circumstances under which you are leaving are not the most positive, make sure you and the space part on good terms. It is part of your responsibility as a magical person.

Travel is another time to connect with the energy of place. A spontaneous ritual upon check-in and check-out of a hotel room helps make your stay a more positive experience and keeps your hotel room a sanctuary. Visiting new places, even heavily trafficked tourist areas, give you the opportunity to work with and learn from energies inherent in those places. You meet people when you travel. Use travel as a time to meet energies, astral beings, and native spirits. It expands your experiences on several planes of existence simultaneously.

Listening is the key. It's not about bursting forth and imprinting your own energy on a place. Imposing your will upon a place you visit is not ethical, even if your intent is good. Ask the spirits of place if they want you to work with and for them. Respect their answer, even if it's not the answer you want. When it's a new home, you need to work with the energies. Does that mean you can't get rid of nasties? Of course, you still can. But listen to them first and find out their stories before you take action.

Greet the energies. Make an offering or a libation. Introduce yourself, and tell them why you're there and what you want to do. And then listen. It's not a monologue—it's a dialogue. Let a house tell you what it needs to feel whole. Let a garden advise on any planting you want to do. Let a sacred site reveal something you can carry with you in your heart. Leave something positive for the next person who sets foot there and experiences the energy of place.

Feather Magic

by Ember

Birds have long been considered sacred to many cultures, and bird imagery has been popular in art and personal adornment for centuries. It's no wonder that humans have always been fascinated with flight, and the beauty and variety of feathers continue to capture our imagination.

Birds, and their flight, are often seen to represent the connection between earth and the heavens, thus earning the birds' divine symbolism. Flight connects earth and sky, and corresponds with any kind of reaching toward new heights, from the physical to the transcendence of the soul.

Feathers have been used in decoration throughout history—in jewelry, clothing, tools, weapons, spiritual symbols, prayer sticks, and wands, just to name a few. But feathers are more than merely decorative, and knowing this can enhance their symbolism in ritual and magic.

Feathers may appear to be delicate but are actually quite strong. When we consider the functions of a feather, we automatically think of flight, but that capability ensures many aspects of the bird's survival. Part of learning feather magic means understanding how feathers serve their owners. Birds spend more than half their time preening and molting. They take care of their feathers, as their survival depends on it. Feathers are not merely for appearance, but for protection, regulating body temperature, and waterproofing.

For these reasons, feathers contain a very powerful symbolism and can be a useful magical tool.

There are many types of feathers. Contour feathers cover the body, streamlining and keeping the bird warm and dry; flight feathers are long and located on the wings and tail; and down feathers are small and fluffy, found underneath contour feathers.

Traditionally, since they are used for flight, feathers are associated with the element of air and lend themselves well to spells involving communication, movement and change, transformation, intellect and creativity, or to represent or invoke the powers of the east.

Feathers can be put in sachets and dream pillows, attached to wands and prayer sticks, or simply held in the hand or placed on an altar. Use your imagination to create unique art using feathers. If you make flower arrangements or wreaths, consider adding feathers. Use them as jewelry, in paintings, or in other forms of art. Adorn you home with them (birds often pull out their own down feathers to line their nests). Look to the cultures of the American Indians and the Celts for ideas. Another useful and simple method is to mediate on a feather, perhaps while listening to music of wind instruments such as flutes.

As your collection grows, you may want to identify what bird the feather came from. Bird identification books can help with this. If you're feeding birds, pay attention to the kind that visit your feeder, and you'll have a good start in identifying your feathers.

If you wish, base a spell on the kind of bird your feather is from. A blue jay's feather would be exceptional for strength, a peacock's feather for beauty, and so on. The feathers of waterfowl have the added bonus of the water element associated with them. Take a walk around a public lake where these particular birds are known to visit, and see what you can find lying on the ground.

To find feathers simply look down, they will come to you. Of course, there are places that are easier to find them—near a bird feeder is a good choice, but look everywhere. I've found lovely feathers in both parks and parking lots. A word of caution: It is generally not permitted to collect items, including feathers, in national parks. Be aware of the regulations and respect them, and get permission if necessary. Unfortunately many birds have been exploited for their feathers, so it's best to use only feathers a bird has lost naturally.

Be careful when storing feathers. I like to keep mine in a small, wide-mouth jar, vase, or similar container. It looks decorative—you can arrange them as you would a floral arrangement, and you can store them in a box or wrap them loosely in natural fabric such as cotton or silk. Treat them with the respect you would give the creature they came from.

Feathers are practical, symbolic, and filled with spiritual magic. Whatever means you choose to incorporate feathers into your life, their gifts will touch you in countless ways.

Feather Dedication

When you find a new feather, you may wish to cleanse it for magical use. One of the best ways is to pass it through the smoke of burning sage. You can consecrate your feather with the four elements in this manner as well—the smoke of burning herbs or incense represents air. Allow it to rest in the Sun for the fire element; sprinkle it with a bit of water; and stick the tip into salt or earth.

Here's a feather spell to shake things up and invite change into your life. For this spell you must be open to any kind of change. The intent is naturally for positive results, but often magic is unpredictable and the results may not be obvious right away, or they may manifest in unexpected ways.

You will need any found feather, a bundle of dried sage, a white or yellow ribbon, and incense of your choice. Tie the sage and feather together with the ribbon. Visualize positive change in your life. Focus on happiness and new opportunities, and feel the excitement of the unknown build within you.

Wave the bundle through the incense smoke as you visualize. Then, when you're ready, tie the bundle outside in a place where it can blow in the breeze. Leave it in place as long as you desire or until your spell manifests. If any of the plants or the feather fall from the bundle, do not replace them—allow the wind to take them. When you are finished, leave the bundle as an offering. Bury it, float it in a stream, or simply let the wind carry it away. Keep the feather if you wish, or send it on as a gift to someone else.

Fall's Harvest

by Laurel Reufner

The following recipes take advantage of the spirit and flavors of the fall to make a bountiful harvest meal.

Spiced Cornbread

1	cup flour
1	cup stone-ground cornmeal
3	Tbl. brown sugar
1	Tbl. baking powder
½	tsp. salt
½	tsp. ground cinnamon
½	tsp. ground nutmeg
½	tsp. ground cloves
2	eggs, slightly beaten
1	cup milk
½	cup vegetable or olive oil

Combine flour, cornmeal, sugar, baking powder, salt, and spices in a mixing bowl. Add the eggs, milk, and oil. Stir until ingredients are moist. Pour into a greased baking pan, and bake at 425º twenty to twenty-five minutes until golden brown. Cool before cutting.

Harvest Lentil Stew

1	pound black lentils, cleaned and soaked
1	stalk celery, chopped fine
2–3	potatoes cut in small cubes
1–2	carrots, shredded
2	cloves garlic, minced, or 1 tsp. dried garlic
1	one-lb. can crushed tomatoes
1	lb. stew meat (optional)
2	beef bouillon cubes (optional)
1	Tbl. summer savory

            1   Tbl. thyme

            1   tsp. sage

            1   Tbl. parsley

If you are using meat in the stew, brown it in a skillet with some garlic before placing everything, except herbs, into a large pot and cover with water. Bring to a boil and reduce the heat to a simmer for an hour. Add the herbs during the last half hour.

Pumpkin Pie Bars

For the base:

            1   yellow cake mix (a Jiffy cake mix is perfect)

            1   egg, lightly beaten

            ½   cup butter, melted

In a large bowl, mix together cake mix, egg, and butter. Press the dough into the bottom of a cake pan. For the filling:

            3   eggs, lightly beaten

            1   thirty-oz. can of pumpkin

            ½   cup sugar

            ½   cup packed brown sugar

            ⅔   cup evaporated milk

            1½ tsp. ground cinnamon

Mix the ingredients and pour over the base mixture. For the topping:

            1   cup cake mix

            ½   cup sugar

            ½   cup butter, softened

            ½   cup chopped nuts, optional

In a small bowl, combine the ingredients until the mixture becomes crumbly. Sprinkle evenly over the top of the pumpkin mixture. Bake in a 350° oven for sixty minutes or until a toothpick inserted into the center of the cake comes out clean. Cool before serving. Serve with whipped cream or a similar topping if desired.

The Lore and the Lure of the Blade

by Magenta Griffith

Knives are one of the oldest human tools. Early stone knives and axes have been dated as far back as 300,000 years. The first knives and axes were chipped from flint, or obsidian. Metal knives go back about 5,000 years. The earliest metal knives were bronze, an amalgam of copper and tin. It was centuries before iron was commonly worked into knives.

Copper ores were easier to find and smelt into useful metal. Meteoric iron, a relatively pure source of the metal, was probably the first iron refined for tools. It was hard to find iron ore, and difficult to carry the ore to a forge for refining, so it must have been nothing short of miraculous to find an iron meteorite sitting on the ground.

Some of the legends about iron chasing away the fairies probably have to do with iron weapons driving out indigenous peoples armed only with bronze weapons. Iron is harder, and an iron sword can break a bronze one.

Shaping metal into knives, swords, and axes would likely seem quite magical to people who had been used to stone implements. The people who work with iron are called blacksmiths because that metal is dark. Whitesmiths, meanwhile, are the people who work with silver and tin. A person who worked metals was called a smith because he or she would "smite" or strike, the metal with his or her hammer. The smith held an important position in society and was believed to know the most powerful magic. The smith tamed iron and kindled the new fire at the Winter Solstice.

The Anglo-Saxons, who settled in England about 1,500 years ago, were originally named after the knives they carried. These

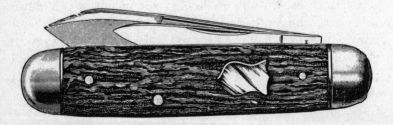

were the "Saxe," a word that still means "knife" in modern north German dialect. The saxe was a single-edged knife that ended in a highly sharpened point. North Germany was where these ancestors of the English came from, and Saxon translates into modern English as the "knife-men." Every Saxon man, woman, or child was buried with a knife. The Saxons saw to it that their dead would not be defenseless in the next world.

In the Middle Ages, people brought their own eating tools with them. A knife was a very personal possession, carried at all times by its owner and used for hunting as well as cutting food.

There are many superstitions about knives. Traditionally, knives and other cutting tools, such as scissors, were considered an ill-omened gift. In many places, the gift of a knife would be interpreted as "cutting off a friendship." However, if the recipient gives the giver a penny for the knife, this makes the gift a purchase, and it no longer unlucky. Related to this is the idea that using cutting tools when opening gifts is also unlucky. Do not tie or wrap gifts in such a way that a knife or scissors will be required to open them.

Other traditions about knives include the idea that a knife placed under the bed during childbirth will ease the pain of labor. A baby was protected by a knife stuck into the headboard of its cradle, usually a iron or steel knife. This was probably because cold iron was considered protection against fairies. Similarly, a house could be protected by a knife being thrust into the front door.

More bits of folklore include that if knives are crossed at the table a quarrel will occur, unless they are immediately separated and straightened so that they lie parallel. It's bad luck to close a pocketknife unless you were the one who opened it. If a knife falls to the ground, it means the arrival of a male visitor. In Newfoundland, it is bad luck to leave a knife blade facing upward.

No matter the folklore about knives, always treat them respectfully and use them with care.

Seeking Your Power Song
by Kristin Madden

The use of voice in shamanic healing is probably more common than even the use of the drum. Otherworldly music and shamanic power songs have been described in nearly all cultures around the world. Vocal sound is used to induce and carry trances, to evoke power, to bind energies, to communicate otherworldly experience, and to heal.

Druids went through extensive training in the bardic schools, and the power of the spoken word was revered among the ancient Celts. Through this vocal ability, Druids could stop battles, lay curses, and cast a variety of spells. It is believed that many of the Celtic musicians learned their craft from the fairy folk. Whether or not this is true, it speaks to our innate recognition of the power of music and its ability to transport us beyond this realm.

Many cultures and magical traditions believe that the spirits do not communicate as we do and therefore are not interested in our everyday manner of speaking. In order to communicate with them we must use an extraordinary method. Song, chant, intonation, and poetry are some of the more common "extraordinary" methods.

Communication with otherworldly beings is the most basic use of the shamanic voice. Many on the shamanic path have learned to dance their power animals. Song is often a part of this dance. To sing your spirit allies while you dance is a powerful combination of communication and shape-shifting.

In modern society, many people lose this natural ability to use the voice. Unless we are small children or trained performers, many of us have blocks in our throat chakras. We grow up to be rather rigid, feeling ridiculous dancing or singing freely, and this limits our ability to communicate honestly and to be open to the otherworlds.

For this reason, it is a good idea to begin by simply finding your voice before seeking your power song. The exercise that follows is designed as a process of steps to be taken over a period of time. Work with each step for a matter of days or months, however long you need. Move on to the next step only when you feel comfortable.

Begin by simply humming a tone to yourself while you are alone. Listen to the tone without judgment and allow it to find its own pitch. Feel your head and throat vibrate with the sound. When you feel comfortable with humming, begin to use simple chants (such as "om" or "awen"). Feel your body vibrate with the tone. Allow your voice to take over as it will, and give yourself freely to the sound without judgment.

Make up a simple song about yourself, your goals, your guides, and your dreams of where the shamanic path will lead you. Sing it as loud as you like and have fun with it. Allow it to create its own energy as you channel your personal energy.

Next, make an offering of thanks, and perhaps sacred herbs or water, to the spirits of this place and to the creator. Ask for their blessings and protection in this work that you are about to do.

Enter a shamanic trance by your usual method. If you prefer, you may count yourself down from ten to one, stopping periodically to take a deep breath and remind yourself to go deeper.

While in your meditative trance state, go deep within your self. Find who you are at your core, beyond your identity and the roles you play in this world. Feel yourself embodying the true you as you are filled with the energy of the multiverse. You are open to healing energy and to communication with spirit guides.

Now, begin to sing from this place of vitality, honesty, and power. Allow all you feel and all that you are to flow into your song. Be aware of any changes in your energy or body as the song becomes part of your being.

When you feel you have experienced what you set out to do, or that your song is complete for now, gives thanks to all those that walk with you, guide you, and enliven you. Sit in silence for a moment and take note of how you feel, then return to normal consciousness.

Healers use power songs to open to spirit guidance and to infuse themselves with the energy needed for healing. This necessarily contributes to the healing of the self. Once you have evoked and merged with your power song, you may call it up whenever you have need. It may change with time as you do, but it will forever be a part of you.

The Charge of the God

by Steven Repko

Most of us are familiar with the popular "Charge of the Goddess," a beautiful and inspiring religious instruction. This divine prose maps out how we are to worship the Goddess to her satisfaction and our benefit.

We learn through the charge that the Goddess protects us and empowers us with the magical arts. She frees us from the bondage of oppression and the inhibitions of societal indoctrination. In return she charges us to be joyous in our exercise of that freedom. Joy and passion is what she expects as our part of religious participation. By worshiping the Goddess we venerate our humanity, and it is through our human intellect that she imparts her mysteries of our religion and a spiritual understanding of the natural world we are a part of.

As Pagan people we envision our deity in both sexes but although most of us can readily embrace the Goddess, the celebration of male deity is not always so easy. The Goddess is humanistic in her methods and motives, so we understand her as we understand our mother, daughter, or the woman next door.

The God is not humanistic; he calls to our primal side, and to the animal instincts we have forgotten in our quest for civilization. He is not supportive, nurturing, or understanding, and therein lies the balance of the natural world.

Just as feminine energy is creative and thoughtful, masculine energy is meant to be flamboyant, destructive, and primitive. It's two rams locking horns over the same square foot of mountain pass for physical and sexual supremacy. The male aspects of nature are beautiful and enticing, but there is always an element of challenge that leaves little room for compromise.

In our modern-day world we forget that only a short time ago mortality was not decided in an emergency room. Divine masculine mystery was dispensed in the forest and field, acts were judged alone. A broken bone or a poorly placed cut was expected to bring death. A poor harvest not only meant personal starvation, but the destruction of a clan or society. When times were abundant humans thrived, and when they were lean we struggled. We misunderstand now that it is not to our detriment that the God challenges us so vehemently. It is for our own protection.

What does the God of Witches expect us to do? He expects us to succeed and fail, to be born, live, die, and to be born again. We are to rise to his challenge, and not take life and the lessons in it for granted. In the same way that the Goddess teaches us how to change what we should not accept, the God helps us accept what we should not change. If we refuse to see the good in every challenge, we miss the real truth in our lessons. We miss the real charge of the God.

With the understanding and experience of these lessons, we built shelters and "stole fire" from the Gods. The climate no longer controlled us—we controlled and we mastered. The lions and wolves were sent teaching us to harvest meat and fowl;

we no longer needed to live on seasonal food alone. With the karma and dharma of a tiger, we were divinely designed to be different.

Our father is the lord of changing light and woods, the guardian of the gates of death and the Summerland.

He protects and defends the laws of the forest and the veil of magic that follows those laws. We become graced by this protection when we embrace those laws and understand them for what they are, our paternal legacy.

He expects us to struggle in our challenges, but he also expects us to rejoice in triumph and victory when we have mastered the lessons.

We all must learn the lessons of life and death. His promise of renewal for the land snatches us from the jaws of death, ensuring there will always be the land and the magic.

Throughout the wheel of the year, the God's charge evolves with the seasons.

At Yule we are reminded of our immortal legacy as the land is reborn every year with the Sun. We are also reminded that although we must learn the lesson of death that we will forever be reborn.

Candlemas, or Imbolc, encourages us to adjust our plan. Once the Pagan day of atonement, February 2 is a scorecard in the calendar of life. If we have worked well in the previous year, we prosper. If not, we suffer. It is the experience of knowing that no opportunity should ever be wasted.

At Beltane, we are sent to seed our physical and spiritual projects. Through the joining of the God and Goddess together we have learned that the spiritual life is not healthy if the physical life is apart from it. This is a time for hope and the optimistic passion that makes life worth living.

Midsummer shows us the lord of light in all his glory. Our lessons now in full practice, this is a time to rejoice in what we have learned and the pain we have endured. The Sun is warm, our bellies are fat, and life is good!

When the sunlight wanes, Lammas, or first harvest, reminds us that there must always be a sacrifice. In his perfect example the lord of the fields gives his physical life that we may live and remember this to the future.

Perhaps the most powerful lesson of the God is at Samhain. This is a day that starts both our new year and the season of death. It is at this time that we remember the struggles and triumphs, and lessons we have learned and failed at. It is through this reflection that we finally see what we yet must study. We see the God as he really is and rejoice at the face of deity that only his children look upon.

Samhain Charge of the God

I am the dark ruler of the world that sheds its skin of life—
The leaves that fall, the season that turns, stories remembered,
Traditions, the lessons of the wheel and all that has passed.

I am the taker of the old and the carrier of the seeds of tomorrow.

Let all who gather in the grove and the field,
Know and understand my worship in death,
For when you have remembered, mourned, and reflected on
What has passed, it is this lesson that takes you to a new morning.

There are no beginnings without endings,
No true wisdom without reflection.
As surely as the world will die, so too shall the Wicca die.
But through my promise of spring, the land will come to be reborn,
And with the land the Wicca, forever.

Hecate

by Ellen Dugan

The earth began to bellow, trees to dance
And howling dogs in glimmering light advance
Ere Hekate came.

—Virgil

Hecate, or Hekate, is the quintessential crone goddess. Often referred to as the "Queen of the Witches," she was a patron deity of seers, midwives, childbirth, and healers. Hecate was for the most part a woman's deity, both for worship and to ask for assistance. She presided over the transitions in life, the transformation of birth and death. For her devotees who lived a balanced life, Hecate brings abundance. She was thought to guide the souls of seekers, though in her aspect as a huntress Hecate not tolerate those silly mortals who do not have their spiritual house in order.

A popular image of Hecate shows a triple goddess carrying torches, a rope, a key, and a dagger. Her three faces were thought to have represented her ability to look to the present, the past, and the future. Hecate is the goddess of intuitive wisdom. Traditionally, those who receive precognitive dreams, who have clairvoyant ability, or are mediums, artists, or psychics, will gain special attention from Hecate. For those of you with psychic ability, try looking a little harder at Hecate.

Associations for Hecate include black dogs, the snake, owl, ravens and crows, bats, and the toad (also a symbol of conception). For herbal and plant correspondences, try the blooming cyclamen, dandelion, lavender, mugwort, mint, and the poppy. Trees associated with Hecate include the yew, cypress, haze, oak, and the willow. Festivals for Hecate include August 13, November 16, called the "Night of Hecate" in Greece, and Hecate's day in Rome on December 31.

Hecate Trevia

Hecate was part of the Greek trinity of Persephone, the maiden, Demeter, the mother, and herself as the crone. To Romans this trio was known as Proserpina, Ceres, and Hecate. (Notice that Hecate's position never changed from one culture to the next; this is a goddess with staying power.) Crossroads where three roads met were sacred to Hecate, earning her the title of "Hekate of the three ways." It was thought that if you left her an offering of food there she would grant you her favors.

Hecate was the oldest form of the Greek triple goddess, presiding over heaven, the underworld, and earth. Even after the worship of other goddesses waned, the ancient people still worshiped her as queen of the underworld and guardian of the three-way crossroad. As Hecate Trevia, her triple images were often displayed at these crossroads, where she was petitioned on the Full Moon for positive magic and on the dark of the Moon for cursing and dark magic.

While this last bit of information sounds a little ominous, keep in mind that Hecate was known by many titles, and is a shape-shifter. Her appearance could and did change often. To some she may appear as a old crone, hunched over a smoking cauldron and draped in a midnight cape. To others she may appear as a dark, beautiful, and mysterious woman with a shimmering crown. To others she may be perceived as a maiden priestess. She was called the "most lovely one," the great goddess of nature, and the queen of the world of spirits. She knew her way around the earth and underworld. The powers of nature, life, and death were at her command.

Intrigued? How about a little guided meditation work? Focus your imagination onto Hecate and on the story below to see what messages Hecate has to tell you.

Hecate Meditation

Picture yourself walking on a quiet clear autumn night along a dark graveled path. It is late, and as you look to the east you see a waning Moon rising slowly over the tree line. The night is quiet and calm. You can hear crickets singing and the mournful hoot of an owl. You walk confidently forward. Enjoying your solitude and the crunch of gravel beneath your feet and the little puffs of white steam that your breath makes in the evening air.

Up ahead you can see a light. It is a torch, mounted to the post marking the crossroads, and as you make your way closer you can make out small offerings of food left neatly at the base of the sign post. Others have been here before you. There is a small basket of apples, a plaque depicting the triple Hecate, and a few loaves of bread. Someone has left what appears to be a small jar of honey. Your hands tighten on the small bundle of homemade bread that you carry. As you approach the crossroads, a breeze picks up and a swirl of autumn leaves rushes by. You stop for a moment to take in the scene and approach the torchlit area with a calm reverence.

Suddenly, the sound of howling dogs shatters the peaceful evening. The light breeze has now grown into a much stronger and colder force. As you push your hair out of your eyes, you hear a growing rumbling noise. You feel the earth tremble beneath your feet, and you instinctively grab at the signpost, dropping your offering as you try to keep yourself upright.

As quickly as it began, the maelstrom fades. Shaken, you right yourself and realize that you have dropped your offering.

Concerned, you pick up the little bundle and brush a few dead leaves from it. You realize that the other offerings, once arranged so neatly, are now in disarray. Without a thought you immediately begin to straighten the mess. A trio of old-fashioned keys catches your eye. Intrigued, you pick them up and admire their shapes. Carefully you place the keys on top of the little jar of honey. Pleased with the results, you look around for any missed items and prepare to rise to your feet.

A prickling at the base of your neck is the first indication that you are no longer alone. As you turn slowly to look behind you, a large black dog comes barreling out of the darkness, running straight at you. There is no time to be afraid, Your eyes widen and the next thing you know the dog has knocked you flat on your back and is affectionately greeting you. Your initial shriek of alarm gives way to helpless laughter as you vainly attempt to get the dog off your chest so you can sit up. After a few moment of laughing struggle, you manage to collar the dog and sit upright again.

"Where did you come from?" you ask your new canine friend. The dog barks once, and his tail whips back and forth. You sling an arm around your new friend and wonder who the animal belongs to. As you give the dogs ears a good scratch, he suddenly become alert and rigidly still. It is then you notice that a woman is now approaching. Her sandaled feet are noiseless on the gravel path, and she is draped from head to ankle in a richly textured, black-hooded cape.

As she approaches, an owl swoops down from the tree line and lands on the top of the sign post. Your heart is hammering in your chest as you rise to your feet to greet the lady. You bow your head and murmur a greeting. As she walks into the flickering torchlight, you see that she is a stately middle-aged woman in a glistening silver crown. But her face shifts. In the next moment she is a young woman, dark and beautiful, then an elderly woman with a mass of wrinkles and a shock of white hair. The only thing that is constant is her eyes.

They are ageless—a deep jet-black, sparkling, and with a radiant wisdom and kindness. No matter which face she shows, her eyes and the expression in them remain the same. Pay attention to how Hecate appears to you.

"Greetings," she says softly, in a voice that rustles like dry leaves. Listen carefully to what she has to say.

After she finishes speaking, Hecate holds out her hand and the three old keys that you were admiring appear in her palm. She hands them to you as her hair whips about in the cold wind. Honored, you close your fist around them.

"I leave you with three gifts," she tells you quietly, "knowledge, intuition, and magic. Hold these close to your heart, and if your ever have need of me know that I will be there. "

You clasp the keys to your chest, and a curious warmth emanates from the keys. Slowly they dissolve and the warmth moves to inside your own body. You bow your head and whisper your thanks.

Hecate pulls up her hood up and smiles at you one last time. As she turns to leave, the dog leaps to her side and follows her down the path. A mist rising from the ground seems to swallow them up as they disappear from your view.

Look around you now, and focus on your image of the sacred crossroads. Keep this visualization in place, and should you ever wish to return here, know that it will be waiting for you. Feel the warmth of Hecate's gifts of knowledge, intuition, and magic burning bright within you. Then take a deep breath, and begin your journey home.

Penny-Finding Luck

by Janina Renée

Most Americans won't bother to stoop and pick a found penny off the ground. However, when you take time for little things you magically affirm that you are a person with time to spare.

Some people maximize the magical potential of both time and money by saving, and even matching, any sum they find until they have enough to donate to charity. You can boost your penny-finding luck by saying a little blessing, such as: "A penny saved is a penny earned, and good luck gained is a favor returned."

You could also try the old European custom of spitting on a found coin for luck. Fortunately, we don't have to worry about getting in trouble for this. My great-grandmother used to tell of how a man back in nineteenth-century East Prussia, delighted with his luck in finding a coin, spat on it and was immediately hauled off to jail. The coin had an image of the kaiser on it. Please don't spit on coins, however, if you intend to pass them on to other people.

A found penny or other coin can also serve as an omen, telling you something about the quality of the day. Using magical numerology, add the numbers in the coin's year date. For example, $2005 = 2 + 0 + 0 + 5 = 7$. (If you get a number higher than 10, as with $1985 = 1 + 9 + 8 + 5 = 23$, add the numbers again, so $23 = 2 + 3 = 5$, until you get a number between 1 and 9.) If your coin's number adds up to 1, this is a good day for getting things started. If 2, you will need to take other peoples' feelings into account. A 3 is good for your creative life. A 4 is for your home life. A 5 is for making changes. A 6 is for a pleasant social interlude. A 7 is for new ideas. An 8 is for organization, and a 9 is for having lots of options.

And here's a little mathematical short cut: With magical addition, any 9 and any numbers adding up to 9 (like 2 and 7) can be tossed out, and the result will be the same. Thus, for 1963, the 9, the 6, and the 3 can be cast out, leaving the 1, which is what $1 + 9 + 6 + 3$ would have come out to if the numbers were added.

Silver Magic

by Dallas Jennifer Cobb

All around me light bounces, energy shimmers. As the circle is cast, the priestess's hands glimmer, flashing brilliance. Small reflected orbs of light brighten the faces of those gathered. Is it some special effect? A technological trick? Or is it magic?

Looking closely at the people near me I see rings, earrings, pendants, and necklaces. At the altar sit magnificent magical objects, fetishes, and sculptures—all made of the magical metal, silver.

Metal Magic

Magically, silver and other metals were used by alchemist as early as 200 BC. Alchemy, from *chyma,* the Greek word for the casting or fusing of metals, was rooted in both magical and scientific practices. Ancient alchemists strove to create the philosopher's stone, rumored to be a magical potion that would transform base metals into gold and creating a by-product elixir that would give immortality and celestial knowledge.

Particular metals were associated with the planets. The metals, often called by their planetary names, were said to contain a celestial power derived directly form the ruling planet—an arcanum. This arcanum could only be released and perfected through alchemical processes.

Alchemists were not the only people who used metals for magic. Ordinary people have long been using metals for rites and rituals, and many of the old magical skills survive as superstition and custom.

The Magical Energies of Silver

Silver, associated with the Moon, has been used as a powerful tool for focusing intuition and ancient knowledge. Facilitating spiritual insight and psychic understanding, it is often used in ritual and for magical practice. The powers and associations of silver the metal and color harness the energies of the Moon and lunar goddesses.

Because of its association with the Moon, silver is sacred to Monday, a day for using silver to aid intuition, psychic dreams, and unconscious wisdom. Using a sacred metal on its power day facilitates the power of the metal to amplify personal power, channeling magical intent. But the use of a sacred metal isn't limited only to its particular day, you can use silver for magical works on other days.

Because silver represents the Moon and the lunar goddesses Isis and Diana, it is closely associated with intuition and sudden insights. The color is associated with visions and a desire for spiritual fulfillment. Used in magic, silver helps to bring your hidden potential to the foreground. It is the magical metal used for psychic development, dream work, intuition, instinctive wisdom, and visions. It is especially powerful when its ruling Moon is full.

For women, silver is particularly significant because of its connection with women's mysteries, beauty, home, and hearth. Worn by Isis, the Egyptian mother goddess, silver has long been used to invoke her and magical feminine energy. Silver bells are used as a special invocation of the power of all mother goddesses.

Because of the cyclical nature of the Moon, silver has also been associated with reincarnation and karma.

Channeling the Moon's magnetic effect on emotions and mental health, silver facilitates emotional balance.

Silver Spells

Though some rituals are suggested here, the creation of a personal ritual using silver will be the most powerful way to channel your own intuition and latent psychic abilities. Let your instincts flow, and craft a splendid personal ritual that will send your magic into the world.

Leave a silver ring in the moonlight, and then place it beneath your pillow before sleep. It will bring psychic dreams that give answers to the problems of the day. You can keep a silver-colored pen by the bed and write down your dream symbology when you awake.

Silver can be used for divination. In the Bible, the seer Joseph used a silver cup as his divinatory tool. You can use a silver cup, filled with water, to scry the future, enhance visions, and understand subtle mysteries.

When you find old quarters made from real silver, hold on to them. Carry these silver coins in your pocket to invoke best results in financial interactions. Toss a silver coin into a sacred body of water under a Full Moon to appease the mother goddess and earn favor.

Medieval superstition said a woman should not pray to God for any special favor. Instead, she should pray to her own deity, the Moon, by means of a piece of silver. Tied to this is the belief, still prevalent in some areas, that a woman should turn a silver coin when making her wish on the Moon.

A woman wanting to conceive should wear a belly chain made of silver during her fertile days to welcome mother goddess energy. Worn during sex, the chain invokes fertility and increases physical sensation and stimulation during intercourse.

Scrying (seeing psychic pictures or receiving impressions) with silver is especially effective on the first clear night of the week of the Full Moon. Use a plain silver object with a rounded surface such as a coffee pot or inverted silver bowl. Alternatively, place circles of thin silver bracelets in a small bowl of clear water, and let the moonlight form ripples on the silvery water. Think of a question and half-close your eyes. You may see images, colors, or shadows in the silver or hear half-formed words. If they do not make sense immediately, write them down or draw them on paper with a silver pen and place them under your pillow. The answer will come to you in your dreams. When you are finished scrying, place the silver vessel near an open window to be recharged by the Moon.

Silver is a symbol of protection and money. In China, infants are given silver lockets to wear at all times to protect against bad dreams and night terrors. In many parts of the world, silver is turned over on the New Moon so that money will come during the month.

Silver magic can be part of your everyday life. Choose a piece of silver jewelry that you can wear at all times—alone, at work, rest or play. On the Full Moon, place the jewelry in the light of an open window to charge it with the powers of the Moon. Wearing the charged silver ring or pendant can help you to invoke the energy of the Moon and of lunar goddesses. This will keep the fertile abilities of intuition and psychic connection alive within you.

When you are out in the world, your silver jewelry may be visible to all you encounter, but the magic of silver will be your private power. Then you, too, can go out into the world and glitter.

Rasputin: Holy Devil

by Denise Dumars

> "I am Russia."
> —Grigori Efimovich Rasputin

In early 2003, some factions of the Russian Othodox Church nominated Grigori Efimovich Rasputin, one of the most controversial figures of the twentieth century, for sainthood. The man, a prominent religious figure named Iliodor and dubbed a "holy devil," seems an unlikely candidate for sainthood, but if one examines the full historical record, the pieces—at least some of them—fall into place.

The myth of Rasputin is perhaps less interesting than the truth. It's untrue that he was an illiterate, unwashed peasant; it is equally untrue that he was a "mad monk." As to his illiteracy, well, Rasputin wrote copious letters and his journals have recently been published in Russia. He may have been unwashed while on religious pilgrimages, but he was also a great fan of the *banya*, the sauna/hot and cold bath combination that has both healing and mystical connotations.

Rasputin was no more "mad" than other psychics, shamanic healers, and religious mystics. In some ways he was an extraordinary example of a common character in Russian society—the *starets*, or wandering holy man. But Rasputin was never a monk, nor a priest, nor an ordained minister in any church. His formal religious training consisted of a few months spent here and there at various monasteries, and he relied greatly on his own visions and inspiration experienced during pilgrimages to sacred sites.

At first, Rasputin was viewed as a true mystic by respected religious leaders. They believed he had experienced a vision of the

Black Madonna and felt that his gifts of prophecy and healing were given by God. They would eventually change their minds.

On the other hand, Rasputin was, by his own admission, a world-class sinner. A drunkard and womanizer, his name is so synonymous with alcohol that at least two brands of liquor are named for him. It is also true that he sometimes took advantage of women who came to him for spiritual guidance—though once he came to prominence many women went to him specifically for what could be called "sexual healing."

The modern view of Rasputin is that of a magician and folk healer more than a Christian religious figure. The film *Rasputin* (2000), with Alan Rickman in the title role, offers the most modern view of Rasputin, exploring both the magical and religious connotations of the mystic's "gifts." Indeed, the role of Rasputin is a coveted one in films, and he has been played by many fine actors, including Lionel Barrymore, Tom Baker, and Christopher Lee.

What ultimately led to Rasputin's assassination was his influence over the royal family of Russia. Rasputin had been introduced to Alexandra, the tsarina—an unpopular "German" empress who was hated all the more once the Russians entered World War I. Alexandra, however, was determined to win the favor of the Russian people after marrying the love of her life, the ineffectual Tsar Nicholas II. She converted to the Orthodox Church and became extremely religious. When her son and the heir to the Romanov dynasty, the Tsarevich Alexei, was diagnosed with hemophilia, she prayed for a cure.

To this day, the inherited blood disorder hemophilia is incurable, although now there are treatments available. In the tsarevich's day, there was little medical science could do. The slightest bruise might cause uncontrollable internal bleeding, and an open wound could cause the boy to bleed to death. The boy suffered terribly whenever he hurt himself in the minor ways that all children do. One day when doctors thought the end was near for Alexei, Alexandra called for Rasputin, who was already known as having healed other children.

He told her to go to the chapel and pray. He sent the doctors away and stayed with the boy. In time, he called for the family and the boy's personal physician. Alexei was now sitting up, his fever

broken, his pain greatly relieved, and the internal bleeding stopped. Needless to say, Rasputin soon became an indispensable part of Romanov life.

Rasputin's healing techniques would not be unfamiliar to today's alternative practitioners. He used what we would call self-hypnosis and guided visualization to calm Alexei, slow the bleeding, and relieve the pain. Doctors at that time thought him a charlatan, but Alexandra believed that he had divine healing powers. As soon as his influence was acknowledged by the royal family, Rasputin's life was in danger.

His influence soon became a political one, and people sought the royal family's favors, both politically and socially, through Rasputin. Soon the mystic was famous and was hated equally by both the ruling class and the revolutionaries. What neither group understood was Rasputin's power over the imagination of the peasants. They believed that the alcoholic, adulterous magician was a gift from God.

Rasputin survived an assassination attempt on June 28, 1914, the same day that Archduke Ferdinand was assassinated in Sarajevo to start World War I. As the war raged and the power of the tsar waned, so, too, did Rasputin's influence. Eventually, the tsar sought to banish him. In the winter of 1916 left for Siberia. He left behind a letter, which was not delivered to the tsarina until after his death. The letter prophesied the end of the monarchy in Russia, and prophesied his own death. He knew he was to be assassinated, and in the letter it stated that if he were to be killed by a member of the royal family instead of by a commoner, the ruling family would be dead within two years.

Rasputin was assassinated on December 16, 1916, by Prince Felix Yusupov and several coconspirators, each one a member of the royal family or a government official. His murder is the stuff of legends—allegedly it took poison, a beating, and a hail of bullets to finish him. He may have also been sexually assaulted. Rasputin's body was thrown into the river. Startlingly enough, an autopsy called the cause of death drowning, as his lungs were filled with water. This fact merely added fuel to the belief in Rasputin's supernatural abilities.

Shortly before his assassination, Rasputin had given interviews to journalists, who quoted him saying: "The fools don't understand who I am. A sorcerer, perhaps, a sorcerer may be. They burn sorcerers, and so let them burn me, too. But there is one thing they do not realize. If they do burn me, Russia is finished; they'll bury us together."

Rasputin's body was disinterred in 1917 and burned on a bonfire. Nicholas and Alexandra and their children were executed on the night of July 14, 1918. The monarchy of Russia was history, as Rasputin had predicted.

The current patriarch of the Russian Orthodox Church called the movement to make Rasputin a saint "madness." Indeed, this group is pro-monarchy, antisemitic, and believes that the fall of Rasputin and the Romanovs were a conspiracy fostered by Western influences.

Rasputin was neither a devil nor an angel. He was merely an extraordinary but greatly flawed human being who continues to haunt our imaginations almost a hundred years after his spectacular death. The magical community should watch the progress of this situation closely, for if Rasputin becomes a saint he will be the first magician canonized since Joan of Arc.

Sabbat Breads

by Lily Gardner

The endless cycle of birth, growth, harvest, and death is the sacred model of Pagan life. We observe this never-ending cycle in the wheel of the year, in the phases of the Moon, in our individual growth, and even in our knowledge of the birth and death of stars. When we make bread, we celebrate this same round of mystery.

Set a bowl of bread dough in a warm spot, and in twenty minutes bubbles form. The bread grows swollen as if pregnant. Push the dough back in the bowl, and it rises again. Shape it and bake it, and the fragrance fills your home with sweet perfume better than any flower.

Goddesses and gods of grain have existed as long as the making of bread. The best-known Greek goddess of grain is Demeter, whose Eleusian festivals tell the story of the seasons. From the Roman Ceres, we get the name "cereal." Durga is a former Hindu grain goddess, and Inari hails from the Shinto faith.

357

What better way to celebrate our holy days than by baking bread? The following recipes are suggestions for sabbat breads.

Imbolc

The original bread of the Scots was an unleavened oatcake cooked in a hot skillet called a bannock. Ancient Scots served a special bannock for each of the holidays.

Imbolc Bannock

1½ cups flour

2 cups rolled oats

½ cup sugar

4 tsp. baking powder

½ tsp. salt

½ cup raisins

1 egg

½ cup butter, melted

⅓ cup buttermilk

Mix together flour, oats, sugar, baking powder, salt, and raisins. Make a well in the center. In a separate bowl whip egg, butter, and buttermilk. Add to dry ingredients and stir until a batter is formed. Scrape onto a well-floured surface and knead lightly. Shape into a ball, then place on a greased baking sheet. Mark a Bridget's cross in the center, using a sharp knife. Bake in a preheated 425° oven for fifteen minutes. Serve warm.

Ostara

Hot cross buns are associated with Good Friday, but originally they were sacramental cakes to honor Demeter, eaten during the Spring Equinox. Eating the buns at this time is said to bring good health for the whole year.

Hot Cross Buns

1 cup milk

½	cup buttermilk
2	Tbl. active dry yeast
1	cup sugar
2	tsp. salt
11	Tbl. unsalted butter, melted and cooled
1	tsp. cinnamon
½	tsp. nutmeg
4	large eggs
4–5	cups flour
1⅓	cups raisins
2	large egg whites
1½	cups powdered sugar
2	Tbl. freshly squeezed lemon juice

Cook milks in small saucepan over medium heat until scalded (just before boiling). Cool to room temperature and pour into a bowl. Add yeast, sugar, salt, butter, cinnamon, nutmeg, and eggs. Gradually add enough flour to create a sticky dough. Knead five minutes, until smooth. Cover with plastic wrap and let rest for thirty minutes. Coat a large bowl with butter. Knead dough about two minutes. Add raisins, and knead until combined. Shape dough into ball and place it in a buttered bowl. Cover tightly with plastic wrap and return to refrigerator. Let it rise overnight. In the morning, let dough sit at room temperature twenty minutes. Butter a cookie sheet. Divide dough into twenty-four portions. Shape into balls and place two inches apart in pan. Cover with plastic wrap and let rise until double in size, approximately two hours. Heat oven to 400°F with rack in center. In small bowl whisk one egg white with one tablespoon water and a pinch of salt. Brush tops of buns with egg wash. With a sharp buttered knife, score crosses on buns. Bake ten minutes, misting oven and buns with water three times. Reduce oven to 350°F. Bake another fifteen minutes. Whisk together remaining egg white, powdered sugar, and lemon juice. Ladle glaze over warm buns.

Lughnasah

Lughnasah is the feast of bread and beer. Some Pagans make a bread man for this very special harvest holiday.

Lughnasah Herb Bread

1   cup whole-wheat flour

1   cup white flour

    Pinch salt

1   tsp. baking powder

2   tsp. cream of tartar

1   tsp. brown sugar

½   Tbl. active dry yeast

½   tsp. caraway seed

1   tsp. dill weed

3   Tbl. soft butter

1   cup yogurt

Mix the dry ingredients. Work in butter with your hands. Add yogurt and mix well. Knead gently on a floured board and form into a round loaf. With a sharp knife, cut a cross on the top of the loaf. Bake on a greased cookie sheet in a 375°F degree oven for thirty minutes.

Pre-Islamic Deities

by Eileen Holland

The most venerated object on this planet is a rock— a broken rock. Believed to be a meteorite, the shattered stone is held together with pitch and silver wire. It is housed in Saudi Arabia in a shrine called the *ka'aba*. Each year millions of Muslims make the *haj* (pilgrimage) to Mecca, where they enact a pre-Islamic ritual of circling this rock. Muslims hold it sacred to their god Allah, but Arabs were making pilgrimages to this and other sacred stones long before Islam.

Arabians once had many gods and goddesses, and the ka'aba was surrounded by images of 360 of them. They had household gods and tribal gods, and most villages had a large stone that represented a deity. The prophet Mohammed syncretized one tribal god (some say goddess), Allah, with the single god of the Jews and the Christians to create Islam. Allah became the supreme god by force of arms, and Mecca became the center of his worship.

Hubal, an oracular god associated with divination by arrows, was lord of the ka'aba before Allah. The meteorite was held sacred to him, and he was also represented by a tall red stone image. Sacrifices were made to Hubal by those who sought his favor, and offerings were made to his image. Hubal can be invoked for lunar magic and for divination, particularly when information or advice is sought about disputes, journeys, new undertakings, marriage, newborns, fidelity, or the dead. He is not mentioned by name in the Koran, the holy book of Islam, but several other deities are.

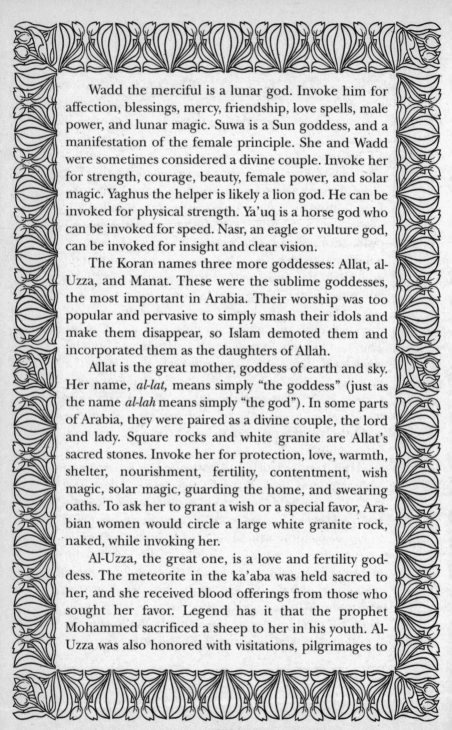

Wadd the merciful is a lunar god. Invoke him for affection, blessings, mercy, friendship, love spells, male power, and lunar magic. Suwa is a Sun goddess, and a manifestation of the female principle. She and Wadd were sometimes considered a divine couple. Invoke her for strength, courage, beauty, female power, and solar magic. Yaghus the helper is likely a lion god. He can be invoked for physical strength. Ya'uq is a horse god who can be invoked for speed. Nasr, an eagle or vulture god, can be invoked for insight and clear vision.

The Koran names three more goddesses: Allat, al-Uzza, and Manat. These were the sublime goddesses, the most important in Arabia. Their worship was too popular and pervasive to simply smash their idols and make them disappear, so Islam demoted them and incorporated them as the daughters of Allah.

Allat is the great mother, goddess of earth and sky. Her name, *al-lat*, means simply "the goddess" (just as the name *al-lah* means simply "the god"). In some parts of Arabia, they were paired as a divine couple, the lord and lady. Square rocks and white granite are Allat's sacred stones. Invoke her for protection, love, warmth, shelter, nourishment, fertility, contentment, wish magic, solar magic, guarding the home, and swearing oaths. To ask her to grant a wish or a special favor, Arabian women would circle a large white granite rock, naked, while invoking her.

Al-Uzza, the great one, is a love and fertility goddess. The meteorite in the ka'aba was held sacred to her, and she received blood offerings from those who sought her favor. Legend has it that the prophet Mohammed sacrificed a sheep to her in his youth. Al-Uzza was also honored with visitations, pilgrimages to

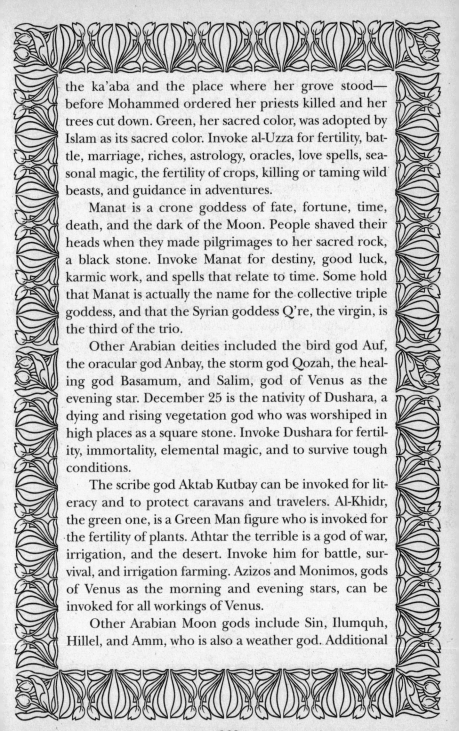

the ka'aba and the place where her grove stood—before Mohammed ordered her priests killed and her trees cut down. Green, her sacred color, was adopted by Islam as its sacred color. Invoke al-Uzza for fertility, battle, marriage, riches, astrology, oracles, love spells, seasonal magic, the fertility of crops, killing or taming wild beasts, and guidance in adventures.

Manat is a crone goddess of fate, fortune, time, death, and the dark of the Moon. People shaved their heads when they made pilgrimages to her sacred rock, a black stone. Invoke Manat for destiny, good luck, karmic work, and spells that relate to time. Some hold that Manat is actually the name for the collective triple goddess, and that the Syrian goddess Q're, the virgin, is the third of the trio.

Other Arabian deities included the bird god Auf, the oracular god Anbay, the storm god Qozah, the healing god Basamum, and Salim, god of Venus as the evening star. December 25 is the nativity of Dushara, a dying and rising vegetation god who was worshiped in high places as a square stone. Invoke Dushara for fertility, immortality, elemental magic, and to survive tough conditions.

The scribe god Aktab Kutbay can be invoked for literacy and to protect caravans and travelers. Al-Khidr, the green one, is a Green Man figure who is invoked for the fertility of plants. Athtar the terrible is a god of war, irrigation, and the desert. Invoke him for battle, survival, and irrigation farming. Azizos and Monimos, gods of Venus as the morning and evening stars, can be invoked for all workings of Venus.

Other Arabian Moon gods include Sin, Ilumquh, Hillel, and Amm, who is also a weather god. Additional

363

goddesses include Nayila, who can be invoked for sex magic, and the Sun goddess Shams, who is invoked for solar magic. Fatimah, the shining one, is a semidivine figure. Islam claims her as the daughter of Mohammed, but she may be a goddess who was assimilated into the new religion. Whatever her origin, Fatimah can be invoked for fate, destiny, protection, hospitality, generosity, strength, goodness, lunar magic, and averting the evil eye. The Hand of Fatimah, a popular charm also known as the hamsa hand, is widely used for protection throughout the Middle East.

Like other monotheists before him, Mohammed found it advantageous to incorporate many features of existing Pagan worship into the new faith.

He and his followers smashed the images of deities, assumed aspects of their worship, executed their clergy, and persecuted their devotees. Muslims tried to erase the memory of the Arabian deities, but these gods and goddesses live on and are available to us still if we need them.

On Prayer

by Diana Rajchel

Back in my Christian days, I listened closely to sermons on the importance of prayer. I believed those sermons—that God wanted to hear from me, wanted a friendship with me.

At the age of fourteen, I began to prepare for bed by taking a shower, dancing to a few songs on the radio, and then pulling my Bible off the bookshelf to read a few chapters and pray. When I prayed, I made petitions both serious and light, mentioned how my day went, and I posed occasional serious questions. My prayers—even the nonpetition ones—did receive answers. I do believe that the regular prayer had a profound effect on me, and helped me handle the particularly nasty social environment of my childhood.

When Wicca found me five years later and I finally relented to the touch of the gods in a new form, I embraced ritual with enthusiasm. I attempted meditation with as few accidental naps as I could manage, and I read the works of Beyerl, Cunningham, Valiente, and other prominent Wiccan authors. Still, I felt like there remained a hole in my practice. In time, I was recognizing what I missed: prayer. I liked prayer. I simply wanted the two-way experience I felt when I prayed as a Christian.

So, lacking the Pagan prayer books only made available in the last three years, I set about making my own prayer book. I scoured the net, I borrowed from Scott Cunningham, and I wrote prayers where I felt inspired or recognized a hole. Once, twice, sometimes three times a day I would light a candle and read aloud from my homemade prayer book.

Since then, I strive never to miss is my daily prayer time—whether simply stating my love for the gods every morning, making an offering, or simply stopping to chat with the divine.

The Practicalities of Prayer

The ritual associations of Pagan practices sometimes seem to crowd out prayer. With all the study and meditation required to gain even the smallest iota of spiritual insight, a person can forget that it's absolutely necessary to open a conversation with the divine. Passive prayer, as taught in religious institutions, is usually not enough. One can't operate on a philosophy of stating it once and forgetting about it. The divine is not a holy cash machine. Prayer demands making contact, having a willingness to take the spiritual relationship into a personal dimension, and speaking to it just as you would your friends and loved ones.

Prayer Practice

Active prayer involves genuine emotion, visualization, and a routine that helps the brain register a sacred time and sacred action (and differentiate it from normal reality). While I find prayer more portable than meditation and ritual practices, a few steps can help you ease into the experience, particularly if prayer is something you rarely have practiced.

First, try to pray at the same time every day. While the divine can listen to you any time, you need to signal to yourself that you are having an important conversation. This will help you treat the communication of prayer as something special.

Try to pray in a regular location. I personally have a foot-locker covered by some old scarves and candle wax. This works well for me both as an altar and as a comfortable prayer spot. Of course, I do not have this option in my workplace. I have absolutely no Pagan or otherwise religious expression anywhere on my desk, and I do not have the luxury of a conference room with a door that locks. In good weather, I simply find a park near my office building in downtown Minneapolis. In bad weather, I find a bench in an indoor lobby and tell any questioners that I'm practicing deep breathing "for medical reasons."

When I can pray aloud—usually at home—I draw from my old prayer book, from immediate needs I recognize around me, from one of the Pagan prayer books presently on the market. When I pray silently, I usually begin by running through one of my favorite litanies, and then I observe where my subconscious—and the divine response—takes me.

Pagans, particularly those using Wiccan ritual formats, borrow freely from the prayer accessories of other faiths. Such accessories include prayer flags, prayer beads (i.e., rosaries or malas), mandalas, spoken prayer revised from popular Christian prayer, and a host of other techniques either inspired by mythologies or outright borrowed from larger modern religions.

Those who prefer to use prayer accessories often prefer meditative format with their prayers. The object provides a focus, either to track how often a mantra is repeated, or to assist in absorbing the person completely in the divine conversation. While prayer beads are at the moment the most popular choice, no one method has more effect than another. As in all divine relationships, the heart and sincerity of the person appealing to the divine is the key.

If you are a little uncertain what to say to initiate prayer, an Internet search can supply a few prayers to begin practice. Most such prayers range from nature worship to direct conversation with specific deity. Others take a more general approach. Still, the most powerful prayers will be those that come from your own heart.

Talismans and Amulets from Scottish Folk Tradition

by Sharynne MacLeod NicMhacha

The rites and customs of Scotland have been preserved and recorded in the last few centuries by historians and folklorists, revealing a rich and vibrant magical tradition. Charms and magical objects were common and plentiful, and were used on the quarter days and sometimes every day. Here are some of the most common magical objects used as talismans and amulets in Scottish folk tradition.

Rowan, Silver, Amber, and Bone

In Scotland, a great number of objects were worn as talismans or used as amulets for protection. They were often chosen for their shape, color, natural qualities, or magical properties. Red was the supreme magical color. Necklaces of red coral or red rowan berries were strung on red thread and worn as amulets. Amber beads strung on red thread worn were also worn as amulets by upperclass women and by fisherwomen in the northeast. Bracelets of leather, copper, plaited hair, or red coral served as protective amulets, and these were either worn, carried on the person, or placed in the house or barn to ward off danger. An amulet of mint, rue, and senna worn as bracelet also averted danger. Charmed necklaces that incorporated lucky stones and pebbles were used to prevent danger or bring luck. A twig of rowan was carried in the pocket for protection.

Colored threads were frequently used in witchcraft in the Highlands. Red thread twisted around the finger served as a simple but potent everyday amulet. Black thread with nine knots in it was tied around a sprained limb to relieve swelling and pain. Blue threads were used as charms to prevent fevers in nursing women. These were handed down from mother to daughter. Blue thread or wool was also used in the divination rites that took place at Samhain. A triple thread of black, white, and red (each one a different thickness) was wound three times around the tail of an ill or bewitched animal.

Other powerful talismanic objects included silver, salt, iron, and bone. Silver was believed to have powerful healing properties. A silver coin or talisman was dipped in water to impart healing powers. The *peigh-inn pisich* (lucky penny) was the name of a coin that was kept in the pocket and turned three times at the first glimpse of New Moon for luck. Salt was often associated with life and good fortune. It was one of the first things moved into a new house. A purification and protection ceremony known as *saining* was often performed with salt, fire, and water. Iron was sometimes used for protection, and small pieces of iron were sewn into the hems of garments. Iron horseshoes were hung with the points up for good luck. Bones of holy or revered people were believed to bestow good luck and were also used as talismans. In some cases they were cased in silver or tied with red thread.

A special amulet of vellum or leather was used with an incantation called the *fath-fidh* to make persons or things invisible. In this form of magic, men were often transformed into horses, bulls, or stags, and women into cats, hares, or hinds. The charm was sometimes used by hunters, warriors, and travellers, as it had the power to make them invisible (or unrecognizable) to enemies or wild animals.

Magical Charm Stones

Many stones were believed to have healing or protective powers. These included large standing stones or dolmens, as well as smaller rocks, pebbles, and crystals. The use of magical healing stones is an ancient custom in Scotland. The chief Druid at the Pictish court at Inverness was reported to have been cured of illness by drinking water in which a white pebble from the River Ness had been dipped. White quartz pebbles have been found at ancient megalithic sites, and white pebbles painted with magical designs or symbols have been unearthed at a number of Pictish sites.

In Scottish folk tradition, certain pieces of white or rose quartz were known as "fever stones." These were put in boiling water to impart special qualities to the liquid. When the water had cooled, peopled washed their arms and legs with the water to prevent arthritis and other illnesses. In Galloway, flat round stones with holes drilled through them were steeped in water that was then sprinkled on sick animals. A similar ritual existed using "fairy arrows" (prehistoric flint arrowheads). Stones that contained a naturally occurring hole (usually from flowing water) were called "elf cups." These were strung in groups of threes on horse hair or string and hung above the door for protection. In addition, if one peered through such a stone on the quarter days, one might be able to see the future.

Certain Highland families were the proud guardians of prized hierlooms: ancient and very magical rock crystal charm stones. These round crystals were set in silver hoops, mounted in silver pendants, or hung on a silver chain. Crystal spheres or balls were also treasured. These crystals could be dipped into healing wells or vessels of water to impart their healing powers, touched to grant wishes, or worn as talismans against the evil eye.

Other magical stones were prized in Scottish folk tradition. Green stones could be carried for protective or healing powers, or to ensure victory. Tribesmen were said to have sworn oaths upon these stones. The green pebbles on Iona were used as amulets and to save people from drowning. Like crystals, green stones or pebbles were also set in silver and worn as protective amulets or pendants. River stones were used as amulets against danger—although, once blackened in the fire, they could also be used in cursing magic. The Strathardle Witches were said to have cherished a particular garnet stone that is now in the Highland Museum at Fort William.

In addition, there was a very mysterious magical stone called the Clach Nathrach ("Serpent Stone"). It was believed to have been formed by the movement of serpents whose secretions gave the stones their power. They were used for healing, as an aid in childbirth, and to protect against enchantment. They were also used to cure illnesses attributed to the bites of adders or other poisonous beasts. These "stones" are actually spindle whorls that were discovered in the fields of heather from time to time. The legend associated with these objects is similar to another account that is almost two thousand years old. In ancient Gaul, the Celts revered an object called a "Druid's egg," which was believed to have been formed from the movement, hissing, and saliva of wriggling serpents. These "eggs" may have actually been Iron Age glass beads, for these are now known in Scottish Gaelic as *glaine nathrach* (serpent's glass).

Tattoo Sigil Magic

by Tammy Sullivan

Tattoos have long held a mystical and magical significance, likely due to the loss of lifeblood during the application. Early tattooing was used to symbolize the fertility of the earth, the preservation of life after death, and many cultural factors. Certain primitive tribes had tattoo magicians. In Tibet, tattooing a mantra onto a moving body part is considered to have the same effect as chanting the mantra

People are again beginning to realize the sacredness of tattoo applications, as well as the ritual possibilities. For instance, it is a common ritual today to undergo a tattoo procedure as a rite of passage into adulthood.

The creation of a personal sigil to be used for a tattoo should not be undertaken lightly. In effect, you are creating a permanent spell with the intention of attaining a lifelong goal. To determine a proper goal, I suggest meditating and vision-questing. You'll want to make sure that the goal you choose is something you wish to strive for throughout your lifetime—and not just a passing fancy. If you take your time choosing your goal, you should be prepared for all consequences.

Once the appropriate goal has been determined there are many ways to create the sigil. In the word method, you write down your goal (a word or short sentence), remove any repeating letters and arrange the remaining letters into a design. In the pictoral method, you choose a picture that represents your goal. In the square of nine method, your written goal is transformed into a series of marks—using a chart of numbers with letter correspondences.

Once you determine your tattoo's design, you have to determine its placement. This may be achieved through meditation, chakra correspondence, or simple instinct. Temporary tattoos of your design may be made by drawing your design on a piece of thermal paper. Just place a bit of gel deodorant on the skin where you wish to apply the tattoo. Press the design firmly on the skin and hold a few seconds. Alternatively, you may wish to create a stencil and apply the temporary tattoo with henna.

You may also want to keep the tattoo temporary and change the goal around to match your needs, creating new sigils and symbols for other spells. If you decide to keep it temporary you will need to charge the sigil in order to imprint it, using meditation, into your subconscious.

The sigil will act as a hidden signal both to your brain and to the universe. The energy you have expended in the creation of the design holds the key to the power, and you need not be the one who inks it on permanently for it to work. The inking will charge the sigil, through the slight pain of the needle. You may wish to meditate and achieve an alpha state while undergoing the application. Placing it on the body activates it, but you will need to feed it, if you decide to go the permanent route.

Sailors of long ago used to feed their tattoos by rubbing rum on them under the light of the Moon. You may do that, or you might wish to incorporate ceremony and smoke incense, anoint the sigil with essential oils or magical waters, and say a blessing or affirmation chant. You will need to use an antibacterial ointment for a day or so after the inking, and it would be beneficial to bless and charge it under a Full Moon beforehand. You may consecrate your design to the four elements, if you wish, or hold a dedication ritual and dedicate yourself to the goal you have set.

Ideally, you should place your sigil on the night of the Full Moon and feed it every Full Moon after. It is fine to go with a date that holds special meaning to you for the original placement, but I would continue the feeding on the nights of the Full Moon.

Afterward, you must work forget the sigil. Make sure the message is hidden in the artwork of the tattoo, as well as ingrained in your subconscious. It is not necessary for the sigil to remain visible to continue the effect.

This type of spell is a long process and a lot of work, but this must be the case—as it is a permanent spell and packs a powerful magical punch. I cannot stress enough the careful consideration you must put into this before attempting. If you take your time, and follow the guidelines, you will enjoy the benefits of the tattoo throughout your lifetime.

Products
and
Services

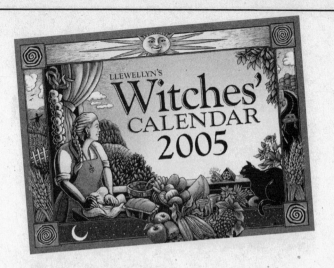

Bewitching Days and Pagan Ways

Wake up each day under the spell of this entrancing calendar of folklore and magic. Colorful original artwork by Kathleen Edwards accompanies a new seasonal topic each month. Barbara Ardinger, Cerridwen Iris Shea, James Kambos, Christopher Penczak, and Raven Grimassi are among the authors contributing their expertise. In addition, the back of the calendar features eight articles including "Honoring Our Ancestors" by Yasmine Galenorn, "The Witch's First-Aid Kit" by K. D. Spitzer, and "Yemaya, Ocean Lady" by Denise Dumars.

LLEWELLYN'S 2005 WITCHES' CALENDAR
36 pp. • 13 x 9½ • 12 full-color illustrations
0-7387-0141-6/J138 • $12.95 U.S. $19.95 Can.
To order call 1-877-NEW WRLD

Read your Future in the Cards

Tarot enthusiasts rejoice! Look for an array of news, advice, and in-depth discussions on everything tarot in Llewellyn's new *Tarot Reader*.

Renowned authors and tarot specialists deliver deck reviews and articles concerning card interpretation, spreads, magic, tarot history, and professional tarot reading. Each year's almanac will also feature a calendar with pertinent astrological information, such as Moon signs and times. This year's *Tarot Reader* includes articles by Ruth Ann and Wald Amberstone, Joan Cole, Mary K. Greer, and James Wells.

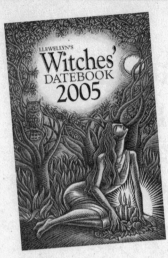

A Planetary Perspective for Our Times

What are the planets saying about our world? Find out in Llewellyn's new *Starview Almanac*. Renowned astrologers provide reliable insight into politics, entertainment, health, and fashion. Forecasts and trends relating to current events and issues, such as homeland security and America's obesity problem, are discussed without astrological terminology. Also included are financial and weather forecasts for 2005, profiles of famous people, facts about living with Mercury-retrograde periods, and a weekly calendar with fun forecasts by Sally Cragin.

LLEWELLYN'S 2005 STARVIEW ALMANAC
288 pp. • 5¼ x 8
0-7387-0539-X / J138 • $8.95 U.S. $11.95 Can.
To order call 1-877-NEW-WRLD

Channel Your Energy

The unseen world of energy is all around us. Becoming aware of your personal energy is the first step toward understanding and channeling its power. The *Energy SourceBook* can help you discover how energy flow is a source of physical health, prosperity, and happiness.

Experienced in both traditional and alternative medicine, Dr. Jill Henry describes how energy manipulation is a terrific tool for self-healing and transformation. She discusses several energy theories in depth, spanning meditation, feng shui, polarity energy balance, and chakra work. The *Energy SourceBook* also teaches the techniques behind the theories, offering more than 150 simple exercises and activities.

ENERGY SOURCEBOOK
The Fundamentals of Personal Energy
Dr. Jill Henry, Ed.D.
216 pp. • 7½ x 9⅛
0-7387-0529-2/J138 • $16.95 U.S. $22.95 Can.
To order call 1-877-NEW-WRLD

Encounter the God of the Wild Wood

Magic and witchcraft begin with self-awareness. A crucial step toward self-awareness is recognizing the many faces of the witches' god. This book provides a clear mythology for those who need assistance in answering the call of wildness within.

High Priestess Ly de Angeles teaches beginning and advanced practitioners about the persona of the gods and the Celtic perspective of sacredness. Going beyond ordinary witchcraft manuals, she explains fundamental concepts, such as logos and mythos, the Tuatha de Danann, the Quicken Tree, immortality, animism, pantheism, and the elements. Also included are urban stories of magical realism, which take readers on a ritual journey to understanding the solstices and equinoxes.

WHEN I SEE THE WILD GOD
Encountering Urban Celtic Witchcraft
Ly de Angeles
288 pp. • 6 x 9 with pronunciation guide
0-7387-0576-4 / J138 • $12.95 U.S. $17.50 Can.
To order call 1-877-NEW-WRLD

Occult Attack!

In this occult novel, myth and magick come to life on the stage of a small London shop. In the heart of Oxford, England, sits Malynowsky's Bookshop, the sort of place that makes people go "oooh" as soon as they step into it. Its books both lure and intimidate, and the clientele come to browse in the knowledge that their needs will be met and their privacy respected. Inside, the myths reenact themselves daily among the customers, employees, and the books themselves.

This collection of six short stories takes you inside this little world of mystery, real magick, and moral lessons. Meet Paul Magwitch, possessed by the spirit of a young girl who compels him to buy expensive things he does not need or want; the Witch in the city, who ekes out a living reading Tarot for strangers in the park; and Eurydice, a shop employee who tragically becomes the victim of a customer's magickal attack.

THE MAGICK BOOKSHOP
Stories of the Occult
Kala Trobe
240 pp. • 6 x 9 with diagrams
0-7387-0515-2/J138 • $15.95 U.S. $21.50 Can.
To order call 1-877-NEW-WRLD